THE CAMBRIDGE BIBLE COMMENTARY

NEW ENGLISH BIBLE

GENERAL EDITORS

P. R. ACKROYD, A. R. C. LEANEY

J. W. PACKER

EZEKIEL

THE
BOOK OF THE PROPHET
EZEKIEL

COMMENTARY BY

KEITH W. CARLEY

Lecturer in Old Testament Studies
Rarongo Theological College, Papua New Guinea

CAMBRIDGE UNIVERSITY PRESS

Published by the Syndics of the Cambridge University Press
Bentley House, 200 Euston Road, London NW1 2DB
American Branch: 32 East 57th Street, New York, N.Y.10022

Library of Congress Catalogue Card Number: 73–94352

ISBNS:
0 521 08653 1 hard cover
0 521 09755 x paperback

First published 1974

Printed in Great Britain
at the University Printing House, Cambridge
(Brooke Crutchley, University Printer)

11-18-75

GENERAL EDITORS' PREFACE

The aim of this series is to provide the text of the New English Bible closely linked to a commentary in which the results of modern scholarship are made available to the general reader. Teachers and young people have been especially kept in mind. The commentators have been asked to assume no specialized theological knowledge, and no knowledge of Greek and Hebrew. Bare references to other literature and multiple references to other parts of the Bible have been avoided. Actual quotations have been given as often as possible.

The completion of the New Testament part of the series in 1967 provides a basis upon which the production of the much larger Old Testament and Apocrypha series can be undertaken. The welcome accorded to the series has been an encouragement to the editors to follow the same general pattern, and an attempt has been made to take account of criticisms which have been offered. One necessary change is the inclusion of the translators' footnotes since in the Old Testament these are more extensive, and essential for the understanding of the text.

Within the severe limits imposed by the size and scope of the series, each commentator will attempt to set out the main findings of recent biblical scholarship and to describe the historical background to the text. The main theological issues will also be critically discussed.

Much attention has been given to the form of the volumes. The aim is to produce books each of which will be read consecutively from first to last page. The introductory material leads naturally into the text, which itself leads into the alternating sections of the commentary.

The series is accompanied by three volumes of a more general character. *Understanding the Old Testament* sets out to provide the larger historical and archaeological background, to say something about the life and thought of the people of the Old Testament, and to answer the question 'Why should we study the Old Testament?'. *The Making of the Old Testament* is concerned with the formation of the books of the Old Testament and Apocrypha in the context of the ancient near eastern world, and with the ways in which these books have come down to us in the life of the Jewish and Christian communities. *Old Testament Illustrations* contains maps, diagrams and photographs with an explanatory text. These three volumes are designed to provide material helpful to the understanding of the individual books and their commentaries, but they are also prepared so as to be of use quite independently.

P. R. A.
A. R. C. L.
J. W. P.

CONTENTS

ILLUSTRATIONS

THE FOOTNOTES TO THE
N.E.B. TEXT

The footnotes to the N.E.B. text are designed to help the reader either to understand particular points of detail – the meaning of a name, the presence of a play upon words – or to give information about the actual text. Where the Hebrew text appears to be erroneous, or there is doubt about its precise meaning, it may be necessary to turn to manuscripts which offer a different wording, or to ancient translations of the text which may suggest a better reading, or to offer a new explanation based upon conjecture. In such cases, the footnotes supply very briefly an indication of the evidence, and whether the solution proposed is one that is regarded as possible or as probable. Various abbreviations are used in the footnotes:

(1) Some abbreviations are simply of terms used in explaining a point: *ch(s).*, chapter(s); *cp.*, compare; *lit.*, literally; *mng.*, meaning; *MS(S).*, manuscript(s), i.e. Hebrew manuscript(s), unless otherwise stated; *om.*, omit(s); *or*, indicating an alternative interpretation; *poss.*, possible; *prob.*, probable; *rdg.*, reading; *Vs(s).*, version(s).

(2) Other abbreviations indicate sources of information from which better interpretations or readings may be obtained.

Aq.   Aquila, a Greek translator of the Old Testament (perhaps about A.D. 130) characterized by great literalness.

Aram.   Aramaic – may refer to the text in this language (used in parts of Ezra and Daniel), or to the meaning of an Aramaic word. Aramaic belongs to the same language family as Hebrew, and is known from about 1000 B.C. over a wide area of the Middle East, including Palestine.

Heb.   Hebrew – may refer to the Hebrew text or may indicate the literal meaning of the Hebrew word.

Josephus   Flavius Josephus (A.D. 37/8–about 100), author of the *Jewish Antiquities*, a survey of the whole history of his people, directed partly at least to a non-Jewish audience, and of various other works, notably one on the *Jewish War* (that of A.D. 66–73) and a defence of Judaism (*Against Apion*).

Luc. Sept.   Lucian's recension of the Septuagint, an important edition made in Antioch in Syria about the end of the third century A.D.

Pesh.   Peshitta or Peshitto, the Syriac version of the Old Testament. Syriac is the name given chiefly to a form of Eastern Aramaic used by the Christian community. The translation varies in quality, and is at many points influenced by the Septuagint or the Targums.

Sam.   Samaritan Pentateuch – the form of the first five books of the Old Testament as used by the Samaritan community. It is written in Hebrew in a special form of the Old Hebrew script, and preserves an important form of the text, somewhat influenced by Samaritan ideas.

Scroll(s)   Scroll(s), commonly called the Dead Sea Scrolls, found at or near Qumran from 1947 onwards. These important manuscripts shed light on the state of the Hebrew text as it was developing in the last centuries B.C. and the first century A.D.

Sept.   Septuagint (meaning 'seventy'; often abbreviated as the Roman numeral LXX), the name given to the main Greek version of the Old Testament. According to tradition, the Pentateuch was translated in Egypt in the third century B.C. by 70 (or 72) translators, six from each tribe, but the precise nature of its origin and development is not fully known. It was intended to provide Greek-speaking Jews with a convenient translation. Subsequently it came to be much revered by the Christian community.

Symm.   Symmachus, another Greek translator of the Old Testament (beginning of the third century A.D.), who tried to combine literalness with good style. Both Lucian and Jerome viewed his version with favour.

Targ.   Targum, a name given to various Aramaic versions of the Old Testament, produced over a long period and eventually standardized, for the use of Aramaic-speaking Jews.

Theod.   Theodotion, the author of a revision of the Septuagint (probably second century A.D.), very dependent on the Hebrew text.

Vulg.   Vulgate, the most important Latin version of the Old Testament, produced by Jerome about A.D. 400, and the text most used throughout the Middle Ages in western Christianity.

[. . .]   In the text itself square brackets are used to indicate probably late additions to the Hebrew text.

(Fuller discussion of a number of these points may be found in *The Making of the Old Testament* in this series)

HISTORICAL TABLE

B.C.	Background events	B.C.	The prophecies
609	– Josiah killed in battle; Jehoahaz soon deposed in favour of Jehoiakim		
604	– Nebuchadrezzar assumes rule in Babylon		
598	– Jehoiachin succeeds to the throne of Judah		
597	– the first exile; Jehoiachin taken to Babylon; Zedekiah made the vassal king of Judah		
594–3	– revolt against Babylon planned by minor states		
		593	– Ezekiel's call and first prophecies (1: 2; 3: 16)
		592	– the vision of corruption (8: 1)
		591	– a history of rebellion (20: 1)
589–8	– Nebuchadrezzar lays siege to Jerusalem	589–8	– Jerusalem a cauldron (24: 1)
588	– Hophra becomes pharaoh		
		588–7	– against Pharaoh (29: 1; 30: 20; 31: 1)
587	– Zedekiah flees Jerusalem; the city is destroyed		
		587–6	– news of Jerusalem's fall reaches Ezekiel (33: 21)
		586	– against Tyre (26: 1); Egypt's demise (32: 1, 17)
585	– Nebuchadrezzar lays siege to Tyre		
		573	– the final vision (40: 1)
		571	– Egypt for Nebuchadrezzar (29: 17)
568	– Nebuchadrezzar invades Egypt		
562	– the death of Nebuchadrezzar; release of Jehoiachin		
539	– Cyrus of Persia captures Babylon		

THE
BOOK OF THE PROPHET
EZEKIEL

✻ ✻ ✻ ✻ ✻ ✻ ✻ ✻ ✻ ✻ ✻ ✻ ✻

WHAT THE BOOK IS ABOUT

When Jerusalem was captured by Babylonian forces in 597 B.C. the city was left intact, but Ezekiel was taken away with the king and certain other leading men, to their captors' homeland. While an exile in Babylonia, Ezekiel saw a vision of God and was commanded to tell his people what God intended to do with them, and why. His activities as a prophet are the subject of the Old Testament book which bears his name. They extended from the time of his call in 593 B.C. until at least 571 B.C., the last date recorded in the book (29: 17). Until the time of the second capture and destruction of Jerusalem by the Babylonians in 587 B.C., he castigated his people for their unfaithfulness to God and foretold the doom of those remaining in Jerusalem and the land of Judah. He may occasionally have uttered an encouraging word for his fellow exiles, but by both acted and spoken prophecies he made it plain that divine judgement had first to fall in punishment for Israel's failure to observe God's laws. With the destruction of Jerusalem, hopefulness began to predominate in his prophecies and he was charged also with the task of being a pastor to individual exiles – encouraging them to right living and warning them when their behaviour was bad. His words included prophecies of doom and success for nations other than his own people Israel, and he envisaged the eventual restoration of the exiles to their homeland.

I

THE ORDER OF THE BOOK

Ezekiel appears to be the most orderly of all the Old Testament prophetic books. As we now have it, chs. 1–3 tell of the prophet's call; chs. 4–24 contain his prophecies of Jerusalem's terrible fate; chs. 25–32 are prophecies against foreign nations; chs. 33–9 encourage the hope of restoration after Jerusalem had fallen in 587 B.C.; while chs. 40–8 present a vision of a new temple, with God dwelling once more among his people. Many of the prophecies are even dated. But appearances can be deceptive. In Ezekiel the dates are not all in chronological order. The latest date occurs in the middle of the book, in a prophecy against Egypt (29: 17). The dates of the remaining prophecies against foreign nations probably once formed an independent series, and some dates appear to have been altered by editors of the book (e.g. see the commentary on 33 : 21). Also, the dates normally only relate to the prophecy immediately following. Sometimes later prophecies or prophetic signs have been included early in the book – because of their importance in the prophet's life (e.g. 3 : 16–21); to soften the harshness of a previous saying (20: 32–8); or to acknowledge a different outcome from that earlier foretold (29: 17–21). Moreover, some material is not from Ezekiel himself but from his followers or from editors of the book. Thus, each passage needs to be examined individually to determine, where possible, its place in the activity of the prophet and the growth of the prophecy as a whole.

HOW DID THE BOOK COME TO BE WRITTEN?

Books were not common in the ancient world. They had to be handwritten and not everyone could read and write. Prophets anyway were speakers of God's word rather than writers of it. But some prophets, at least from the time of Amos in the mid-eighth century B.C., either wrote, or had written for them, accounts of their activities. There are specific references to the recording of Isaiah's words so that their fulfilment might prove their truth (Isa. 8: 1f. and 30: 8). And Jeremiah used a scribe to record his prophecies so that they could be communicated to a wider audience at a later time (Jer. 36), since what prophets said on one occasion could be applied to other situations as well. Both of these motives may have persuaded Ezekiel of the importance of providing a written account of what he had said, done and felt as a prophet. This was not composed at a single sitting nor as a single connected narrative. There was a considerable period during which the prophet recorded and worked over accounts of his activities, adding pieces here, correcting passages there. Sometimes there is repetition in the form of doublets – sayings having the same meaning but put in slightly different ways. Sometimes his sayings are not prophecies at all, but sermons encouraging people to learn the lessons that God intended the exile to teach them. The dated prophecies concerning Jerusalem and Israel (chs. 1: 1 – 3: 15; 3: 16 and chs. 4–5 (which were originally introduced by 3: 16); chs. 8–11; 20; 24; 33: 21f.; and 40–8) probably formed a general framework for chs. 1–24 and 33–48 of the book we know. Among these prophecies were added collections of sayings on particular themes (e.g. false prophecy, ch. 13; the sword, ch. 21), often related to the time sequence of the dated passages only insofar as prophecies of doom were largely included prior to ch. 24 and those of hope were added between chs. 33 and 40. The prophecies against foreign nations are likely to have been one such separate collection. The insertion of it, with its dated sayings, between chs. 24 and 33 gave rise to the most obvious point of disorder in the book. Ezekiel may have played little part in assembling the book in its present form. The work of editors is apparent in a number of the minor collections (e.g. see the commentary on 6: 13f.) and the book as a whole has undergone considerable editorial revision (e.g. see on 3: 16–27). But between Ezekiel's own recording and revision of his prophecies and the editorial activity that has resulted in the present book, there have been extensive attempts to reinterpret and apply the prophecies to the situations of later periods by the followers of the prophet.

EZEKIEL AND HIS DISCIPLES

It seems very likely that just as Elijah and Elisha, Isaiah and Jeremiah had disciples who assisted in their work (2 Kings 2: 3; 6: 1; Isa. 8: 16 footnote; Jer. 36: 4), Ezekiel too had his followers. The disciples are not mentioned, but the very preservation of the prophet's words, as well as their continuing exposition, implies that they struck a responsive chord among some of Ezekiel's contemporaries, who saw to it that his prophecies were not forgotten. Who these people were we will never know. Among them may have been some of the elders who came to sit before the prophet in his house to inquire of God's will (e.g. 8: 1). The kind of emphasis the disciples have contributed to the book suggests that there were priests among them, some of whom were concerned to make the prophecy an instrument of their desire to dominate the priesthood of the restored Israel (44: 15–31). Others wished to ascribe Israel's punishment and its hope for the future solely to God's concern for his holy name (36: 16–32). Often they have adopted the language and style of Ezekiel himself, to elaborate his words or to add prophecies intended to complete his work.

Often we cannot say whether Ezekiel or one of his followers was responsible for a particular passage. It may be clear enough that a word or saying has been added later. Sometimes it is an expansion of, or a natural supplement to, what has already been said. Sometimes it contradicts a previous saying or gives quite a new meaning to what was said earlier. And while it is important to determine, where we can, what Ezekiel's own words were, it is no less important to try and determine the reasons for their reinterpretation, whether by the prophet or his disciples. For in the book of Ezekiel there is preserved not the words of one man alone, but evidence of the response to, and continuing exposition of, his words within a living community. For example, in ch. 1 Ezekiel's account of the living creatures consisted of verse 5 and parts of verses 6 and 11. His disciples have added further details. In ch. 12 a prophecy of the second exile has been revised in the light of the actual event, possibly by Ezekiel himself. Ch. 23: 36–49 illustrates the reinterpretation of the prophet's words to counter a specific evil of a later time.

Of Ezekiel's life we learn only incidentally. Since his behaviour constituted a 'sign' for his contemporaries (12: 6; 24: 24), personal experiences became the substance of his prophecies. But we should beware of reading the book of Ezekiel as a biography of the prophet. It was intended primarily as a record of the word of God. We do learn of Ezekiel's likely age (1: 1), of his priestly descent (1: 3), of his apparent seizure, so that he was unable to speak or move at some time during his prophetic ministry (see on 3: 22–7), and of the death of his wife whom he loved deeply (24: 15–24). Beyond that, his origins, physical circumstances and fate are unknown. His prophecies do indicate, however, his wide knowledge of his people's heritage and his desire to recall them to their responsibilities as God's people. He combines a prophet's deep sensitivity to moral injustice with a priest's concern for appropriate religious observance. And so intensely does he assert God's control of history that he attributes the worst deeds of his people to God's deliberate plan to punish them for their earlier bad behaviour (20: 25f.). Throughout the book there is repeated the phrase – 'that they may know that I am the LORD'. All that was promised through the prophet would show to Israel and the nations the nature of Israel's God and his power to act among them. For sympathetic understanding of the prophecy, some appreciation is necessary of Ezekiel's passion to vindicate and proclaim anew God's justice and holiness, and to affirm his lordship over all.

FROM BABYLON TO JERUSALEM

A feature of the prophecy which is puzzling to most readers is Ezekiel's reports of having been taken by a spirit from his home among the exiles to Jerusalem and back. That was a distance of about 700 miles in each direction, by way of the Euphrates valley and Syria (see map, p. 169). The difficulty has sometimes been solved by supposing that Ezekiel really lived in Jerusalem during the first part of his prophetic activity, or that he made a number of journeys between Jerusalem and Babylon in an orthodox manner. The references to the spirit are thus simply figures of speech. But there are several points at which the prophecy suggests Ezekiel was conscious, with great intensity, of unseen forces such as are mentioned in the prophecies of Elijah and Elisha 300 years earlier. Those prophets sometimes found their physical powers increased (1 Kings 18: 46) or believed themselves removed from one place to another (1 Kings 18: 12; 2 Kings 2: 16). They described this in terms of 'the hand of the LORD' being upon the prophet, or of 'the spirit of the LORD' lifting and bearing the prophet away. We hear little of such experiences from the prophets from the time of Amos onward, but outside the Bible, particularly in Arabic literature, we find similar accounts of such experiences. In present-day Papua New Guinea, there are numerous reports of men who claim to have flown astonishing distances to effect healing, to give counsel or simply observe conditions in other places. Ezekiel, aware of such feelings of removal (see on 11: 1f.), appears to have used the terms of the earlier prophets – 'the hand of the LORD came upon [me]', 'the spirit lifted me and took me' (cp. e.g. 1: 3; 3: 14) – to describe them.

EZEKIEL AND OTHER PARTS OF THE OLD TESTAMENT

Beside the links with the early prophets, Ezekiel displays knowledge of the so-called 'writing prophets', especially

Isaiah, Hosea and Jeremiah. Like Isaiah he knew the common belief that Jerusalem, with its temple, was protected against all enemies because it was the dwelling-place of God. The prophecies of Hosea, though he was from the northern kingdom of Israel, are reflected at a number of points; this may have been partly due to Jeremiah's influence, for Jeremiah was most intimate with Hosea's message and Ezekiel in turn was familiar with many parts of Jeremiah's prophecy. Jeremiah may even have been known to Ezekiel personally before the latter's exile. Although neither prophet mentions the other, Ezekiel adapts numerous sayings of Jeremiah and may well be termed a disciple of his elder contemporary.

Like other prophets, the basis of Ezekiel's work was the belief that Israel was responsible to obey the law of the covenant made between his people and God. His prophecies of doom illustrated the inevitable outcome of behaviour which broke that agreement. The Ten Commandments and the Book of the Covenant (Exod. 20 and 21–3 respectively) were early forms of covenant law. Another law-code, in the form of material now incorporated in Deuteronomy, had been made much of in the religious and political reform of King Josiah toward the end of the seventh century B.C. (see on 6: 1–14). Ezekiel was aware of the code of Deuteronomy and shows evidence of agreement with some of its provisions. But he more often appeals to the covenant law now found in Lev. 17–26 as the basis for judgements of individuals or the nation of Israel. This so-called 'Holiness Code' calls Israel to obey the law so that it might be 'holy, because I, the LORD your God, am holy' (Lev. 19: 2). Ezekiel's familiarity with its tradition of law, though not with the code as a written document, suggests it may have derived from the priesthood of Jerusalem – or a group within that priesthood – with which Ezekiel was associated because of his priestly descent. There are also links in the book with the material in the Pentateuch (the first 'five books' of the Bible, Genesis to Deuteronomy), which came from what is termed the 'Priestly' author or

7

authors. This is composed of a narrative interspersed with earlier traditions of Israel's origins and – like the Holiness Code – was written down in exile. The Holiness Code is from the sixth century and the Priestly material possibly from the sixth, continuing into the fifth century B.C. (On these writings see also *The Making of the Old Testament*, pp. 108ff., in this series.)

THE STYLE, TEXT AND HISTORY OF THE BOOK

The literary style of Ezekiel is diverse. The prophet has employed a great range of imagery, some familiar from other parts of the Old Testament, some remarkably fresh and vivid. That which he has borrowed is often dramatized or its symbolism is drawn to almost bizarre lengths. In debate he follows the typical Near-Eastern fashion of exaggeration and seeming crudity in his frankness. He is a master of allegory and of fine poetry, but often words and phrases are repeated over and again for the sake of emphasis, and his painstaking elucidation of legal cases may seem irksome if thought is not given to the importance of the decisions to be reached.

If Ezekiel's work has links with the Pentateuch, it also has points of contrast. It is reported that when discussion took place about the composition of the Hebrew Bible some time prior to A.D. 70, Ezekiel's position within the Jewish scriptures was secured only after the rabbi Hananiah ben Hezekiah had burned 300 jars of oil, studying the prophecy in order to explain the differences between it and the already accepted laws of the Pentateuch. Even then, according to Jerome, a biblical scholar of the late fourth century A.D., rabbis forbade persons under thirty years of age to read the beginning or the end of the book. Speculation concerning the appearance of God and the other symbolism of the opening vision was regarded as dangerous. Within the Christian Church, how-ever, the book's authority as scripture has been unchallenged, and although it is rarely referred to elsewhere in the New

Testament, extensive use is made of its imagery in the book of Revelation.

At numerous points the Hebrew text of Ezekiel is extremely difficult to understand. As the N.E.B. footnotes indicate, the Hebrew is often 'obscure', the English rendering 'probable' but not certain. Fortunately the Greek version, the Septuagint, was translated from an earlier and shorter form of the Hebrew text than any we now possess. So we can see, by comparing the Greek and Hebrew, many places where the latter has been expanded or altered by scribes in the course of copying the text. In this short commentary only a few passages can be noted where this is important for showing that the Hebrew text has been expanded and elaborated by later scribes. However, the Greek translation is not correct throughout and cannot be solely relied upon to restore the original Hebrew. Help sometimes comes from Hebrew manuscripts dating from the ninth century A.D. onwards, or versions of the text in other languages may throw light on the meaning of words or phrases (see pp. ixf.). A complication with older Hebrew writing was that no vowels were used, nor were there any divisions into verses or chapters. Sometimes these factors have led to misunderstanding of words and the inadvertent reading into the text of words which scribes had added in the margin to help readers understand the themes of passages. Some instances are noted in the commentary.

✳   ✳   ✳   ✳   ✳   ✳   ✳   ✳   ✳   ✳   ✳   ✳   ✳   ✳

Ezekiel's call to be a prophet

✳ The first three chapters describe the awesome vision of God's glory and the command Ezekiel receives to prophesy. Parallels to the vision and call of Isaiah (ch. 6) are numerous. ✳

THE SETTING OF THE PROPHET'S CALL

1 ON THE FIFTH DAY of the fourth month in the
thirtieth year, while I was among the exiles by the
river Kebar,[a] the heavens were opened and I saw a vision
2 of God. On the fifth day of the month in the fifth year
3 of the exile of King Jehoiachin, the word of the LORD
came to Ezekiel son of Buzi the priest, in Chaldaea, by
the river Kebar, and there the hand of the LORD came
upon him.

✷ 1. *in the thirtieth year*: the date in this verse has been interpreted in a variety of ways. One suggestion is that it indicates
the prophet's age. If so, it establishes his authority as a priest,
since according to Num. 4 members of priestly families could
undertake priestly duties from the age of thirty. *the river
Kebar*: or Kebar canal, was a broad waterway which left the
river Euphrates near Babylon and flowed south-eastward
through the city of Nippur to rejoin the Euphrates near
Erech (see map, p. 169). *the heavens were opened*: Ezekiel would
have shared the idea common in his day of a 'three-decker'
universe, with the flat earth sandwiched between heaven and
the underworld (or Sheol). A close parallel to the image of the
sky opening to reveal God is found in Isa. 64: 1: 'why didst
thou not rend the heavens and come down?'
     2. *the fifth day of the month in the fifth year*: here the number of
the month has dropped out of the text (cp. 'the fourth month'
in verse 1). Most of the dates in the book mark the time of
exile of King Jehoiachin, implying that Ezekiel regarded him
as still the rightful ruler of Jerusalem, although he reigned only
three months after the death of his father, Jehoiakim (2 Kings
24: 8). In Babylon Jehoiachin was placed under some form of
arrest until the death of Nebuchadrezzar in 562 B.C. (2 Kings

[a] *Or* the Kebar canal.

25: 27f.). The months are reckoned according to the Babylonian calendar in which the new civil year began in the spring (cp. on 40: 1). The year was divided into twelve lunar months of thirty days each. By the periodic addition of an extra month, the calendar was made to correspond with the solar year, but only approximate dates can therefore be given in terms of present-day reckoning.

The fifth year of Jehoiachin's exile was 593 B.C. and the month June–July.

3. *Ezekiel son of Buzi the priest*: the words 'the priest' may refer to either Ezekiel or his father. *Chaldaea*: the southern Mesopotamian basin, dominated at this time by Chaldaeans from the Syro-Arabian desert. The Chaldaean kings Nabopolassar (625–605 B.C.) and his son Nebuchadrezzar (604–562 B.C.: written thus in Jeremiah and Ezekiel, elsewhere usually as Nebuchadnezzar) ruled the territory from Babylon. This verse is the only one in the book in which Ezekiel's experiences are described by someone else. We have to allow here for the editing of the book by Ezekiel's disciples. The book may once have begun with the first half of this verse: *the word of the LORD came to Ezekiel* ... Then followed the account of Ezekiel's experiences as if the prophet himself was describing them. As already mentioned (p. 2) such disorder is not uncommon in this book. The second half of the verse, *and there the hand of the LORD came upon him*, probably should read 'the hand of the LORD came upon me'. The same phrase occurs in four other places in the book (3: 22; 8: 1; 37: 1; 40: 1) and introduces accounts of visions.

Together these verses establish the book's worth. Not only was Ezekiel a priest, or the son of a priest, and so well versed in the traditions and religious practices of his people, but he had experienced a prophet's calling by vision (cp. Isa. 6; Jer. 1) and bore *the word of the LORD*. The problem of authority is crucial. The very nature of the things Ezekiel had to communicate to his people required that his authority be of the highest. If, as has been suggested, the book originally opened with the phrase *the word of the LORD came to Ezekiel*, its claim to be read as prophecy, commanding the attention of all who heard or read it, was established from the outset. For possession of the word of God marked out those who communicated the divine will to the people of Israel at large (so 2: 4f.). Also, the practice of dating prophetic passages seems to be related to the question of authority. Dates emphasized the truth of the divine word in particular situations of crisis or debate. But if the claim to bear the word of God is commonly found in Old Testament prophecy (cp. also Amos 7; Hos. 1), we read little of *the hand of the LORD* coming upon prophets. Where it is said to come upon Elijah and Elisha, however, it is related to times in those prophets' lives when something extraordinary happened to them. They were granted unusual physical power and endurance (1 Kings 18: 46) or were enabled to see things hidden from other men (2 Kings 3: 15). In the present case, Ezekiel saw a vision of something quite 'out of this world'. And he goes on to describe it. ✳

THE LIVING CREATURES

4 I saw a storm wind coming from the north, a vast cloud with flashes of fire and brilliant light about it; and within was a radiance like brass,*[a]* glowing in the heart of the
5 flames. In the fire was the semblance of four living
6 creatures in human form. Each had four faces and each
7 four wings; their legs were straight, and their hooves were like the hooves of a calf, glittering like a disc of
8 bronze. Under the wings on each of the four sides were
9 human hands; all four creatures had faces and wings, and their wings touched one another. They did not turn as
10 they moved; each creature went straight forward. Their

[a] *Mng. of Heb. word uncertain.*

faces were like this: all four had the face of a man and the face of a lion on the right, on the left the face of an ox and the face of an eagle. Their wings*[a]* were spread; each [11] living creature had one pair touching its neighbours',*[b]* while one pair covered its body. They moved straight [12] forward in whatever direction the spirit*[c]* would go; they never swerved in their course. The appearance of the [13] creatures was as if fire from burning coals or torches were darting to and fro among them; the fire was radiant, and out of the fire came lightning.*[d]*

✻ This and the two following sections show evidence of much reworking, in the course of which more and more details have been added to the original account of the vision. Indeed, some scholars believe it is no longer possible to find the prophet's own description of the vision. The N.E.B. has gone some way to providing a text less encumbered with repetitions and obscurities. But though suggestions will be given below about the possible original form, they should not be thought to represent a final solution to the many problems of this chapter. Ch. 10 has also been expanded by Ezekiel's followers, largely in dependence on this vision.

Attempts to picture the vision can only be tentative. Yet as some of the difficulties of the text are unravelled, the reader of today should not fail to appreciate the vision as most will have done through the centuries. That is to say, we should take seriously the visionary nature of Ezekiel's experience and appreciate these verses as a kind of moving, changing dream, fantastic in some features and obscuring as much as it reveals of the divine glory.

[a] So Sept.; Heb. adds and their faces.
[b] its neighbours': prob. rdg.; Heb. unintelligible.
[c] Or wind.
[d] Prob. rdg., cp. Sept.; Heb. adds (14) and the living creatures went out (prob. rdg.; Heb. obscure) and in like rays of light.

The living creatures call to mind the two cherubim set at either end of the ark of the covenant in the temple of Jerusalem (1 Kings 8: 6f.). The wings of the cherubim covered the ark, which was a wooden chest approximately 44 inches (111 cm) long, 26 inches (67 cm) wide and 26 inches high, and was thought of as the throne or as the footstool of Israel's God (1 Sam. 4: 4; 1 Chron. 28: 2).

4. *a storm wind. . .a vast cloud with flashes of fire*: the appearance of God is linked with the wind, cloud and lightning flashes of storms in a number of other places in the Old Testament (e.g. Exod. 19: 16). *coming from the north*: according to Babylonian mythology the home of the gods was in the north (cp. Isa. 14: 13). It is implied here that Israel's God retains his power, even though he chooses to live for a time in the traditional dwelling-place of the Babylonian deities. *and within was a radiance like brass, glowing in the heart of the flames*: this half-verse anticipates what is described in verse 27 and is one of the later expansions of the narrative.

5. *four living creatures*: the number *four* has special significance in Ezekiel and suggests the idea of completeness, as it does in the phrase 'the four corners of the earth' (Isa. 11: 12; cp. the four wings of the living creatures in the following verse; the four scenes of false worship in ch. 8; the four plagues in ch. 14).

6b, 11b. *and each (had) four wings. . .one pair (of each) touching its neighbours', while one pair covered its body*: these words represent the earliest material in verses 6–11. The reason for separating these half-verses from the rest is that they belong together on account of their subject-matter (the four wings of each living creature) and they contain a noun with a feminine suffix relating to the living creatures – literally 'their bodies' (fem.). While the cherubim of the ark of the covenant were two in number, and each of those cherubim had two wings, the number of individuals and wings is double in Ezekiel. The freedom of the prophets to adapt such traditional sacred imagery is further illustrated in Isa. 6, where in similar circumstances an unspecified number of seraphim, each with six wings, are described. Possibly Ezekiel was influenced by foreign religious symbolism, for reliefs and statuettes of four-winged creatures have been found in the Tigris–Euphrates region. While one pair of wings were for flight, the pair of wings which covered the body of each living creature served the same purpose as the pair which, for the sake of modesty, covered the legs or private parts of the seraphim in Isa. 6.

6a, 7–11a. Masculine suffixes relating to the living creatures in the first half of verse 6, and from verse 7 to the first half of verse 11, perhaps intentionally mark this material off from verses 6*b* and 11*b*. The details of the creatures' faces, feet, etc., which have been added at different times, succeed largely in confusing the general description of the creatures' 'human form' given in verse 5.

6a. Each had four faces: four-faced statuettes of gods have been found in Babylon.

7. their legs were straight: literally 'their legs (plural) were a straight leg (singular)' (see the following verse). *glittering like a disc of bronze*: this part of the description may owe something to verse 27 where 'glowing brass' is referred to.

8. Under the wings on each of the four sides were human hands: as with the number of feet in the previous verse we are left in some uncertainty about the number of hands. Did each face of each creature have hands and feet? The reference to *human hands* may have come from 10: 7.

10. the face of a man...of a lion...of an ox...(and) of an eagle: together with man, the three noblest and strongest creatures of the bird and animal worlds are represented in the service of God. The four appear again in the New Testament in Rev. 4: 7, which depends on this passage; later still they come to be symbols of the four evangelists: Matthew (man), Mark (lion), Luke (ox), John (eagle).

11a. Their wings were spread: i.e. the uppermost pair. The phrase calls to mind the outspread wings of the cherubim of the ark (Exod. 25: 20).

12. *They moved straight forward. . .; they never swerved in their course*: this is part of the earliest account of the vision. *in whatever direction the spirit would go*: these words do not appear even in the later material of verses 9 and 17, where motion is also mentioned.

13f. As the N.E.B. footnotes show, the Septuagint does not contain verse 14, and verse 13 is also later material calling to mind the 'smoking brazier' and 'flaming torch' which passed between the divided pieces of Abram's sacrifice in Gen. 15: 17. This represents an attempt by Ezekiel's disciples to establish the authority of the prophet's words by drawing on imagery of another, and perhaps by this time venerated, vision. (See also on 10: 2.) ✵

THE WHEELS BESIDE THE CREATURES

15 As I looked at the living creatures, I saw wheels on the
16 ground, one beside each of the four.[a] The wheels[b] sparkled like topaz, and they were all alike: in form and
17 working they were like a wheel inside a wheel, and when they moved in any of the four directions they never
18 swerved in their course. All four had hubs and each hub had a projection which had the power of sight,[c] and the
19 rims of the wheels were full of eyes all round. When the living creatures moved, the wheels moved beside them; when the creatures rose from the ground, the wheels
20 rose; they moved in whatever direction the spirit[d] would go; and the wheels rose together with them, for the
21 spirit of the living creatures was in the wheels. When the one moved, the other moved; when the one halted,

[a] one. . . four: *prob. rdg.; Heb. obscure.*
[b] *So Sept.; Heb. adds* and their works.
[c] the power of sight: *prob. rdg.; Heb.* fear.
[d] *Or* wind.

the other halted; when the creatures rose from the ground, the wheels rose together with them, for the spirit of the creatures was in the wheels.

✶ The report of the vision originally went directly on to describe the throne of God above the heads of the living creatures (verses 22–8*a*). But there has been inserted a somewhat puzzling description of wheels beside the creatures. The wheels may symbolize a mobile platform on which the ark of the covenant could be moved about (cp. 2 Sam. 6: 3ff.). When describing the interior of the temple, the late passage 1 Chron. 28: 18 actually refers to a 'chariot' in association with the ark. It is not surprising to find that the interest roused by Ezekiel's vision has led to the scene's elaboration by those who preserved and handed on his prophecy. It would have been done with reverent intent, to complete the vision by including in it other articles associated with the temple worship. There are secondary expansions even within this section. Verse 17 anticipates the movement of the wheels referred to in verses 19f.; verse 18 elaborates the appearance of the wheels; and verse 21, which is absent from some manuscripts, largely repeats verses 19f.

15. *on the ground*: it is now assumed that the living creatures were resting on the ground.

16. *topaz*: or some kind of precious, gold-coloured stone. *a wheel inside a wheel*: the interpretation usually given is that each of the four wheels appeared to have another smaller wheel bisecting it at right angles. Thus the possibility of movement forward, backward or to either side was indicated. Yet the wheeled platform, suggesting movement along the ground in a conventional manner, contrasts sharply with the throne borne through the air by the winged creatures.

18. Translation is difficult, but the verse conveys the idea of perpetual watchfulness over the world, just as the wheels within wheels suggest the presence of God in every place.

20. *the spirit*: the life force of the creatures, harmonizing their movement with the movement of the wheels. The source of the spirit is God himself (see on 2: 2). ✳

THE APPEARANCE OF GOD'S GLORY

22 Above the heads of the living creatures was, as it were, a vault glittering like a sheet of ice, awe-inspiring, stretched
23 over their heads above them. Under the vault their wings were spread straight out, touching one another, while
24 one pair covered the body of each.*ᵃ* I heard, too, the noise of their wings; when they moved it was like the noise of a great torrent or of a cloud-burst,*ᵇ* like the noise of a crowd or of an armed camp; when they halted
25 their wings dropped. A sound was heard above the vault over their heads, as they halted with drooping wings.
26 Above the vault over their heads there appeared, as it were, a sapphire*ᶜ* in the shape of a throne, and high above
27 all, upon the throne, a form in human likeness. I saw what might have been brass glowing like fire in a furnace from the waist upwards; and from the waist downwards
28a I saw what looked like fire with encircling radiance. Like a rainbow in the clouds on a rainy day was the sight of that encircling radiance; it was like the appearance of the glory of the LORD.

✳ The climax of the vision is the description of 'the appearance of the glory of the LORD' (verse 28a). The word for 'glory' was a technical term used when speaking of the presence of Israel's God among his people. Tradition had it that

[a] *So some MSS.; others repeat* one pair covered the body of each.
[b] *Or* of the Almighty.
[c] *Or* lapis lazuli.

to look on the face of God meant death (Exod. 33: 20), but his presence could be described in terms of a light or fire of blinding brightness, within a protective cloud (Exod. 19: 16–18; 40: 34–8). After the building of the Jerusalem temple, 'the glory of the LORD', signified by its protective cloud, was said to dwell in the holy of holies or innermost sanctuary of the temple, as a symbol of God's presence (1 Kings 8: 10f.). This came to mean in popular belief that God himself dwelt in the temple. Hence the protest, ascribed to Solomon by a later writer on the occasion of the dedication of the temple: 'Heaven itself, the highest heaven, cannot contain thee; how much less this house that I have built!' (1 Kings 8: 27).

A remarkable feature of this first chapter of Ezekiel is that the earthly manifestation of God ('the glory of the LORD') appears to the prophet far away from the temple in Jerusalem. The importance of this event can hardly be exaggerated for those who were accustomed to link the presence of God with a particular country or building. Until that time Ezekiel, like the rest of the exiles, would have felt himself, removed as he was from the central religious symbols of his faith, terribly isolated from all that gave meaning to life. Now, with the presence of God among the exiles quite evident, religious life and meaningful worship became a vital new possibility (cp. on 11: 16, and the encouragement in Jeremiah's letter to the exiles, Jer. 29: 1–9). Now there were not simply memories of worship in the Jerusalem temple, but there was the possibility of experiencing God's presence in a foreign land. The novelty of the event is emphasized by the use five times in the chapter of a word translated 'semblance' or 'like(ness)' or 'as it were' (verses 5, 10, 22). To some degree the word conveys the eerie half-knowledge of a dream, and in part its use reflects the respect due the divine majesty. As though it was too bold to speak, except in veiled terms, of the manifestation of God in Babylon, the appearance of his glory and all that accompanied it is described as an image or symbol of the reality itself.

Verses 23–6 elaborate the earlier description of the living creatures. The prophet himself describes a platform ('vault') on which God's throne rested, and on the throne sat the mysterious 'form in human likeness'.

22. *vault*: the word is used in Gen. 1: 6–8 to signify a hemisphere of hammered metal, separating the heavens from the water over the earth. Here a flat surface seems to be indicated. *awe-inspiring*: hardly fitting at this point and absent from the Septuagint.

23–5. The first of these verses partly repeats verse 11; the second shares the interest of 10: 5 in the sound of the creatures' wings; and the third anticipates the voice originally introduced in verse 28. All are later additions.

26. *sapphire*: Exod. 24: 10 describes 'a pavement of sapphire' under God's feet.

28*a*. *a rainbow in the clouds*: an image used later by the Priestly authors as a sign of God's covenant with mankind (Gen. 9: 12–17). *

A MESSAGE OF WOE

28*b* When I saw this I threw myself on my face, and heard
2 a voice speaking to me: Man,*ª* he said, stand up, and let
2 me talk with you. As he spoke, a spirit came into me and
3 stood me on my feet, and I listened to him speaking. He said to me, Man, I am sending you to the Israelites, a nation of rebels who have rebelled against me. Past generations of them have been in revolt against me to this
4 very day, and this generation to which I am sending you is stubborn and obstinate. When you say to them, 'These
5 are the words of the Lord GOD', they will know that they have a prophet among them, whether they listen or
6 whether they refuse to listen, because they are rebels. But

[a] *Lit.* Son of man *and so throughout the book when Ezekiel is addressed.*

you, man, must not be afraid of them or of what they
say, though they are rebels against you and renegades,
and you find yourself sitting on scorpions. There is
nothing to fear in what they say, and nothing in their
looks to terrify you, rebels though they are. You must 7
speak my words to them, whether they listen or whether
they refuse to listen, rebels that they are. But you, man, 8
must listen to what I say and not be rebellious like them.
Open your mouth and eat what I give you.

Then I saw a hand stretched out to me, holding a scroll. 9
He unrolled it before me, and it was written all over on 10
both sides with dirges and laments and words of woe.
Then he said to me, 'Man, eat what is in front of you, **3**
eat this scroll; then go and speak to the Israelites.' So I 2
opened my mouth and he gave me the scroll to eat. Then 3
he said, 'Man, swallow this scroll I give you, and fill
yourself full.' So I ate it, and it tasted as sweet as honey.

✳ Raised from the ground, where he had fallen at the sight
of God's glory, Ezekiel receives his prophetic commission.
At this point the narrative becomes quite explicit. Jer. I: 9
describes God stretching out a hand and putting his words in
Jeremiah's mouth. In Ezekiel the same action occurs, but with
much additional detail. The words are contained in a written
scroll, which must be unrolled, its contents described, and
then consumed. Thus there seems to be a restatement of
Jeremiah's account of his call, heavily dramatized in a fashion
typical of Ezekiel. It is God's voice which addresses the prophet, first warning him of Israel's obstinacy and assuring him
of divine protection. Such ideas appear in the commissionings
of Isaiah and Jeremiah also, but there is here another emphasis
characteristic of Ezekiel's prophecy. His people's past is one
of almost unrelieved rebellion. The accusation that Israel is a

rebellious nation recurs time and again in chs. 1–24, which are mostly devoted to declaring the woeful message of the scroll. There are only minor expansions of the text in this section.

28*b*. *I threw myself*: literally 'I fell', suggesting that the prophet did not merely lie prostrate on account of reverence for God, but that he was so shocked by the vision that he collapsed on the ground. This has been thought by some scholars to confirm evidence elsewhere in the prophecy (e.g. 3: 15; 33: 22) that Ezekiel was prone to some kind of periodic seizures or fits. In any event, his state of shock seems apparent and though he is commanded to stand, it is 'a spirit' which actually stands the prophet on his feet (see on 2: 2).

2: 1. *Man*: see N.E.B. footnote. The name emphasizes the humble status of the prophet as a mere mortal, before the divine majesty of the Creator. The meaning of the name 'man' or 'son of man' in Ezekiel should be clearly distinguished from its meaning in Dan. 7: 13f., where it is used of a figure of great power, a meaning of importance in the New Testament.

2. *a spirit came into me*: the Hebrew word for *spirit* (*rūaḥ*) may mean 'wind' or 'breath'. These were both thought to originate from God but they lacked the close association with God that the term 'the spirit of the LORD' has later in Ezekiel (see on 37: 1). Here it is *spirit* – undefined – which raises Ezekiel to his feet, supplements and revives his physical powers, like a fresh 'breath of life' (cp. Gen. 2: 7).

4. *the Lord GOD*: the Hebrew word normally translated 'the LORD' was originally used alone throughout the prophecy. When the custom developed of not pronouncing that Hebrew name, since it was too holy, another title for God was added beside it. This occurs frequently in Ezekiel.

6. *though they are rebels against you and renegades*: it seems preferable to read for the difficult text here, 'though thorns surround you'. The people are rebels against God; their rebellion may bring hostility, both verbal and physical, against his messengers.

9f. Scrolls usually contained writing on just one side. But this scroll was so full of words of judgement, which would bring deep grief, that the writing overflowed to cover the back as well. The image of the scroll serves to dramatize the fact that the words Ezekiel speaks are not his own but are given to him by God, and it is evidence of the growing importance of writing as a means of communicating God's word. It may even reflect knowledge of Jeremiah's scroll, with its warnings that awaited fulfilment (Jer. 36: 1–4).

3: 3. *it tasted as sweet as honey*: not a sign that the prophet took a morbid delight in his woeful task. Rather the phrase affirms the saying found elsewhere that God's word was sweet (Ps. 19: 10; 119: 103). That word became part of the prophet's life, expressed in all that he said and did. Sensations of taste within visionary experiences are reported in other literature. ✳

DUMBFOUNDED AMONG THE EXILES

Man, he said to me, go and tell the Israelites what I have 4 to say to them. You are sent not to people whose speech is 5 thick and difficult, but to Israelites. No; I am not sending 6 you to great nations whose speech is so thick and so difficult that you cannot make out what they say; if however I had sent you to them they would have listened to you. But 7 the Israelites will refuse to listen to you, for they refuse to listen to me, so brazen are they all and stubborn. But 8 I will make you a match for them. I will make you as brazen as they are and as stubborn as they are. I will 9 make your brow like adamant, harder than flint. Never fear them, never be terrified by them, rebels though they are. And he said to me, Listen carefully, man, to all 10 that I have to say to you, and take it to heart. Go to your 11 fellow-countrymen in exile and speak to them. Whether they listen or refuse to listen, say, 'These are the words of the Lord GOD.'

12 Then a spirit*a* lifted me up, and I heard behind me a fierce rushing sound as the glory of the LORD rose*b* from
13 his place. I heard the sound of the living creatures' wings brushing against one another, the sound of the wheels
14 beside them, and a fierce rushing sound. A spirit*a* lifted me and carried me along, and I went full of exaltation,
15 the hand of the LORD strong upon me. So I came to the exiles at Tel-abib who were settled by the river Kebar.*c* For seven days I stayed with them, dumbfounded.

✵ Having received his commission Ezekiel is now sent to prophesy, encouraged by the promise of strength to meet all resistance.

4. *the Israelites*: literally 'the house of Israel'. Ezekiel never uses this term of the people of northern Israel as distinct from those of the southern kingdom of Judah. Most frequently it refers to the people of Jerusalem and Judah, who claimed the honoured title after the fall of Samaria, the northern capital in 722 B.C. But sometimes it refers to both northern and southern kingdoms, including past generations of Israelites (cp. 2: 3), which suggests that the prophet used it of all the people who had joined in the covenant with God (hence the term 'the God of Israel', Exod. 24: 10). Ezekiel's mission was ultimately to the whole contemporary generation of Israelites, whether in Jerusalem and Judah or in exile. Although, as verse 11 indicates, his immediate audience was his fellow-exiles, Ezekiel does not always distinguish clearly between the Israelites in Judah and in Babylon. They share equally the guilt of their whole nation. He often seems quite unconscious

[a] *Or* wind.
[b] rose: *prob. rdg.; Heb. obscure.*
[c] *So some MSS.; others add* and where they were living.

of the miles that separated them. His prophecies against Jerusalem are spoken and acted out with implicit belief in their fulfilment, even though they were observed only by the exiled representatives of Israel.

5f. *thick and difficult*: to Israelite ears foreign languages sounded guttural and heavy. But since he speaks their own tongue, Ezekiel's listeners will not have the excuse of failing to comprehend his message.

7. Like Isaiah (Isa. 6: 9f.), Ezekiel is warned that there will be no favourable response to his mission, though the possibility of such a response is indicated (2: 5; 3: 11).

8f. Jeremiah's account of his call is again reflected in these verses. As he was fortified (Jer. 1: 18), so too is Ezekiel. There may also be a word-play on the prophet's name, for Ezekiel means 'God makes strong or hard'.

11. *Go to your fellow-countrymen in exile*: see on verse 4.

13. This later addition, partly based on 1: 23f., explains the 'fierce rushing sound' of the previous verse.

14f. It is implied that the site of the vision was some distance from the exile settlement, for it is to the latter place that Ezekiel now returns. The prophet's intense awareness that he was undergoing an abnormal experience is indicated by his reference to *the hand of the LORD* being strong upon him. Again it is *A spirit* which transports the prophet in his visionary experience, as a result of which he remains for a week overwhelmed and speechless. *full of exaltation*: literally 'in the heat of my spirit', that is with a feeling of great excitement. *Tel-abib*: the exiles apparently used this as the name of their settlement, and it has been used (written Tel Aviv) for a city of the modern state of Israel. The word 'Tel' is used of a mound covering a deserted city. *

APPOINTED AS A WATCHMAN

16 At the end of seven days the word of the LORD came to
17 me: Man, I have made you a watchman for the Israelites;
you will take messages from me and carry my warnings
18 to them. It may be that I pronounce sentence of death
on a wicked man:[a] if you do not warn him to give up
his wicked ways and so save his life, the guilt is his;
because of his wickedness he shall die, but I will hold you
19 answerable for his death.[b] But if you have warned him
and he still continues in his wicked and evil ways, he
shall die because of his wickedness, but you will have saved
20 yourself. Or it may be that a righteous man turns away and
does wrong, and I let that be the cause of his downfall; he
will die because you have not warned him. He will die for
his sin; the righteous deeds he has done will not be taken
into account, and I will hold you answerable for his death.
21 But if you have warned the righteous man not to sin and
he has not sinned, then he will have saved his life because
he has been warned, and you will have saved yourself.

✻ Later in Ezekiel's life he received another commission, to
exercise a pastoral function among his people. He was to be
responsible for warning the wicked individually of approaching punishment. This second, and novel, task for the prophet
seems to have arisen in response to the exiles' despair after the
fall of Jerusalem. It is announced more fully in ch. 33, and
verses 16*b*–19 of the present chapter are essentially the same as
33: 7–9. So it seems that an editor has introduced 3: 16*b*–21
at this point to invest Ezekiel's later role with the same auth-

[a] *Prob. rdg.; Heb. adds* if you do not warn him.
[b] *Lit.* I will require his blood from your hand.

ority as his initial call and to give a glimpse of the more hopeful task of the prophet's later life. Verse 16*a*, *At the end of seven
days*, originally introduced the prophecy of 4: 1ff. The remainder of this section will be dealt with in the commentary
on ch. 33. ✶

The impending ruin of Jerusalem

✶ The N.E.B. has made three divisions of chapters 3 : 22 – 24:
27, but the titles of each must be regarded with caution. For
any one of the three titles – *The impending ruin of Jerusalem*
(3 : 22 – 7: 27), *Jerusalem's guilt and punishment* (chs. 8–11) and
Jerusalem's downfall certain (chs. 12–24) – could apply as well
to another or to all the divisions. The point is important, for
the reader should not assume a growing awareness on
Ezekiel's part that the words he spoke would be fulfilled.
Ezekiel appears to have envisaged from the beginning of his
prophetic activity the certain downfall of the city whose sin
was so gross that God had to act against it for his own
honour's sake. The themes by which the diverse elements of
3: 22 – 7: 27 are linked editorially are the portrayal of
Jerusalem and Judah under siege and under threat from three
plagues. But these themes are much less apparent in chs. 6 and
7, for both chapters focus on other topics – the corrupt places
of worship in the countryside and the approaching 'end'
respectively. The passage 3: 22 – 5: 17 contains the first in a
series of prophecies which Ezekiel is commanded to act out.
Examination of this kind of prophecy elsewhere indicates
that the divine instruction may be given, mention made of
its execution and then an interpretation given of its meaning
(e.g. Jer. 13: 1–11). And even where each of these three stages
is not mentioned their fulfilment may be inferred. Thus,
although Ezekiel frequently mentions only the command to
perform an acted prophecy, the fact that he does perform it
may be taken for granted. ✶

BOUND AND SPEECHLESS

22 THE HAND OF THE LORD CAME UPON ME there, and he said to me, Rise up; go out into the plain, and
23 there I will speak to you. So I rose and went out into the plain; the glory of the LORD was there, like the glory which I had seen by the river Kebar, and I threw myself down
24 on my face. Then a spirit came into me and stood me on my feet, and spoke to me: Go, he said, and shut yourself
25 up in your house. You shall be tied and bound with ropes, man, so that you cannot go out among the people.
26 I will fasten your tongue to the roof of your mouth and you will be unable to speak; you will not be the one to
27 rebuke them, rebels though they are. But when I have something to say to you, I will give you back the power of speech. Then you will say to them, 'These are the words of the Lord GOD.' If anyone will listen, he may listen, and, if he refuses to listen, he may refuse; for they are rebels.

✻ As in the previous section, a later event in the prophet's life is reflected in these verses. Some time before the fall of Jerusalem, Ezekiel lost the power of speech. This was regarded as a sign to the exiles of the speechless shock they would feel at the news of Jerusalem's destruction (24: 15–27). Ezekiel's original commission was to declare God's word to the exiles and chs. 4–24 are evidence that he did so. But like 3: 16*b*–21, these verses prepare the way for a subsequent event of major significance for the prophet, although they are confusing in their present context. The complicated interweaving of several elements of the prophecy suggests that Ezekiel's followers, handling the material with a considerable degree of freedom, have been responsible for these verses and their insertion here.

28

22–24*a*. The allusions to the first vision of the prophet are borrowed from other passages. The location in *the plain* derives from 37: 1.

24*b*–25. The command that the prophet should retire to his house and be bound with ropes is related to the acted prophecy of 4: 4–8, which was probably performed later in Ezekiel's life than is suggested by its position at the beginning of the book.

26. The connection of these verses with Ezekiel's later dumbness has already been mentioned. The apparent contradiction between dumbness at this early stage and the fulfilment of his calling is explained in verse 27 by the periodic restoration of speech to enable the delivery of prophecies. The theme of dumbness is used to underline the point that the word which the prophet speaks is God's, not his own. ✻

A SIGN OF SIEGE

Man, take a tile and set it before you. Draw a city on it, **4** the city of Jerusalem: lay siege to it, erect watch-towers 2 against it, raise a siege-ramp, put mantelets in position, and bring battering-rams against it all round. Then take 3 an iron griddle, and put it as a wall of iron between you and the city. Keep your face turned towards the city; it will be the besieged and you the besieger. This will be a sign to the Israelites.

✻ Originally 3: 16*a* (see p. 27) introduced these verses. After sitting dumbfounded for seven days the prophet receives the first command to perform an acted prophecy. There are two distinct prophetic signs here. Verses 1–2 describe the siege of a city portrayed in clay. In the first half of verse 3 an iron plate is employed to symbolize God's determination not to withdraw punishment from the city. But the second half of the verse combines the two images, holding them to be a single sign, and indeed they have a single ominous meaning.

1. *a tile*: clay bricks were commonly used for building construction in Babylon. Before baking, the soft clay surface was suitable for writing or drawing, and architects' plans were sometimes sketched on bricks. *the city of Jerusalem*: an explanatory note, anticipating the subsequent interpretation of the sign.

2. Around the brick Ezekiel is to model the weapons of siege that will give an enemy access to the city.

3. *Keep your face turned*: in Ezekiel, the turning of God's face toward a person or thing implies that God's power is active, whether for good or for evil, in respect to the object of his gaze. In the present case evil is clearly intended as the prophet, representing God, faces the city he has sketched in clay. ✳

A BEARER OF INIQUITY

4 Now lie on your left side, and I will lay Israel's iniquity on you; you shall bear their iniquity for as many days
5 as you lie on that side. Allowing one day for every year of their iniquity, I ordain that you bear it for one[a] hundred and ninety days; thus you shall bear Israel's iniquity.
6 When you have completed all this, lie down a second time on your right side, and bear Judah's iniquity for
7 forty days; I count one day for every year. Then turn your face towards the siege of Jerusalem and bare your
8 arm, and prophesy against it. See how I tie you with ropes so that you cannot turn over from one side to the other until you complete the days of your distress.

✳ A very complex process of growth underlies these verses. The passage originated with the instruction to Ezekiel in

[a] *So Sept.; Heb.* three.

verse 4 to lie on his side and bear the iniquity of Israel. There may be reflected here a period of confinement and physical restraint, related to the prophet's period of dumbness before the fall of Jerusalem (24: 27; 33: 22). Whatever the actual circumstances were, Ezekiel regarded the event, like everything else that happened to him, as a sign from God for his people. His followers have linked the sign, by way of verses 7f., with the symbolic siege Ezekiel mounted against the city in verses 1–3. His time of physical restraint, in which he saw himself as suffering on behalf of Israel, thus became an unspecified period during which he was compelled to maintain the acted prophecy of siege. At a later stage the kind of additional material we have already seen in ch. 1 has been added, first in verse 5. The interest of the prophet's followers at this point was to calculate the period of the nation's iniquity. The Hebrew text preserves one calculation – the iniquity of Israel extended back for 390 years (see the footnote). The Greek text, followed by the N.E.B., represents another calculation of 190 years. Complicating the passage even further is the assignment of a separate period of punishment for Judah in verse 6. Ezekiel himself believed his people's iniquity began even before the exodus from Egypt (20: 8). But when it is realized that these calculations originated with his followers, there is no need to resort to the explanations sometimes given, by appeal to prolonged seizures or the powers of Hindu yogis, of how the prophet could have lain so long on his side.

4. *left*: since directions were taken from the east, facing the rising sun, the left is the northern side, the direction of the northern kingdom. This word was added only after the distinction had been made between the two kingdoms. *Israel*: this originally referred to the people of Judah and Jerusalem (see on 3: 4). *you shall bear their iniquity*: the image of one person suffering in place of many is more fully elaborated in the theme of the Suffering Servant in the exilic prophecies of the Second Isaiah (e.g. Isa. 52: 13 – 53: 12), a theme that was so important for Jesus' understanding of his

task. But here it represents an important development in prophecy, for Ezekiel no longer stands over against his people as God's representative, but is fully identified with them, even bearing punishment on their behalf. *iniquity*: as well as meaning the offence or wickedness itself, the Hebrew word so rendered could mean 'the guilt, or punishment of iniquity'.

5f. *one day for every year*: compare the penalty calculated by Priestly authors on the basis of 'a year for each day' in Num. 14: 34. *one hundred and ninety days*: the Hebrew text's figure of 'three hundred and ninety days', or years, covered in Israelite reckoning the period from the consecration of Solomon's temple until its destruction in 587 B.C. Ezekiel's observation of great corruption in the temple (ch. 8) may have suggested this period. With the distinction between Israel and Judah created by the addition of verse 6, however, the Greek text's 'one hundred and ninety days', or years, seems intended to cover the period from the exile of the northern kingdom to the fall of Jerusalem (approximately 150 years), plus 40 years' exile for Judah. For by the addition of these verses the sign of the prophet's suffering has become a prediction of the end of the exile in Babylon. 'Forty years' could serve as a general term for a generation, a generation which was to suffer for its sins just as once Israel wandered 'forty years' in the wilderness on account of its earlier iniquity (see again Num. 14: 34). The Israelites from the north, in exile from their homeland for nearly 190 years, and those from the south, in exile for about 40 years, will be freed together. *right side*: towards the south.

7. Like the turning of the prophet's face (verse 3), the 'bared arm' is a sign of God's activity (Isa. 52: 10).

8. Unlike the other prophecies of chs. 4–5, it is God who acts here and not the prophet. This verse precludes the possibility of Ezekiel turning from side to side, and it must therefore be earlier than the allocation of a separate period of punishment for Judah in verse 6. ✻

LIFE UNDER SIEGE

Then take wheat and barley, beans and lentils, millet 9
and spelt. Mix them all in one bowl and make your
bread out of them. You are to eat it during the one[a]
hundred and ninety days you spend lying on your side.
And you must weigh out your food; you may eat 10
twenty shekels' weight a day, taking it from time to
time. Measure out your drinking water too; you may 11
drink a sixth of a hin a day, taking it from time to time.
You are to eat your bread baked like barley cakes, using 12
human dung as fuel, and you must bake it where people
can see you. Then the LORD said, 'This is the kind of 13
bread, unclean bread, that the Israelites will eat in the
foreign lands into which I shall drive them.' But I said, 'O 14
Lord GOD, I have never been made unclean, never in
my life have I eaten what has died naturally or been
killed by wild beasts; no tainted meat has ever passed my
lips.' So he allowed me to use cow-dung instead of 15
human dung to bake my bread.

Then he said to me, Man, I am cutting short their 16
daily bread[b] in Jerusalem; people will weigh out anxiously
the bread they eat, and measure with dismay the water
they drink. So their food and their water will run short 17
until they are dismayed at the sight of one another; they
will waste away because of their iniquity.

✻ The next acted prophecy, in verses 9*a* and 10f., involves
careful rationing of food, which will be necessary under the
impending siege. An attempt has been made in verse 9*b* to

[a] *So Sept.; Heb.* three.
[b] *Lit.* breaking the stick of bread.

link the prophecy with the previous section, and verses 12–15 portray the conditions of exile rather than of siege. Verses 16f. are an independent prophecy, but their evident connections with the sign of rationing food have led to their insertion at this point.

9*a*. Every available grain is gathered to provide food, even the small millet seed and spelt, an inferior kind of wheat.

9*b*. *You are to eat it. . .*: this represents the same stage of tradition as verse 5 in the previous section. There is no distinction between Israel and Judah and no reference to which side the prophet is to lie on.

10f. The picture is one of great scarcity. The ration of the poor-quality bread is about 8 ounces (228 gm) daily, to be eaten at set times. Access to water, as well as to the fields, is restricted, so a daily water ration of $1\frac{1}{3}$ pints (0.76 litres) is allowed.

12–15. The words *where people can see you* (verse 12) indicate that this further acted prophecy belongs to the kind found in ch. 12, which are signs of exile. We are not told of any observers of the signs of siege in chs. 4–5.

12. *barley cakes* were baked on stones (1 Kings 19: 6), heated with a fuel of animal dung, often mixed with straw. *human dung* was ritually unclean and was always buried to prevent defilement (Deut. 23: 12–14).

13. This later interpretative statement interrupts the command to the prophet (verse 12) and his response (verse 14). It specifies the impurity of the exiles' food by reason of its contact, however indirectly, with human dung. And it calls to mind the belief that in countries where Israel's God was not worshipped the land and its produce were also unclean (Hos. 9: 3).

14. Ezekiel's protest emphasizes the importance to him of ritual purity. For the prohibitions concerning animals which had died naturally or been killed by beasts, see Deut. 14: 21 and Exod. 22: 31 respectively. *tainted meat*: the meat of shared-offerings three days old (Lev. 19: 5–8).

34

15. A concession is made – at least to the prophet – in the matter of cooking with human dung. But the stigma of eating in an unclean land still attaches to the prophecy. This suggests there were well-recognized degrees of impurity. It is interesting to compare in the New Testament the very different reply to Peter's request that he be allowed to avoid unclean food: 'it is not for you to call profane what God counts clean' (Acts 10: 15).

16f. The interpretation of the acted prophecy of rationing, which follows in 5: 5ff., is anticipated here. The words *anxiously* and *with dismay* have been added from 12: 19. ✲

THE OUTCOME OF THE SIEGE

Man, take a sharp sword, take it like a barber's razor and 5 run it over your head and your chin. Then take scales and divide the hair into three. When the siege comes to 2 an end, burn one third of the hair in a fire in the centre of the city; cut up one third with the sword all round the city; scatter one third to the wind, and I will follow it with drawn sword. Take a few of these hairs and tie 3 them up in a fold of your robe. Then take others of them, 4 throw them into the fire and burn them, and out of them fire will come upon all Israel.

✲ The third acted prophecy of siege (verses 1f.) envisages the fate of the besieged people. Over a century earlier Isaiah had prophesied a time when Judah would be shaved by the razor of Assyria (Isa. 7: 20). Ezekiel is told to act out that prophecy, so giving it fresh meaning for the immediate future. Among many peoples human hair can represent the person from whom it comes. It is carefully disposed of and care is taken to prevent it falling into the hands of enemies, for what happens to the hair is believed to become the fate of its original owner. In the prophecy, Ezekiel's hair symbolizes the hair of those under the siege portrayed in clay (4: 1f.). The addition in verses 3f. is from a time after the fall of Jerusalem.

2. The verse contains a number of additions of minor importance. Originally it read 'burn one third of the hair in a fire; cut up one third with the sword; and scatter one third to the wind'. The fire represented death from the hardships of the siege; the sword, death at the hands of those besieging the city; and the wind was a figure of exile for those who survived the siege.

3–4*a*. These verses alleviate the disastrous outcome of the preceding prophecy. Some exiles will be protected from harm. Tying hairs in a robe alludes to God's care of those whom he wraps up and puts with his own treasure (1 Sam. 25: 29). But there will also be a further act of judgement in terms of consuming fire. This parallel with the prophecy of a new exodus (20: 32–8) suggests that these verses concern the whole exiled community and not only those who escape the siege. They are, moreover, an indirect exhortation to obedience, illustrating the way the prophet's earlier words were adapted to a changed situation, either by the prophet himself or by his followers.

4*b*. *and out of them fire will come upon all Israel*: these words are best accounted for by assuming the verse has been altered in the light of 19: 14, 'fire bursts forth from its own branches'. The Septuagint reads: 'and you shall say to the whole people of Israel', implying that originally the phrase served to introduce 5: 5ff. ✳

THE MEANING OF THE SIEGE SIGNS

5 These are the words of the Lord GOD: This city of Jerusalem I have set among the nations, with other countries
6 around her, and she has rebelled against my laws and my statutes more wickedly than those nations and countries; for her people have rejected my laws and refused to conform to my statutes.

7 Therefore the Lord GOD says: Since you have been

more ungrateful than the nations around you and have
not conformed to my statutes and have not kept my laws
or even the laws of the nations around you, therefore, 8
says the Lord GOD, I, in my turn, will be against you; I
will execute judgements in your midst for the nations to
see, such judgements as I have never executed before 9
nor ever will again, so abominable have your offences
been. Therefore, O Jerusalem, fathers will eat their 10
children and children their fathers in your midst; I will
execute judgements on you, and any who are left in you
I will scatter to the four winds. As I live, says the Lord 11
GOD, because you have defiled my holy place with all
your vile and abominable rites, I in my turn will consume
you without pity; I in my turn will not spare you. One 12
third of your people shall die by pestilence and perish
by famine in your midst; one third shall fall by the sword
in the country round about; and one third I will scatter
to the four winds and follow with drawn sword. Then 13
my anger will be spent, I will abate my fury against them
and be calm; when my fury is spent they will know that
it is I, the LORD, who spoke in jealous passion. I have 14
made you a scandal*a* and a reproach to the nations
around you, and all who pass by will see it. You*b* will be 15
an object of reproach and abuse, a terrible lesson to the
nations around you, when I pass sentence on you and do
judgement in anger and fury. I, the LORD, have spoken.
When I shoot the deadly arrows of famine against you,*c* 16
arrows of destruction, I will shoot to destroy you. I will
bring famine upon you and cut short your daily bread;*d*

[a] *Or* desolation   [b] *So Sept.; Heb.* She.   [c] *Prob. rdg.; Heb.* them.
[d] *Lit.* and break your stick of bread.

¹⁷ I will unleash famine and beasts of prey upon you, and they will leave you childless. Pestilence and slaughter will sweep through you, and I will bring the sword upon you. I, the LORD, have spoken.

✻ Having made it clear that complete disaster was going to overtake the inhabitants of the besieged city, it remained only for Ezekiel to declare the city's identity. Sustaining the sense of drama evident throughout the prophecies of siege, he announces briefly: 'This is Jerusalem!' The reason for the prophecies (verses 5-6*a*) and God's sentence on the city (verses 8f. and 14f.) then follows. There is no attempt to interpret specific features of the acted prophecies, except in the additional material from Ezekiel's disciples. Unexpected changes of number, person and gender are evidence of the complicated growth of the passage.

5. Jerusalem was believed to be the centre of the world (cp. 38: 12), and such claims for their capitals have been made by other nations. In Jerusalem's case the claim was founded on God's gift to Israel of his law, which was intended to make the nation among whom God had his dwelling-place an example to all peoples (cp. Isa. 2: 2-4; Mic. 4: 1-3).

6*a*. *laws*: conditional laws of the type, 'if or when you do so-and-so, then such-and-such must follow' (cp. Exod. 21: 1ff.). *statutes*: unconditional commands or prohibitions, familiar from the so-called Ten Commandments, 'you shall or you shall not do this or that' (cp. Exod. 20: 3ff.).

6*b*-7. *for her people have rejected. . .*: Ezekiel's followers, in a restatement of the charge, have sought to emphasize the comparative wickedness of Israel. *and have not kept. . .even the laws of the nations*: Israel has not even followed the common standards of justice, let alone obeyed God's commands.

8f., 14f. The sentence on the city is all the more forceful for its brevity. The nations that should have been able to see in Israel a people whose life was governed by God's law will instead see an example of God's judgement executed against her proud capital. For *I have made you a scandal* (verse 14), read 'I will make you . . .'.

10. The threat of enforced cannibalism is made elsewhere in the Old Testament and the eating of children is attested in the siege of Samaria (2 Kings 6: 29). The thought that children should eat their parents was especially repulsive in a society that put much stress on honouring parents (Exod. 20: 12). The scattering of those who remain reflects 5: 2.

11–13. Here the allusions to the fate of the besieged in 5: 1f. are interpreted. An important formula, which characterizes the book of Ezekiel, is first found in verse 13*b*: *they will know that it is I, the LORD*. The phrase indicates that God's power and purpose will be recognized by the fulfilment of his words to the prophet.

16f. A further attempt to specify the means of destruction in terms of traditional lists of plagues – famine, wild beasts, pestilence and war. The number four suggested the completeness of the punishment, as in 14: 13–21. ✳

AGAINST ISRAEL'S MOUNTAINS

These were the words of the LORD to me: Man, look **6**₁,₂ towards the mountains of Israel, and prophesy to them: Mountains of Israel, hear the word of the Lord GOD. ₃ This is his word to mountains and hills, watercourses and valleys: I am bringing a sword against you, and I will destroy your hill-shrines. Your altars will be made ₄ desolate, your incense-altars shattered, and I will fling down your slain before your idols. I will strew the corpses ₅ of the Israelites before their idols, and I will scatter your bones about your altars. In all your settlements the blood- ₆ spattered altars*ᵃ* shall be laid waste and the hill-shrines

[a] blood-spattered altars: *or* cities.

made desolate. Your altars will be waste and desolate and your idols shattered and useless, your incense-altars hewn

7 down, and all your works wiped out; with the slain falling about you, you shall know that I am the LORD.

8 But when they fall,[a] I will leave you, among the nations, some who survive the sword. When you are scattered in

9 foreign lands, these survivors, in captivity among the nations, will remember how I was grieved because their hearts had turned wantonly from me and their eyes had gone roving wantonly after idols. Then they will loathe themselves for all the evil they have done with their

10 abominations. So they will know that I am the LORD, that I was uttering no vain threat when I said that I would bring this evil upon them.

11 These are the words of the Lord GOD: Beat your hands together, stamp with your foot, bemoan your vile abominations, people of Israel. Men will fall by sword,

12 famine, and pestilence. Far away they will die by pestilence; at home they will fall by the sword; any who survive or are spared will die by famine, and so at last

13 my anger will be spent. You will know that I am the LORD when their slain fall among the idols round their altars, on every high hill, on all mountain-tops, under every spreading tree, under every leafy terebinth, wherever they have brought offerings of soothing odour for

14 their idols one and all. So I will stretch out my hand over them and make the land a desolate waste in all their settlements, more desolate than the desert of Riblah.[b] They shall know that I am the LORD.

[a] when they fall: *prob. rdg.; Heb. obscure.*
[b] *Prob. rdg.; Heb.* Diblah.

✳ There are three separate prophecies here. The first (verses 1–7), addressed to Israel's mountains, concerns the country sanctuaries outlawed during Josiah's reform of 621 B.C., on the basis of the deuteronomic law found in the temple (2 Kings 22–3). The second (verses 8–10), from a later period, presupposes the existence of survivors from Judah and Jerusalem. The third (verses 11–13*a*) is addressed to the people of Israel and has been loosely associated with the first prophecy by an editor's addition of verses 13*b*–14.

2. For looking toward a person or place, see on 4: 3. Visual contact with the subject of prophecy is excluded in this case. *the mountains of Israel*: the whole land of Israel is meant, as the next verse indicates.

3f. *hill-shrines*: although they were not necessarily built in high places (Jer. 7: 31) they generally conveyed a sense of nearness to the heavenly dwelling-place of the gods. Originally Canaanite sanctuaries, they were apparently acceptable places of worship in Israel's early period (1 Sam. 9: 12; 1 Kings 3: 4). Animal offerings were slaughtered on the *altars*, on top of which were sometimes set small *incense-altars* or stands where fragrant-smelling gums and spices were burnt. The favourite Hebrew word in Ezekiel for *idols* is a – probably intentional – pun on the word for 'dung'. Whether or not Josiah's reform was as thorough as 2 Kings 23: 8 gives us to believe, Ezekiel testifies to a resurgence in his own time of worship regarded as utterly false and blasphemous. The ideal of Deuteronomy (ch. 12), that worship at country sanctuaries should cease and there be only one place of sacrifice for Israel, would have been most attractive to a member of Jerusalem's priesthood. That may have been one reason for Ezekiel's opposition to the hill-shrines. But also, while country sanctuaries preserved some elements of Israelite belief and worship, many seem to have been the scenes of various religious practices judged unworthy of Israel. There is evidence of the worship of the gods of other nations, of the veneration of female divinities, and of worship before figures representing God or gods. Hence the damning prophecy of these verses, which is characteristic in its sweeping condemnation of all worship at the hill-shrines.

5–7*a*. An expansion, reinforcing the prophecy largely by an address to the Israelites. The idols and altars would be defiled and unsuitable for worship with human blood and bones strewn over them.

6. *your works*: probably the idols that craftsmen had made (cp. Hos. 13: 2).

7*b*. *you shall know*...: the conclusion of the original prophecy.

8–10. The words *sword* and *idols* have served as links between the preceding prophecy of disaster and these later words of Ezekiel which were added at this point for the same reason that 5: 3–4*a* was placed in its present position, to alleviate a judgement of overwhelming disaster and to encourage obedience.

9. *remember*: the word implies more than the recollection of past events. The exiles will actively seek to restore their relationship with God by repenting of their former waywardness. *I was grieved*: the Hebrew reads, 'I have been broken'. There is probably a textual error here. It was God who broke his sinful nation's heart (or caused it to grieve), rather than the nation who broke God's heart. So read: '... will remember me, when I have broken their heart, which had turned wantonly from me ...' *hearts* and *eyes* signify the whole man, in his inward being and in his contact with the world. *abominations*: a favourite term of Ezekiel's for practices that lead to religious impurity; used mainly of idolatry, but sometimes of adultery.

11. From the Hebrew text it is clear that it is the prophet, not the people of Israel, who is told to *beat* (*his*) *hands together* and *stamp with* (*his*) *foot*. Like looking toward the mountains (verse 2), these more expressive gestures symbolized God's activity against his people. They are gestures of rage, of great anger about to vent itself in judgement. In view of this

the word *bemoan* in the N.E.B. is perhaps more aptly rendered by the cry 'Woe (to you! because of) your vile abominations.'

12. The terms *Far away* and *at home* (literally 'far' and 'near') do not refer, as has sometimes been thought, to the exiles on the one hand and to those dwelling in Jerusalem on the other. Together they simply mean 'everywhere'. The prophecy concerns the besieged city of chs. 4–5, as the three-fold plagues of sword, famine and pestilence indicate. That may be the reason for the chapter's position in the book.

13*b*–14. *when their slain fall. . .*: an editor has here expanded the prophecy of verses 11–13*a* in order to unify the chapter. He refers back to the worship on the mountains that was the subject of the first prophecy, and also adds phrases common to the descriptions of such worship in the books of Deuteronomy, Kings and Jeremiah. *terebinth*: a large, common tree, of sacred significance in this context. *more desolate than the desert of Riblah*: it is more likely that 'from the desert to Riblah' was intended to be read here. Such a phrase describes the extent of the whole land, from the southern-desert border with Egypt to an ideal northern border in Syria. ✲

THE COMING END

The word of the LORD came to me: Man, the Lord GOD 7 1, 2 says this to the land of Israel: An end is coming, the end is coming upon the four corners of the land.[a] The end is 3 now upon you; I will unleash my anger against you; I will call you to account for your doings and bring your abominations upon your own heads. I will neither pity 4 nor spare you: I will make you suffer for your doings and the abominations that continue in your midst. So you shall know that I am the LORD.

[a] *Or* earth.

5 These are the words of the Lord GOD: Behold, it comes,
6 disasters one upon another;[a] the end, the end, it comes,
7 it comes.[b] Doom is coming upon you, dweller in the land;
   the time is coming, the day is near, with confusion and
8 the crash of thunder.[c] Now, in an instant, I will vent my
   rage upon you and let my anger spend itself. I will call
   you to account for your doings and bring your abomina-
9 tions upon your own heads. I will neither pity nor spare;
   I will make you suffer for your doings and the abominations that continue in your midst. So you shall know that
   it is I, the LORD, who strike the blow.

✲ Ch. 7 comprises three poems of judgement. The text is
confused by obscurities and additional commentary, so that the
N.E.B. has understandably presented it as prose. There
appear originally to have been two prophecies. The first
(verses 2–4) takes the form of a personal address to the land of
Israel. The second (verses 5f. and 10–27) describes in an
impersonal style the effects of the judgement. Within the
second prophecy another has been added, similar to the first
but addressed to the 'dweller in the land' (verse 7).

2–4. *An end is coming*: Amos, in his vision of summer fruit,
referred by word-play to the coming of 'an end' upon the
people of Israel (see the footnote to Amos 8: 2). It is that
theme of final disaster which is elaborated in this chapter.
Ezekiel's portrayal of the 'end' has been further developed in
Dan. 8–12. *the four corners of the land*: the whole territory of
Judah. The land is addressed as if it was a person. Ezekiel has
in mind the strong sacramental bond that was felt to exist
between land and people. The inhabitants are only directly
referred to in the phrase *So you shall know. . .* (verse 4). It is

[a] disasters . . . another: *so some MSS.; others* one disaster, a disaster.
[b] *Prob. rdg.; Heb. adds* it wakes up, behold it comes.
[c] and the crash of thunder: *prob. rdg.; Heb. unintelligible.*

therefore preferable to read with the Hebrew text, 'upon your own head' (singular) in verse 3.

5f. The major poem, continued in verses 10–27, begins: 'These are the words of the Lord GOD: the end has come.' The second half of verse 5 and the repetition in verse 6 are absent from the Septuagint.

7–9. The evident similarities between verses 3f. and 8f. suggest that this is a variant form of the first prophecy, more pointedly directed to the people. It has actually been added between verses 3 and 4 in the Septuagint.

7. *the day*: 'the day of the LORD' was once looked forward to as a time when God would bring about the defeat of all Israel's enemies and give his people peace and prosperity. But Amos had rejected that happy prospect of 'the day'. He portrayed it as a time when God would destroy his own people, in punishment for their misdeeds (Amos 5: 18–20; cp. Zeph. 1: 14–18). Ezekiel develops this theme more fully in verses 10–27.

8. *heads*: read the singular as in verse 3, since the subject of the prophecy ('dweller', verse 7) is singular. ✶

BEHOLD, THE DAY!

Behold, the day! the doom is here, it has burst upon them. 10
Injustice buds, insolence blossoms, violence shoots up 11
into injustice and wickedness. And it is all their fault,
the fault of their turmoil and tumult and all their restless
ways.[a] The time has come, the day has arrived; the buyer 12
has no reason to be glad, and the seller none for regret,
for I am angry[b] at all their turmoil. The seller will never 13
go back on his bargain while either of them lives; for the
bargain will never be reversed because of the turmoil,

[a] and all their restless ways: *so Vulg.; Heb. unintelligible.*
[b] I am angry: *so Targ.; Heb. anger.*

and no man will exert himself, even in his iniquity, as
14 long as he lives.*a* The trumpet has sounded and all is
ready, but no one goes out to war.*b*

15   Outside is the sword, inside are pestilence and famine;
in the country men will die by the sword, in the city
16 famine and pestilence will carry them off. If any escape
and take to the mountains, like moaning doves, there
17 will I slay them, each for his iniquity, while their hands
18 hang limp and their knees run with urine. They will go
in sackcloth, shuddering from head to foot, with faces
19 downcast and heads close shaved. They shall fling their
silver into the streets and cast aside their gold like filth;
their silver and their gold will be powerless to save
them on the day of the LORD's fury. Their hunger will
not be satisfied nor their bellies filled; for their iniquity
20 will be the cause of their downfall. They have fed their
pride on their beautiful jewels, which they made into
vile and abominable images. Therefore I will treat their
21 jewels like filth, I will hand them over as plunder to
foreigners and as booty to the most evil people on earth,
22 and these will defile them. I will turn my face from them
and let my treasured land be profaned; brigands will
come in and defile it.

23   Clench your fists, for the land is full of bloodshed*c* and
24 the city full of violence. I will let in the scum of nations
to take possession of their houses; I will quell the pride of
the strong, and their sanctuaries shall be profaned.
25 Shuddering will come over them, and they will look in

[a] as long as he lives: *poss. mng.; Heb. obscure.*
[b] *So Sept.; Heb. adds* for I am angry at all their turmoil.
[c] bloodshed: *prob. rdg.; Heb.* the judgement of bloodshed.

46

vain for peace. Tempest shall follow upon tempest and 26
rumour upon rumour. Men will go seeking a vision from
a prophet; there will be no more guidance from a priest,
no counsel from elders. The king will mourn, the prince 27
will be clothed with horror, the hands of the common
people will shake with fright. I will deal with them as
they deserve, and call them to account for their doings;
and so they shall know that I am the LORD.

* This poem once began with verses 5f. and takes up the
joint themes of Amos – the coming end and the day of the
LORD. The precise nature of Hebrew poetry can prove a
matter for intense debate, but scholars are agreed that a basic
element of it is the presentation of ideas that may be similar
or stand in contrast to one another. For example, in verse 12
we have: 'The time has come / the day has arrived; the
buyer has no reason to be glad / and the seller none for regret.'
In this chapter, so far as the original form of the poem may be
conjectured, Ezekiel has built up, with an economy of words
but great vividness of imagery, a comprehensive picture of
life in the day of final judgement. Sometimes explanations
of words or ideas which do not appear in the Septuagint
reveal the work of later commentators. Other expansions
cannot be attributed confidently either to Ezekiel or his
followers. But there is a prose addition in verses 21–4, probably
from Ezekiel himself, that should be dated after 587 B.C. An
impersonal style predominates. No one is addressed and God
speaks of his own activity only in verse 27.

10f. *Injustice buds, insolence blossoms*: the reason for the
end of God's patience, which has issued in the end of the
nation, is given in illustrations from nature. It goes without
saying that the fruit of injustice and insolence will be more
violence and wickedness, deserving God's wrath. But the
point has nonetheless been made explicit in an expansion of
the poem in verse 11.

12f. The apparent meaning of the first of these verses is that no emotion will be felt at gain or loss in trade. But the contrast between the gladness of the buyer and the regret of the seller should not be pressed. The figure is of all normal activities ceasing, and with that men will no longer experience natural emotions. *for I am angry at all their turmoil*: these words, together with verse 13, are comments added by later hands. Verse 13 elaborates on the cessation of normal activities, pointing out that business agreements cannot be remade because evil men (literally 'one whose life is in his iniquity') will die.

14–16. Courage flees before the forces of God. A picture is drawn in verses 14–15*a* of a people under siege, with none prepared to fight in defence of them. *all is ready* may mean 'weapons are at hand'. *in the country men will die*, etc. (verses 15*b*–16): further commentary describing the outcome of the now familiar three-fold plagues. Notice how the word *outside* is misunderstood. The sword no longer menaces those within the city but those who are literally 'outside' *in the country* or the fields.

17f. Signs of terror and mourning are everywhere apparent, and panic deprives men of self-control. Sackcloth and shaven heads commonly signified grief and mourning (cp. 27: 31).

19f. The poem probably read simply:

> they shall fling their silver into the streets
> and cast aside their gold like filth;
> their hunger will not be satisfied
> nor their bellies filled.

The uselessness of wealth is underlined in the comment which follows the first two lines of the poem, and again in verse 20 which introduces the theme of pride. *for their iniquity will be the cause of their downfall*: the Hebrew may be understood to imply that greed for wealth was the source of their iniquity. The phrase is characteristic of Ezekiel and his followers (cp. e.g. 14: 3f., 7).

21–4. In this prose addition God speaks of what he will do and, if the N.E.B. rendering of the difficult text is correct, he commands the prophet to make another gesture of threatening rage (verse 23). The plundering of the city and the defilement of the land and sanctuaries described here suggest that the actual fate of Jerusalem was known to the author.

21f. *foreigners. . .the most evil people on earth. . .brigands*: all three denote the Babylonians. Elsewhere Ezekiel uses the expression 'the most ruthless of nations' (e.g. 28: 7). The more disparaging terms here are not so much intended to abuse the invaders as to show how low Israel has fallen for God to send against those chosen to be his holy people men who make no pretence of maintaining just and right behaviour. In several Psalms the phrase 'the wicked of the earth' (which is a literal rendering of the second of the above terms) refers in a general sense to the impious (cp. Ps. 101: 8, where it is used of impious Israelites). *I will turn my face from them*: here the turning of God's face toward or away from his people must be understood in terms of the priestly blessing which invokes God to 'make his face shine upon you . . . (and) look kindly on you' (Num. 6: 25f.). Now God turns away his face so that a curse and not a blessing may fall on his land or temple. *my treasured land* interprets an ambiguous term (literally 'my secret thing or place') which may also mean the temple or the most holy place within the temple (for which see 41: 3f.).

25–26a. The major poem resumes, describing the people's vain search for comfort and guidance in the day of the LORD. *peace*: the Hebrew *shālōm* or wholeness, which embraced the ideas of physical and mental well-being, economic prosperity and harmonious relations between man and man, and between man and God. *Tempest. . .upon tempest*: one tragedy after another.

26b. *Men will go seeking. . .*: the vain search for peace is elaborated here in terms which directly contradict the words attributed to the people in Jer. 18: 18: 'there will still be priests to guide us, still wise men to advise, still prophets to proclaim the word'. None of the traditional guides in faith or prudent behaviour will be able to assist. The author of the addition in Ezekiel was dependent on Jeremiah's saying. The change of reference from the prophet's 'word' to his *vision* is not significant since God's word could come in the form of a vision. But Ezekiel's use of the term *elders* in place of Jeremiah's 'wise men' as the source of wise counsel reflects the growing importance of the eldership during the exile, as we shall have cause to notice again in the next chapter.

27. *The king will mourn*: these words do not appear in the Septuagint and have been added to explain the term *prince*, which Ezekiel prefers to use for the ruler of Judah (see on 37: 21-3). Only in the second half of this verse does the poem refer to God himself as the source of all these horrors. It is no foreign power that by its own might has brought Israel to this state but Israel's God, who has used a foreign nation to punish justly his own people. ✲

Jerusalem's guilt and punishment

✲ Chs. 8-11 are presented as an account of a single vision of Jerusalem's corruption and destruction, and of God's departure from the city. However, much of ch. 10 is the result of later attempts to harmonize features of this vision with ch. 1. And in ch. 11, verses 1-13 are an account of a separate vision, while verses 14-21 were originally quite independent of Ezekiel's visionary experiences. ✲

CARRIED TO JERUSALEM

8 ON THE FIFTH DAY OF THE SIXTH MONTH in the sixth year, I was sitting at home and the elders of Judah were with me. Suddenly the hand of the Lord GOD

2 came upon me, and I saw what looked like a man. He

seemed to be all fire from the waist down and to shine
and glitter like brass from the waist up. He stretched out 3
what seemed a hand and seized me by the forelock. A
spirit[a] lifted me up between heaven and earth, carried me
to Jerusalem in a vision of God and put me down at the
entrance to the inner gate facing north, where stands the
image of Lust to rouse lustful passion. The glory of the 4
God of Israel was there, like the vision I had seen in the
plain. The LORD said to me, 'Man, look northwards.' 5
I did so, and there to the north of the altar gate, at the
entrance, was that image of Lust. 'Man,' he said, 'do 6
you see what they are doing? The monstrous abominations which the Israelites practise here are driving me far
from my sanctuary, and you will see even more such
abominations.'

✻ In this chapter the four scenes within the vision reveal
increasingly greater acts of apostasy as the prophet is taken
from a position outside the city to stand in the temple court
itself. The whole is carefully constructed to heighten the
dramatic impact at each successive stage. We cannot confirm
the existence in Jerusalem of all the alien forms of worship
observed by Ezekiel. But Jeremiah described the decline of
worship after the death of King Josiah (7: 1–15) and the
political pressures of later years could quite conceivably have
led to the adoption of foreign religious practices, known to
Ezekiel before his exile or described to him in Babylon.

1. The date is August–September 592 B.C., fourteen months
after the first vision. The same setting, within the prophet's
house with elders sitting before him, is described in 14: 1 and
20: 1. The last of these passages confirms that the reason for the
elders' attendance on Ezekiel was that he might give them

[a] *Or* wind.

guidance from God. The elders were the heads of families, or at least of the most influential families of Israelite communities. With the dislocation of life in the early sixth century B.C. the elders recovered something of the importance they had prior to the establishment of the monarchy. Jeremiah addressed them, along with the priests and prophets, as those worthy of special mention among the exiles (Jer. 29: 1) and we have noted their importance as advisers of the people according to Ezek. 7: 26.

2f. The man cannot be God himself for Ezekiel always refers to his 'glory' when speaking of God's appearance. The further description of the man in the second half of verse 2 is an erroneous expansion borrowed from 1: 27. The mysterious figure seems intrusive, since in the following verse a spirit is the agent of the prophet's movement and the instructions to the prophet come from God. But his action serves to affirm the reality of Ezekiel's feeling of physical removal, despite the strong qualification of the experience as visionary. Later the prophet Zechariah reports being guided in visions by heavenly messengers or angels (e.g. Zech. 1: 9) and the apocryphal Daniel, Bel, and the Snake describes an angel lifting up the prophet Habakkuk 'by his hair' and transporting him from Judaea to Babylon (Daniel, Bel, and the Snake verse 36). A fragment preserved in quotation by the church father Origen from an apocryphal gospel 'according to the Hebrews' has the words 'the Saviour said: "Just now my mother the Holy Spirit took me by one of my hairs and carried me away to the great mountain Tabor"', thus attributing such experiences also to Jesus (cp. the temptation descriptions of the Gospels, e.g. Matt. 4: 5–10). *the inner gate*: the Septuagint does not have the word *inner*. The reference is to the north gate of the city not the inner gate of the temple precincts, which is mentioned in verse 14. *where stands the image of Lust. . .*: an addition anticipating the command to look to the north in verse 5.

4. One of a number of editorial additions intended to link this vision with the first.

5. The prophet is commanded to observe the first example of pagan worship, presumably the offering of gifts on an altar. The second half of the verse should read: 'and there to the north was the altar of the image of Lust'. In the Hebrew the word for *gate* has become wrongly associated with the term for *altar*, and *at the entrance* is an addition based on verse 3 but absent from the Septuagint. *image of Lust*: the N.E.B. rendering here and in verse 3*b* assumes that the altar was dedicated to the goddess of fertility, Asherah. Josiah had removed the symbol of that goddess from the temple (2 Kings 23: 6), but she formerly had a considerable following in Israel and a resurgence of such worship is not unlikely. The more common rendering 'image of jealousy' understands some unspecified image or idol, of whose prohibition Israel had been told many times. For Israel's God was provoked to jealousy by all images (Exod. 20: 3–5). ✳

MORE SUCH ABOMINATIONS

Then he brought me to the entrance of the court, and I 7 looked and found a hole in the wall. 'Man,' he said to me, 8 'dig through the wall.' I did so, and it became an opening. 'Go in,' he said, 'and see the vile abominations they 9 practise here.' So I went in and saw figures of reptiles, 10 beasts, and vermin, and all the idols of the Israelites, carved round the walls. Seventy elders of Israel were 11 standing in front of them, with Jaazaniah son of Shaphan in the middle, and each held a censer from which rose the fragrant smoke of incense. 'Man,' he said to me, 'do 12 you see what the elders of Israel are doing in darkness, each at the shrine of his own carved image? They think that the LORD does not see them, or that he has forsaken the country. You will see', he said, 'yet more monstrous 13 abominations which they practise.'

14 Then he brought me to that gateway of the LORD's house which faces north; and there I saw women sitting
15 and wailing for Tammuz. 'Man, do you see that?' he asked me. 'But you will see abominations more mon-
16 strous than these.' So he took me to the inner court of the LORD's house, and there, by the entrance to the sanctuary of the LORD, between porch and altar, were some twenty-five men with their backs to the sanctuary and their faces to the east, prostrating themselves to the
17 rising sun. He said to me, 'Man, do you see that? Is it because they think these abominations a trifle, that the Jews have filled the country with violence? They provoke me further to anger, even while they seek to appease
18 me;[a] I will turn upon them in my rage; I will neither pity nor spare. Loudly as they may cry to me, I will not listen.'

✷ 7f. The second scene of the vision commences with the prophet inside the city, standing before the entrance to the great court which encircled both the temple and the palace of Solomon. The curious procedure by which Ezekiel gained access to the room of the elders according to the Hebrew text – digging through the wall when he had already found a hole in it – is explained by reference to the Septuagint, where verse 7b (*and I looked. . .wall*) is completely missing and verse 8 reads simply '"Man," he said to me, "dig." I did so, and there was a door.' What has happened is that a Hebrew word which means 'look carefully' has been understood in its second sense of 'dig'. This has led to the later expansion of these verses in terms of 12: 1–7, where the prophet is told to act out a prophecy of exile by digging a hole through a wall. Originally Ezekiel's attention was called to a door within the complex of buildings around the gate of the great court.

[a] seek. . .me: *lit.* hold twigs to their nostrils.

54

10f. Within the room were carved reliefs of *vermin, and all the idols of the Israelites.* 'Vermin' were fish without fins or scales, winged creatures with four legs, and all forms of lizard (Lev. 11: 10, 20, 29f.). They were regarded as unclean and were not to be eaten. But here they are worshipped, along with other unspecified images, in complete defiance of basic Israelite laws. *figures of reptiles, beasts, and*: an addition based on Deut. 4: 16–18, absent from the Septuagint. The precise nature of the elders' practices is not known. Possibly it was some form of Egyptian worship, since King Zedekiah of Jerusalem was at this time making political overtures to Egypt. The adoption of Egyptian worship, with its animal gods, would thus have been natural. The *Seventy elders* could represent all the laymen of Israel (cp. Exod. 24: 1, 9; Num. 11: 16), so that the idolatry of all is implied by the scene. *with Jaazaniah son of Shaphan* (literally 'standing') *in the middle*: 'standing' here has the mundane sense of standing upright, but earlier in the verse the words *standing in front* are a technical phrase for 'worshipping'. Whoever added the reference to Jaazaniah to the vision appears to have ignored this, and we have the picture of Jaazaniah standing casually among men who are all in an attitude of worship. The addition is, for some unknown reason, intended specifically to implicate in the disreputable practices even the once-respected family of Shaphan. Shaphan was the first to read to Josiah the book of the law which became the basis of the king's reform of worship in 622 B.C. (2 Kings 22: 10).

12. *in darkness*: like the references to digging through the wall in verse 8, this is an expansion based on 12: 1–7. The second part of the verse should be read as a direct quotation of the elders' words: 'They say, "The LORD does not see us; he has forsaken the country".' Since it was believed that Israel's God had deserted his land and left it in the control of other nations, he could not see the people's devotion to other nations' gods, from whom the worshippers sought protection.

14. The site of the third abomination is the northern gate-

way to the temple court. *Tammuz*: a central figure of an ancient and widespread belief in a dying and rising god. Essentially representing the cycle of the seasons, this vegetation deity was held to have been betrayed and killed in the summer, when the land became parched and plant life died away. But his sister Ishtar freed him from the underworld and they married, giving rise to the new growth of vegetation in the spring. At the time of his death each year women mourned in a customary display of grief, but that was in the month called 'Tammuz' (June–July) and not, as here in the vision, two months later. Tammuz is an Assyrian name (the equivalent of Baal in Syria and Damuzi in Babylon) and the worship associated with him was introduced to Israel during the eighth and seventh centuries. It also involved sexual rites promoting the fertility of fields and herds, and it stands in starkest contrast to the worship of Israel's 'living God', whose control of nature was quite independent of a heavenly consort and of stimulation by the sexual activity of his people.

16. Finally Ezekiel observes men worshipping the sun, with their backs turned to the sanctuary (rather than facing it so as to intercede with God for their people, cp. Joel 2: 17). It is likely that the men represent priests, for the idolatry of the laymen and the women has already been described, and the scene has now moved right to the entrance of the temple proper. Egyptian reverence for the sun god seems to be reflected here, though symbols of sun worship were earlier removed from the temple by Josiah (2 Kings 23: 11). *twenty-five men*: 'twenty men' should be read, with the Septuagint; the Hebrew here has been altered to agree with 11: 1.

17. One of the expansions of this difficult verse that already appears in the Septuagint is: *the Jews have filled the country with violence*. It derives from 7: 23, but *violence* signifies social evil rather than idolatry, which is the topic of this chapter. *they seek to appease me*: as the footnote indicates, the literal meaning is 'hold twigs to their nostrils'. The meaning of the ritual is uncertain, but it is more likely to represent some

further form of pagan worship, insulting to God, than an attempt to placate him. *Jews*: literally 'the house of Judah'. The word 'Jews' in the Old Testament is largely a post-exilic term for the inhabitants of Judah and their descendants, whether living in Palestine or in captivity.

18*b. Loudly as they may cry. . .*: an addition, mistakenly understanding the 'loud voice' of 9: 1 as a cry of the people rather than as the sound of God's voice. ✶

THE DESTROYERS COME

A loud voice rang in my ears: 'Here they come, those **9** appointed to punish the city, each carrying his weapon of destruction.' Then I saw six men approaching from the 2 road that leads to the upper northern gate, each carrying a battle-axe, one man among them dressed in linen, with pen and ink at his waist; and they halted by the altar of bronze. Then the glory of the God of Israel rose from 3 above the cherubim.*ᵃ* He came to the terrace of the temple and called to the man dressed in linen with pen and ink at his waist. 'Go through the city, through 4 Jerusalem,' said the LORD, 'and put a mark on the fore-heads of those who groan and lament over the abomina-tions practised there.' Then I heard him say to the others, 5 'Follow him through the city and kill without pity; spare no one. Kill and destroy them all, old men and 6 young, girls, little children and women, but touch no one who bears the mark. Begin at my sanctuary.' So they began with the elders in front of the temple. 'Defile 7 the temple,' he said, 'and fill the courts with dead bodies; then go out*ᵇ* into the city and kill.'

[a] *So Sept.; Heb.* cherub.
[b] *So Sept.; Heb. adds* and they will go out.

8 While they did their work, I was left alone; and I threw myself upon my face, crying out, 'O Lord GOD, must thou destroy all the Israelites who are left, pouring
9 out thy anger on Jerusalem?' He answered, 'The iniquity of Israel and Judah is great indeed; the land is full of murder, the city is filled with injustice. They think the LORD has forsaken this country; they think he sees
10 nothing. But I will neither pity nor spare them; I will
11 make them answer for all they have done.' Then the man dressed in linen with pen and ink at his waist came and made his report: 'I have done what thou hast commanded.'

✶ There are evident parallels between this chapter and the story of the destruction of the Egyptian first-born in Exod. 12. Here there are several angels of death, but as in the earlier narrative they are told to 'go through' and 'kill' those who are not marked with a protective sign. Thus the contrast between God's action then and now is heightened. For once he acted as an angel of death to bring his people freedom from their oppressors. Now he sends his destroyers to punish his people for their wrongdoings.

2. Six men appear carrying weapons and a seventh carries a 'scribe's case' containing reed pens and ink. The origin of the seven figures is uncertain but there was a Babylonian belief in seven evil spirits who worked in association. Alternatively, there may be an allusion here to the seven Babylonian planet gods, for among those gods was one, called Nabû, who served as a heavenly scribe and compiled a Book of Fate. As a priest, *dressed in linen* (cp. Lev. 16: 4), the scribe had the responsibility of distinguishing the righteous from the unrighteous (see on 18: 1–9) and so marking them. The notion of seven angels recurs in later Jewish literature (Tobit 12: 15) and in the New Testament (Rev. 15: 6). *the upper northern gate:* the elevated

gate of the temple court already mentioned in 8: 14. *the altar of bronze*: this stood between the northern gate and the great altar referred to in 8: 16 (see also 2 Kings 16: 14 and plan, p. 271).

3. The verse once read: 'Then he (i.e. the LORD) called to the man . . .' The reference to the glory of God is an addition, anticipating its appearance on the temple terrace in 10: 18.

4. In view of the general depravity reported in the previous chapter, and the prophecies of wholesale destruction earlier, this verse comes as something of a surprise. We cannot identify those who groaned and lamented over the idolatry practised in Jerusalem. Ezekiel was almost certainly aware of Jeremiah's continuing fierce loyalty to God, but his words of sweeping condemnation were typical of Old Testament prophecy in admitting no exceptions to the general state of injustice and guilt. This feature of the vision revives an element of the story of Elijah, when a remnant of 7000 Israelites, unknown to the prophet, are judged to have been faithful to God (1 Kings 19: 18). As suddenly as the pious remnant is mentioned, it is forgotten. Wherever else survivors from Jerusalem are spoken of they share the guilt of those who have perished. *a mark*: or 'a cross' (**X**); the last letter of the old Hebrew alphabet (*tau*) was so written in the earlier form of the script. This probably suggested to the author of the book of Revelation the idea of marking the foreheads of the faithful with the name of Christ (Rev. 14: 1).

6f. The temple had formerly been a place of refuge from violence. Now a holy war of pitiless extermination (cp. 1 Sam. 15: 3) is to begin there. *the elders*: no mention was made in 8: 16 of the sun-worshippers being elders. The absence of these words in some texts of the Septuagint supports the assumption that they were added to avoid implicating the priesthood in the corrupt practices. The original text probably read simply: 'So they began with the men in front of the temple.'

8. One of the important tasks of prophets was to act as

intercessors. In his concern for the innocent – the remnant *who are left* – Ezekiel pleads for their preservation. God's immediate answer was to restate the general charge against the land and people. But the return of the man clothed in linen (verse 11) implies the protection of the innocent by the mark put upon them.

9. *murder*: literally 'blood', meaning violence which leads to bloodshed. No specific mention is made in this verse of corrupt worship. There was no need to mention it since Ezekiel saw social evils as signs of a basically wrong relationship between God and men, of which social evils and corrupt worship were twin manifestations. To speak of one implied the existence of the other. ✳

DESTRUCTION BY FIRE

10 Then I saw, above the vault over the heads of the cherubim, as it were a throne of sapphire*ᵃ* visible above them.
2 The Lord said to the man dressed in linen,*ᵇ* 'Come in between the circling wheels under the cherubim*ᶜ* and take a handful of the burning embers lying among the cherubim; then toss them over the city.' So he went in before my eyes.
3 The cherubim stood on the right side of the temple as
4 a man enters, and a cloud filled the inner court. The glory of the Lord rose high from above the cherubim*ᶜ* and moved on to the terrace; and the temple was filled with the cloud, while the radiance of the glory of the Lord
5 filled the court. The sound of the wings of the cherubim could be heard as far as the outer court, as loud as if God
6 Almighty were speaking. Then he told the man dressed

[a] *Or* lapis lazuli.   [b] *So Sept.; Heb. adds* and he said.
[c] *So Sept.; Heb.* cherub.

in linen to take fire from between the circling wheels
and among the cherubim; the man came and stood by a
wheel, and a cherub from among the cherubim put its 7
hand into the fire that lay among them, and, taking some
fire, gave it to the man dressed in linen; and he received
it and went out.

✻ The vision originally continued in verses 2, 4 and 7, where
the Hebrew word for 'cherubim' appears as a collective
singular (cp. the English words 'flock', 'people') rather than a
plural. The people of Jerusalem having been slain, the city
is now to be destroyed by coals of fire strewn about by the
man clothed in linen. The chief intent of the remaining
verses is to identify the cherubim with the living creatures of
ch. 1. They are later additions and, like most of ch. 10,
contrast markedly, in their carefully detailed description of
the cherubim and their movements, with the bold, dramatic
style of the two previous chapters.

1. Cp. 1: 26.

2. *circling wheels*: Hebrew *galgal*. In 10: 6 these are identified
with the 'wheels' (Hebrew *'ōphannīm*) of ch. 1. It is unclear
whether they were part of the mobile platform of the ark
(see on 1: 15–21) or belonged to a separate wheeled brazier
within the temple. *cherubim*: the name means 'intercessors'.
In Babylon they took the form of winged, human-headed
bulls and were set at temple entrances as guardians and
minor divinities who interceded for men with the great gods.
In the Old Testament they still serve as guardians of God's
throne (see on 1: 4–14), but, though winged, they have human
bodies. *burning embers*: the association of the cherubim with fire
here has given rise to the addition of 1: 13, although, as already
noted, the imagery of 1: 13 derives from another tradition
altogether. *lying among the cherubim*: the plural 'cherubim' is
used in this addition. *toss them over the city*: not to purify it, as
Isaiah was purified for service (Isa. 6: 6f.), but to destroy it.

3. According to the previous verse the man went into the temple to take the embers from the cherubim. According to this verse the cherubim were in the court, outside the temple proper.

4. The original vision continues with the first mention of God's glory, which moves from within to the entrance of the temple. The meaning of the word rendered *terrace* is uncertain. Some kind of pedestal or platform is indicated by its use in 1 Sam. 5: 4f. But in Ezek. 46: 2 and 47: 1 the common rendering 'threshold' or *terrace*, as here, is more suitable.

5. Cp. 1: 24. The prophet was in the inner court so could hardly have made this observation.

6. This instruction has already been given.

7. Omitting additions, the verse may be read: *and a cherub ...put its hand into the fire..., and, taking some fire,...* One of the guardians of the fire hands over the embers to the man. Quite in accordance with the Hebrew style of story-telling, the execution of the man's commission does not require narration. ✳

THE CHERUBIM AND WHEELS

8 Under the wings of the cherubim there appeared what
9 seemed a human hand. And I saw four wheels beside the cherubim, one wheel beside each cherub. They had the
10 sparkle of topaz, and all four were alike, like a wheel
11 inside a wheel. When the cherubim moved in any of the four directions, they never swerved in their course; they went straight on in the direction in which their heads
12 were turned, never swerving in their course. Their whole bodies, their backs and hands and wings, as well as the wheels, were full of eyes all round the four of them.[a]
13, 14 The whirring of the wheels sounded in my ears. Each

[a] *Prob. rdg.; Heb. adds* their wheels.

had four faces: the first was that of a cherub, the second that of a man, the third that of a lion, and the fourth that of an eagle.

Then the cherubim raised themselves up, those same 15 living creatures I had seen by the river Kebar. When the 16 cherubim moved, the wheels moved beside them; when the cherubim lifted their wings and rose from the ground, the wheels did not turn away from them. When the one 17 halted, the other halted; when the one rose, the other rose; for the spirit of the creatures was in the wheels. Then the 18 glory of the LORD left the temple terrace and halted above the cherubim. The cherubim lifted their wings and raised 19 themselves from the ground; I watched them go with the wheels beside them. They halted at the eastern gateway of the LORD's house, and the glory of the God of Israel was over them.

These were the living creatures I had seen beneath the 20 God of Israel at the river Kebar; I knew that they were cherubim. Each had four faces and four wings and the 21 semblance of human hands under their wings. Their 22 faces were like those I had seen in vision by the river Kebar;[a] they moved, each one of them, straight forward.

* The entire section, except for parts of verses 18 and 19, is a later description of the circling wheels and accompanying cherubim of 10: 2, 4 and 7 in terms of the wheels and living creatures of Ezekiel's first vision. This has involved considerable confusion of imagery. The bodies of the cherubim are said to be covered with eyes (verse 12) and the circling wheels are described as having four faces (verse 14). The disorder and repetitions within the narrative indicate that its growth,

[a] *Prob. rdg.; Heb. adds* and them.

like that of 1: 15–21, has been piecemeal. Some verses have been introduced to provide links with the general scene of ch. 1 (verses 15, 20, 22). Others explicitly identify the circling wheels and the wheels of ch. 1 (verse 13) or explain difficulties presented by the original vision of 10: 2, 4 and 7 (verse 8). The intense interest of Ezekiel's followers in harmonizing the various features of the visions in chs. 1 and 10 accounts for the remarkable expansion of the present section. The stages of this development are not clearly discernible, but the major expansion in 10: 9–12 and 16f. has been interrupted by the later insertion of verses 13–15. And verses 15, 20 and 22 are part of the editors' attempts to trace a unified theme throughout the book (cp. 3: 23; 8: 4; 43: 3).

8. This explains the location of the cherub's hand. Cp. 1: 8.

9–12. Cp. 1: 15–18. Both these and verses 16f. vary only slightly from 1: 15–21 in the description of their subjects. But the more complicated text in ch. 1 suggests that this is the earlier version.

13. The Hebrew reads: 'the wheels were called in my hearing "the circling wheels"'.

14. *cherub* appears in mistake for the 'ox' of 1: 10.

15. The first half of the verse anticipates verse 19.

16f. Cp. 1: 19–21.

18f. These verses belong, with 11: 23–5, to the conclusion of the first temple vision. Their position within the description of the circling wheels and cherubim has led to considerable expansion of the text. The vision originally continued from verse 7 with the words: *Then the glory of the LORD left the temple terrace...(and it) halted at the eastern gateway of the LORD's house.* The eastern gateway faced the front of the temple. The scene implies God's abandonment of his sanctuary.

20–2. Cp. 1: 6 and 8f. ✵

NO SAFETY IN JERUSALEM

A spirit[a] lifted me up and brought me to the eastern gate **11**
of the Lord's house, the gate that faces east. By the doorway were twenty-five men, and I saw among them two
of high office, Jaazaniah son of Azzur and Pelatiah son of
Benaiah. The Lord said to me, Man, it is these who are 2
planning mischief and plotting trouble in this city, saying 3
to themselves, 'There will be no building of houses yet
awhile; the city is a stewpot and we are the meat in it.'
Therefore, said he, prophesy against them, prophesy, O 4
man. Then the spirit of the Lord came suddenly upon 5
me, and he told me to say, These are the words of the
Lord: This is what you are saying to yourselves, you
men of Israel; well do I know the thoughts that rise in
your mind. You have killed and killed in this city and 6
heaped the streets with the slain. These, therefore, are the 7
words of the Lord God: The bodies of the slain that you
have put there, it is they that are the meat. The city is
indeed the stewpot, but I[b] will take you out of it. It is a 8
sword that you fear, and a sword I will bring upon you,
says the Lord God. I will take you out of it; I will give 9
you over to a foreign power; I will bring you to justice.
You too shall fall by the sword when I judge you on the 10
frontier of Israel; thus you shall know that I am the Lord.
So the city will not be your stewpot, nor you the meat 11
in it. On the frontier of Israel I will judge you; thus you 12
shall know that I am the Lord. You have not conformed
to my statutes nor kept my laws, but you have followed
the laws of the nations around you.

[a] *Or* wind.   [b] *So some MSS.; others* he.

13   While I was prophesying, Pelatiah son of Benaiah
fell dead; and I threw myself upon my face, crying aloud,
'O Lord GOD, must thou make an end of all the Israelites
who are left?'

✲ This is a separate vision of circumstances in Jerusalem before
587 B.C. Its inclusion at this point within the vision commencing in ch. 8 is confusing, for what it describes would logically
have taken place before the destruction of the city in chs.
9–10. The setting within the temple, where the prophet is
borne by a spirit (verse 1), is the probable reason for its
present position in the book. The original vision, in verses
1–8 and 13, has been expanded in the light of the actual fate
of Jerusalem's leaders.

1f. *A spirit lifted me up and brought me*: these words indicate
that another experience of removal from Babylon to Jerusalem is involved. For a fuller description of such an experience
see 8: 3. But it is significant that this account, like 37: 1–14,
is not specifically stated to be a visionary experience, as are
those commencing in 8: 1 and 40: 1. It seems the prophet
may here have been unable to distinguish whether he was
physically transported to Jerusalem or whether he had a vision
in which it seemed to him as if he were there. Paul reports
a similar lack of certainty in 2 Cor. 12: 1–4. Speaking of the
visions and revelations granted to him he records that he was
caught up as far as the third heaven, 'whether in the body or
out of it, I do not know – God knows'. The prophet's feeling
of bodily involvement in this removal over a long distance
seems to have been unusually intense. Although waking
visions should be distinguished from dreams, perhaps the
experience of an exceptionally vivid dream, from which we
awake feeling 'I was really there!', is the closest most people
come to appreciating this kind of sensation. *the eastern gate*:
see on 10: 18f. The public gathering of men, including some
of high office, suggests that a council of city authorities is in
progress. The words *plotting trouble* render the literal 'give

evil counsel'. *Jaazaniah son of Azzur*: not the son of Shaphan
mentioned in 8: II. Nothing more is known of him or
Pelatiah, but they must have been familiar figures to Ezekiel.

3. This difficult verse is best understood as an expression of
unjustified pride and confidence. The image of the *stewpot* or
cauldron represented the protection from attack that the city
offered its inhabitants, particularly the proud councillors
discussing affairs together. Meat was a valuable commodity
and the figure of men as meat is not necessarily disparaging or
threatening as it later becomes when Ezekiel himself uses it
(24: I-I4). For the first half of the verse, *There will be no
building of houses yet awhile*, the Septuagint reads: 'have not
the houses recently been rebuilt?' Rather than suggesting lack
of confidence in the future of the city, the men boast of their
success in restoring the damage done at the time of King
Jehoiachin's capture. This agrees with the expressions of self-
confidence elsewhere imputed to the inhabitants of Jerusalem
(e.g. in Jer. 28).

5. At a later period the spirit was thought to convey God's
word to men (e.g. I Chron. 12: 18, which is post-exilic), but
there is no evidence of the idea elsewhere in Ezekiel. The verse
probably began: *These are the words*, etc. *you men of Israel*:
the prophecy is addressed to the Israelites in general. The
twenty-five men (verse 1) represent all those who commit
acts of violence.

7f. Taking up the imagery of verse 3, the prophet asserts
that the victims' dead bodies are more worthy of the city's
protection than are the lives of their slayers. The latter will be
taken outside the city to their doom.

9f. This first expansion reflects knowledge of the events
recorded in 2 Kings 25: 18–21, when the leading men of
Jerusalem were taken to Nebuchadrezzar's headquarters at
Riblah and there executed. Since that was seen as the appropriate fulfilment of the prophecy, Ezekiel or a follower has
interpreted earlier words by repeating some of them (*I will
take you out of it*) and specifying their outcome.

11f. There are two subsequent expansions here. The first (verses 11–12a) explicitly denies the words of the councillors in verse 3. The second, *You have not conformed* ... (verse 12b), further establishes the basis of judgement in terms already found in 5: 7.

13. The original account of the vision resumes. There are several examples of prophecies of death being more or less promptly fulfilled in the Old Testament (1 Kings 13: 20–4; 2 Kings 7: 1f., 17–20; Jer. 28: 15–17). But the death of Anan-ias, immediately after Peter challenges his behaviour (Acts 5: 5), is the outstanding parallel to the present verse. It is true that the death of Pelatiah takes place in a vision and we are not told whether the councillors even heard Ezekiel speaking. Yet the thought of a prophet's word causing death would have held no problems for the people of the time, whether the death occurred far away or, as here, in a vision in which the prophet is involved. However, Ezekiel was not prophesying immediate death. Rather was he telling of the men's fate upon their imminent removal from the city, so Pelatiah's untimely death in one way disproved his words. This confirms the genuine-ness of the verse, the real importance of which lies not in the death of Pelatiah at the time Ezekiel was speaking, but in the impact upon Ezekiel himself, when the disaster he was prophesying was foreshadowed in such a remarkable way, for the name Pelatiah meant 'God delivers (a remnant)'. At this symbol of complete annihilation Ezekiel reacts as in 9: 8, interceding again for the remnant of his people. ✳

A NEW HEART AND SPIRIT

14,15 The word of the LORD came to me: Man, they are your brothers, your brothers and your kinsmen, this whole people of Israel, to whom the men who now live in Jerusalem have said, 'Keep your distance from the LORD; 16 the land has been made over to us as our property.' Say therefore, These are the words of the Lord GOD: When I sent them far away among the nations and scattered them in many lands, for a while I became their sanctuary in the countries to which they had gone. Say therefore, 17 These are the words of the Lord GOD: I will gather them[a] from among the nations and assemble them[a] from the countries over which I have scattered them,[b] and I will give them[a] the soil of Israel. When they come into it, 18 they will do away with all their vile and abominable practices. I will give them a different[c] heart and put a 19 new spirit into them;[a] I will take the heart of stone out of their bodies and give them a heart of flesh. Then they 20 will conform to my statutes and keep my laws. They will become my people, and I will become their God. But 21 as for those whose heart is set upon[d] their vile and abominable practices, I will make them answer for all they have done. This is the very word of the Lord GOD.

✳ As if in response to Ezekiel's cry in 11: 13, this once-independent prophecy describes a bright future for that remnant which dwells in exile. Ezekiel's dominant attitude toward the exiles before 587 B.C. was one of damning criticism on account of their continuing disobedience. But one cannot therefore deny the possibility of him also speaking words of encouragement to them. Like 11: 1-13, this passage challenges the assumptions of those still living in Jerusalem and anticipates the great prophecies of renewal collected in chs. 34-7.

15. *this whole people of Israel*: the exiles are meant here. The

[a] *So Sept.; Heb.* you.
[b] I have scattered them: *so Sept.; Heb.* you have been scattered.
[c] *So Sept.; Heb.* a single.
[d] *Prob. rdg.; Heb. adds* the heart of.

unusual stress on their being the *whole* people indicates the prophet's belief that the future of Israel now lies entirely with them. *Keep your distance*: scribes have probably misunderstood the Hebrew text by reading these words as a command. With a change only of the later Hebrew vowel signs, they may be read: 'they are far (from the LORD)'. The inhabitants of Jerusalem believed the exiles, by their removal from the temple in punishment for their sins, had lost every claim to the land once given them by God. They were no longer the people of Israel's God but were under the power of the gods of Babylon. Ezekiel's prophecies frequently begin with quotations against which the prophet argues.

16. The prophecy confirms that God brought the exiles *far away* from the temple but denies that they are far from him. This very important verse affirms the presence of God with this people independently of any sacred building or land (cp. John 4: 21). Israelites had long thought of the temple as the primary meeting-place with God. Now the exiles are reminded that God had met with them 'to some extent' (a more suitable rendering than *for a while*) even in their foreign dwelling. A *sanctuary* was not necessarily a building but a place of meeting between God and man, or even the personal presence of God (cp. Lev. 19: 30; 26: 2, where 'revere me' can be understood for 'revere my sanctuary'). Although they were far from the chosen sanctuary of Jerusalem, where God had been encountered most fully, God had not forsaken his exiled people altogether, but through such prophets as Jeremiah and Ezekiel he had made his will known to them by vision and word. This made possible the attainment of life through obedience to the law (see ch. 18), and the simple acts of worship which eventually flowered into the devotion of the synagogue, though we have no clear evidence to suggest that the institution of the synagogue – originally primarily a place of instruction rather than of worship – is to be traced to the exilic age. The prophecy is an apt counterpart to the vision in which it is now set. For the vision describes the

departure of God's glory from Jerusalem and those who dwelt there had no reason to boast of their nearness to God. On the other hand, those exiles who lamented their remoteness from the temple were far nearer the divine presence than those who continued to worship in their homeland.

17f. These verses are introduced by a fresh instruction to prophesy. Their secondary character is also indicated by the form of direct address in the second person in verse 17 (see the footnotes). The first verse answers the assertion that the exiles have lost all claim to their former land. Verse 18, along with verse 21, reflects the period of the return from exile and renewed interest in worship purified of former faults.

19f. The original prophecy continued with the promise of complete renewal. The terms *heart* and *spirit* are complementary. While they could both be regarded as the sources of emotions, intellectual activity and voluntary action, the heart was more the seat of understanding and responsible behaviour and the human spirit more the seat of the disposition or of moods over which the individual had little control. Together they described the will and temperament of man. Jeremiah's prophecy of a new covenant written on people's hearts (Jer. 31: 31–4) ultimately underlies the conception of renewal here. But so entrenched are the exiles in their old habits of life (Ezek. 14: 1–8) that Ezekiel distrusts the capacity of their stubborn and unresponsive *heart of stone*, even knowing God's law, to obey it. He envisages instead the replacement of the very springs of the exiles' attitudes and actions, enabling them to fulfil God's commands and become his people once more. The same theme appears in 36: 26. The words, *I will become their God*, imply the restoration of that close relationship between God and Israel that was formerly experienced most fully in the worship of the temple (cp. on verse 16).

21. See on verses 17f. ✳

THE GLORY DEPARTS

22 Then the cherubim lifted their wings, with the wheels beside them and the glory of the God of Israel above
23 them. The glory of the LORD rose up and left the city, and
24 halted on the mountain to the east of it. And a spirit[a] lifted me up and brought me to the exiles in Chaldaea. All this came in a vision sent by the spirit of God, and then
25 the vision that I had seen left me. I told the exiles all that the LORD had revealed to me.

✲ Continuing from 10: 19, the vision of chs. 8–10 concludes with the scene of God's departure from Jerusalem and the return of the prophet to Babylon.

22. In order to link the previous scene of the same vision with this, editors have repeated part of 10: 19.

23. From the eastern gateway the glory of God ascends, to halt again beyond the city, a sign that not only the sanctuary but the city had lost the divine presence and the protection it offered. Jerusalem was prey to all the destructive forces of alien nations and their gods. *the mountain to the east*: the Mount of Olives.

25. When he returns to his normal state he tells the exiles, presumably by way of their representative elders who were sitting before him (8: 1), of what he has seen in the vision. Its meaning was that any pride or hope the exiles had in their capital and its remaining inhabitants was completely groundless. ✲

[a] Or wind.

Jerusalem's downfall certain

✴ A variety of material is contained in the next thirteen
chapters (12–24). Most is intended to prophesy the fall of
Jerusalem and its king, although it is apparent that many of
Ezekiel's words have been reinforced or morals drawn from
them in the light of their fulfilment in the events of 587 B.C.
There are wide-ranging surveys of Israel's past in chs. 16, 20
and 23, and ch. 18 deals with a major theme of the prophecy,
the responsibility of each individual before God. Ch. 24,
which ends the first major part of the book, closes on a note
of expectancy, as news from Jerusalem is awaited to confirm
Ezekiel's harsh message. ✴

A JOURNEY INTO EXILE

THE WORD OF THE LORD CAME TO ME: Man, you **12**1,2
live among a rebellious people. Though they have
eyes they will not see, though they have ears they will
not hear, because they are a rebellious people. Therefore, 3
man, pack up what you need for a journey into exile, by
day before their eyes; then set off on your journey. When
you leave home and go off into exile before their eyes, it
may be they will see that they are rebels. Bring out your 4
belongings, packed as for exile; do it by day, before their
eyes, and then at evening, still before their eyes, leave
home, as if you were going into exile. Next, before 5
their eyes, break a hole through the wall, and carry your
belongings out through it. When dusk falls, take your 6
pack on your shoulder, before their eyes, and carry it out,

with your face covered so that you cannot see the ground. I am making you a warning sign for the Israelites.

7 I did exactly as I had been told. By day I brought out my belongings, packed as for exile, and at evening I broke through the wall with my hands. When dusk fell, I shouldered my pack and carried it out before their eyes.

8 Next morning, the word of the LORD came to me: 9 Man, he said, have not the Israelites, that rebellious 10 people, asked you what you are doing? Tell them that these are the words of the Lord GOD: This oracle concerns the prince in Jerusalem, and all the Israelites therein.[a] 11 Tell them that you are a sign to warn them; what you have done will be done to them; they will go into exile 12 and captivity. Their prince will shoulder his pack in the dusk and go through a hole made to let him out, with his face covered so that he cannot be seen nor himself see[b] 13 the ground. But I will cast my net over him, and he will be caught in the meshes. I will bring him to Babylon, the land of the Chaldaeans, though he will not see it; and 14 there he will die. I will scatter his bodyguard and drive all his squadrons to the four winds; I will follow them 15 with drawn sword. Then they shall know that I am the LORD, when I disperse them among the nations and 16 scatter them through many lands. But I will leave a few of them who will escape sword, famine, and pestilence, to tell the whole story of their abominations to the peoples among whom they go; and they shall know that I am the LORD.

[a] therein: *prob. rdg.; Heb.* among them.
[b] he cannot. . .see: *so Sept.; Heb.* he cannot see.

✻ The first half of this chapter has been thought by a number of scholars to indicate that Ezekiel's activity took place, partly at least, in Jerusalem. They have argued that an illustration of a journey into exile would have been most meaningful if observed by the inhabitants of that city. But, as the interpretation of the sign in verses 8–16 shows, this acted prophecy was intended primarily for the exiled Israelites. It warned them not to place their faith in Jerusalem nor to expect a sudden end to their own exile. And although the prophet's action was performed in a foreign country it was believed that it would nonetheless help, as a visible expression of God's intent, to bring about the events portrayed. An important feature of the prophecy is its revision in the light of the actual circumstances that befell Jerusalem in 587 B.C. Again, this is clearest in the interpretation where the capture and blinding of Zedekiah, the prince, is referred to. But verses 5f. repeat the instruction of verse 4 to go out, as into exile, in conditions similar to those described in the more obvious revision of verses 10 and 12–14. The prophecy originally concerned the impending exile of the inhabitants in general.

2f. The charge that their people were blind and deaf to what God intended was made by a number of prophets. But again Ezekiel acknowledges the possibility of their seeing and understanding (see on 3: 7).

4. *your belongings*: obviously only the most essential, such as could be easily carried over a long distance. *at evening*: that is, when the heat of the day was over.

5. *break a hole through the wall*: this instruction, referred to again in verse 7, alludes to the secret escape of the prince. Walls of houses, made of sun-dried bricks in Babylonia, could easily enough have been broken through.

6. *with your face covered*: that is, in disguise; this is explicit in verse 12, where a similar phrase is followed by the words 'so that he cannot be seen'. *so that you cannot see the ground*: an allusion to the blinding of the prince, see on verse 12.

7. The report of Ezekiel's execution of the sign has been

expanded by reference to the prince's secret escape: *I broke through the wall. . .When dusk fell.*

10. *and all the Israelites therein* recalls the original subject of the prophecy.

11. The Hebrew reads literally: 'Say, "I am a sign for you (the exiles); as I have done, so it shall be done to them (the Jerusalemites)."' The change of pronoun is important, for it indicates that the subject of the prophecy and those who heard its interpretation were different.

12. *Their prince*: namely Zedekiah. The incident is related in 2 Kings 25: 3–7. Zedekiah fled Jerusalem by night with an armed escort to avoid capture by the Babylonians. Captured nonetheless, he was taken to Nebuchadrezzar at Riblah where his eyes were put out so that he could not *see the ground. with his face covered. . .*: see on verse 6.

13f. These verses are dependent on 17: 20f. The figure of an ensnaring net as a divine instrument used against the prince (see also 17: 20) probably originated with the prophecy of 19: 8. The ground or land, which the prince was unable to see according to verses 6 and 12, was Chaldaea. *there he will die*: this and 17: 16 are the only Old Testament references to Zedekiah's death in Babylon.

15. This concludes the prophecy made-after-the-event in verses 12–14 and the earlier associated verses. Ezekiel himself may have been responsible for the revision of the original prophetic action in the light of the prince's actual fate.

16. This prophecy has a quite different tone, emphasizing the function of a small surviving group in making known to the nations the reason for God's judgement. It is an editorial addition, possibly dependent on 14: 21–3. ✲

TREMBLE AS YOU EAT

17,18 And the word of the LORD came to me: Man, he said, as you eat you must tremble, and as you drink you must
19 shudder with dread. Say to the common people, These

are the words of the Lord GOD about those who live in
Jerusalem and about the land of Israel: They will eat with
dread and be filled with horror as they drink; the land
shall be filled with horror because it is sated with the
violence of all who live there. Inhabited cities shall be   20
deserted, and the land shall become a waste. Thus you
shall know that I am the LORD.

❋ The acted prophecy about the fate of those who dwelt in
Jerusalem (verses 1–16) is now followed by one concerning all
those living in the cities of Israel and the countryside round
about. The people will live in quaking terror at the devasta-
tion of their land. An addition which misunderstands the more
general subject and relates the prophecy also to the inhabitants
of Jerusalem appears in verse 19.

19f. *the common people*: literally 'the people of the land'.
Although it is unusual to find the exiles addressed in this way,
there is irony in this use of the term. It referred to the common
people of both town and country, and the former leaders of
Judah are reminded by it of their present humble status.
about those who live in Jerusalem and about (literally 'in') *the
land of Israel*: an editorial addition. The subject of the prophecy
is implicit in the interpretation which follows: the former
inhabitants of the deserted cities and wasted land. *filled with
horror*: rather 'stripped of its contents' because of the violence
(cp. 7: 11) of the people. ❋

THE TIME IS NEAR

The word of the LORD came to me: Man, he said, what is   21, 22
this proverb current in the land of Israel: 'Time runs on,
visions die away'? Say to them, These are the words of   23
the Lord GOD: I have put an end to this proverb; it
shall never be heard in Israel again. Say rather to them,

24 The time, with all the vision means, is near. There will
be no more false visions, no specious divination among the
25 Israelites, for I, the LORD, will say what I will, and it
shall be done. It shall be put off no longer: in your life-
time, you rebellious people, I will speak, I will act. This
is the very word of the Lord GOD.

26,27 The word of the LORD came to me: Man, he said, the
Israelites say that the vision you now see is not to be
fulfilled for many years: you are prophesying of a time
28 far off. Say to them, These are the words of the Lord
GOD: No word of mine shall be delayed; even as I speak
it shall be done. This is the very word of the Lord GOD.

✻ These two separate sayings (verses 21–5 and 26–8) take up
words of the people as if to debate them. They introduce the
theme of false prophecy which is dealt with in the next chapter.
Both sayings emphasize that prophecy was related in the first
place to the immediate future. With the lapse of time after
the first conquest of Jerusalem, Ezekiel's contemporaries
allayed their anxieties about the future by telling one another
that the prophecies of Jeremiah, Ezekiel, and possibly other
individuals of whom we have no record, were either empty
threats or concerned some far-off time. There was no need to
fear the prophets' words of judgement, nor to mend one's
ways on account of them. But as the true prophet's words
were words of God himself there was no question of them
going unfulfilled. This would be proved once and for all when
Ezekiel's prophecy of Jerusalem's destruction (e.g. in ch. 7)
shattered the illusory hopes of both Jerusalem's inhabitants
and the exiles.

22. *proverb*: here used simply of a popular saying. *visions
die away*: perish, or lose their power. The word for 'visions'
here is not the same as that for the 'visions of God' seen in a
trance-like state in chs. 1 and 8. The word has a more general

meaning, including things heard as well as seen, and sometimes referring to the whole of a prophet's experience and the
record of it.

24. This is a later addition alluding to the exclusion of false
prophets from the people (see on 13: 8f.). ⁕

FALSE WORDS AND LYING VISIONS

The LORD said to me, Man, prophesy of the prophets of **13**1,2
Israel; prophesy,[a] and say to those who prophesy out of
their own hearts, Hear what the LORD says: These are the 3
words of the Lord GOD: Oh, the wicked folly of the
prophets! Their inspiration comes from themselves; they
have seen no vision. Your prophets, Israel, have been like 4
jackals among ruins. They have not gone up into the 5
breach to repair the broken wall round the Israelites, that
they may stand firm in battle on the day of the LORD. Oh, 6
false vision and lying divination! Oh, those prophets who
say, 'It is the very word of the LORD', when it is not the
LORD who has sent them; yet they expect their words to
control the event. Is it not a false vision that you prophets 7
have seen? Is not your divination a lie? You call it the
very word of the LORD, but it is not I who have spoken.

These, then, are the words of the Lord GOD: Because 8
your words are false and your visions a lie, I am against
you, says the Lord GOD. I will raise my hand against the 9
prophets whose visions are false, whose divinations are a
lie. They shall have no place in the counsels of my people;
they shall not be entered in the roll of Israel nor set foot
upon its soil. Thus you shall know that I am the Lord
GOD.

[a] *So Sept.; Heb.* who prophesy.

* Ch. 13 contains two sayings against prophets (verses 1–9 and 10–16) and two similarly constructed sayings against women who prophesy (verses 17–21 and 22f.). Those against the prophets have been extensively elaborated in later periods. The N.E.B. follows the Hebrew paragraph division, but the first saying ends with verse 9. Verses 4, 6 and 9 are not parts of the original.

So-called 'false prophecy' raises complicated issues, for the truth or falsity of prophets' words could only be determined in the end by looking back later to see whether their words had been fulfilled (Deut. 18: 21f.). Jeremiah was attacked as a false – or at least as an inferior – prophet by those who opposed his understanding of God's will (Jer. 28); and he in turn attacked those who were 'prophesying lies' in God's name (Jer. 14: 14; 23: 25). Moreover, in the additions to his letter to the exiles, Jeremiah opposed those prophets in Babylon who encouraged rebellion and the expectation of an early end to the exile (Jer. 29: 8f., 15, 21–3). Such passages as these remind us that there was a wide variety of prophetic activity in ancient Israel, of which we have only indirect – and often disparaging – information.

2. *prophets of Israel*: it is not specified whether Ezekiel has in mind prophets in Jerusalem or fellow-exiles. *to those who prophesy out of their own hearts*: these words really belong to verse 3 but, by a scribal error, have been added in here. The false prophets are not sent as messengers from God. They cannot even claim to have been used by God to mislead the people, like the 400 prophets who spoke at the inspiration of a lying spirit sent by God (1 Kings 22: 23). They are simply wishful thinkers who make up their words themselves.

3. *Oh, the wicked folly . . . from themselves*: words added as a result of the scribal error in verse 2. Originally the verse here read: 'Woe to those who prophesy out of their own hearts.'

4. The verse is addressed to Israel, not the prophets. Its addition may have been suggested by the image of Jerusalem's decay in verse 5.

5. The verse should begin: 'You have not gone up, etc.' The accusation is addressed to the prophets. *the broken wall*: not an actual stone wall but the people's spiritual defences (cp. the 'wall of defence' in Ezra 9: 9).

6. Both God and the prophets are now spoken of in the third person. The verse expands on the first half of verse 7. *divination*: in this context, any method of telling the future by omens, a widely practised art in the ancient world, which could involve the use of a large range of objects (see on 21: 21f.). A crude modern analogy is tea-cup fortune-telling. Divination was outlawed in Deuteronomy (18: 14) but it seems to have persisted in practice. The false prophets made the same claims as others to bear 'the word of God'. *to control the event*: this is an apt rendering of the phrase 'to be fulfilled'. Insofar as prophets attempted to influence the future for their own purposes they could be classed as sorcerers or magicians. The true prophets, who acted as the messengers of God, believed that God himself controlled events. Their words and actions were powerful in themselves only because they represented what God intended to do.

8f. The brief sentence of doom (*I am against you*) in verse 8 has been expanded in verse 9 to specify the false prophets' exclusion from the community. The prophets are again spoken of in the third person. The three-fold privileges of the people of God are: a share in the decision-making of the community, enrolment as a citizen of Israel, and return to Palestine. If this verse comes from Ezekiel himself it is from the period after 587 B.C., when he openly acknowledged the possibility of the exiles' return to their homeland. ✴

THEY HAVE MISLED MY PEOPLE

Rightly, for they have misled my people by saying that 10 all is well when all is not well. It is as if they were building a wall and used whitewash for the daubing. Tell these 11

daubers that it will fall; rain will pour down in torrents, and I will send hailstones hard as rock streaming down and
12 I will unleash a stormy wind. When the building falls, men will ask, 'Where is the plaster you should have
13 used?' So these are the words of the Lord GOD: In my rage I will unleash a stormy wind; rain will come in torrents in my anger, hailstones hard as rock in my fury,
14 until all is destroyed. I will demolish the building which you have daubed with whitewash and level it to the ground, so that its foundations are laid bare. It shall fall, and you shall be destroyed within it; thus you shall know
15 that I am the LORD. I will spend my rage on the building and on those who daubed it with wash; and people[a] will say, 'The building is gone and the men who daubed it
16 are gone, those prophets of Israel who prophesied to Jerusalem, who saw visions of prosperity when there was no prosperity.' This is the very word of the Lord GOD.

✻ The reason for this second prophecy is given in verse 10. The sentence of judgement occurs in verses 13f. The prophets have misled the people by proclaiming peace, and their attractive but superficial contribution to Israel's life will not protect the nation from punishment.

10. The Hebrew text begins 'Because, yes, because they have misled . . .', indicating the start of a new saying. *all is well*: or simply 'peace' (*shālōm*, see on 7: 25–6a). The prophet Micah, in the eighth century B.C., had attacked the prophets who led God's people astray, giving promises of peace in return for gifts (Mic. 3: 5). In Ezekiel's own period Jeremiah spoke of prophets who assured people that all was well and failed to warn them of the deep disorder of their lives (Jer. 6: 14; cp. 23: 17). Ezekiel takes up the same theme, illustrating

[a] *Prob. rdg.; Heb.* I.

it, as in verse 5, by reference to a wall which the prophets
have not constructed adequately. Here the wall is not that of
the city but may be a kind of fence built of loosely packed
stones. A different Hebrew word, normally used of the walls
of houses, is used in verses 12ff. Whitewash may have added
to the wall's appearance but added nothing to its strength.

11f. An addition repeating part of the judgement of verses
13f. and reinforcing it with a scornful question.

13f. The failure of the prophets of peace to strengthen the
nation's life will be exposed. *It shall fall, and you shall be
destroyed within it*: the pronoun 'it' is feminine, but the word
for 'wall', to which 'it' refers, is masculine. The phrase is
thus an addition, specifying the destruction of the prophets
as stated in verse 15. The figurative destruction of the prophets
of peace would indeed have coincided with Jerusalem's fall,
for that event disproved their earlier words of hope and showed
that they had been speaking without divine authority.

15f. The first of these verses takes up the question of verse
12 and together they reflect the prior destruction of Jerusalem. ✶

YOU HUNT MEN'S LIVES

Now turn, man, to the women of your people who 17
prophesy out of their own hearts, and prophesy to them.
Say to them, These are the words of the Lord GOD: I 18
loathe you, you women who hunt men's lives by sewing
magic bands upon the[a] wrists and putting veils over the
heads of persons of every age; are you to hunt the lives
of my people and keep your own lives safe? You have 19
violated my sanctity before my people with handfuls
of barley and scraps of bread. You bring death to those
who should not die, and life to those who should not live,
by lying to this people of mine who listen to lies. So these 20

[a] *So some MSS.; others* my.

are the words of the Lord GOD: I am against your magic bands with which*ᵃ* you hunt men's lives for the excitement of it. I will tear them from your arms and set those lives at liberty, lives that you hunt for the excitement of 21 it. I will tear up your long veils and save my people from you; you shall no longer have power to hunt them. 22 Thus you shall know that I am the LORD. You discouraged the righteous man with lies, when I meant him no hurt; you so strengthened the wicked that he would not aban- 23 don his evil ways and be saved; and therefore you shall never see your false visions again nor practise your divination any more. I will rescue my people from your power; and thus you shall know that I am the LORD.

✻ Although spoken of as those who 'prophesy', the women who are the subject of these verses hardly deserve the honoured title 'prophetess', which is elsewhere applied to such figures as Miriam (Exod. 15: 20), Deborah (Judg. 4: 4) and Huldah (2 Kings 22: 14). Rather, witchcraft and divination typify their activities and 'sorceress' would be a more apt title for them. Verses 17-21 are similar to verses 2-9, with their introductions followed by a cry of woe or loathing (which includes the reason for the judgement), and then the judgement itself. Verses 22f. are parallel to verses 10-14, with the reason for the judgement given in a brief direct statement (verse 22).

18f. *hunt men's lives*: the allusion seems to be to the control of people's lives by sorcery. The sorceresses have no need to fear for themselves. They *keep (their) own lives safe* by protective magic. *magic bands* and *veils* could be obtained in exchange for gifts of food, to protect people from misfortune brought about by evil spirits or sorceresses in the pay of enemies.

[a] with which: *so Pesh.; Heb.* where.

You have violated my sanctity: this suggests the holy name of
God was invoked in the women's acts of sorcery. Like the
false prophets, the sorceresses acted not as the agents of some
foreign deity but in the name of Israel's own God. *You bring
death . . .*: the power of sorcerers to kill or preserve life is
unquestioned wherever sorcery is widely practised. Sorcery
was forbidden in Deut. 18: 10 since it implied service of
powers other than God. But it was common in the ancient
world and persists in various forms among many peoples
today, including some of those of Africa and the South
Pacific. Ps. 91 invests God with power over the evil forces
employed by sorcerers, but remnants of belief in magic
persisted throughout the biblical period. An interesting
counterpart to the New Testament legend of Peter's shadow
healing people (Acts 5: 15) is the current New Guinean belief
that a sorcerer's shadow can cause death if it falls on a person.
by lying to this people . . .: the Hebrew indicates that these
words refer to the activities of men rather than women.
They are a later addition specifying the falsehood of sorcery.
Ezekiel does not deny the power of sorcery but proclaims
the greater power of God.

20f. *for the excitement of it . . . lives that you hunt for the
excitement of it*: the first phrase is absent from the Septuagint.
The meaning of the word it represents is uncertain and both
phrases are probably later additions. According to the previous
verse the women practised their sorcery as a profession
whereby they earned a meagre living. *liberty*: freedom from
the fear of magic.

22f. The good man is discouraged by his fear of sorcery.
But the evil man finds in sorcery a means of extending his
wickedness and avoiding the punishment that might bring
about his repentance. So the people's rescue from the sorceresses' power is foretold, in words which recall their earlier
rescue by God from the oppressive power of Egypt (Exod.
18: 9f.). ✲

IDOLATRY AMONG THE EXILES

14 Some of the elders of Israel came to visit me, and while
2, 3 they sat with me the LORD said to me, Man, these people
have set their hearts on their idols and keep their eyes
fixed on the sinful things that cause their downfall. Am I
4 to let such men consult me? Speak to them and tell
them that these are the words of the Lord GOD: If any
Israelite, with his heart set on his idols and his eyes fixed
on the sinful things that cause his downfall, comes to a
prophet, I, the LORD, in my own person,*a* shall be con-
5 strained to answer him, despite his many idols. My answer
will grip the hearts of the Israelites, estranged from me as
6 they are, one and all, through their idols. So tell the
Israelites that these are the words of the Lord GOD: Turn
away, turn away from your idols; turn your backs on all
7 your abominations. If any man, Israelite or alien, renoun-
ces me, sets his heart upon idols and fixes his eyes upon
the vile thing that is his downfall – if such a man comes to
consult me through a prophet, I, the LORD, in my own
8 person, shall be constrained to answer him. I will set my
face against that man; I will make him an example and a
byword; I will rid my people of him. Thus you shall
9 know that I am the LORD. If a prophet is seduced into
making a prophecy, it is I the LORD who have seduced
him; I will stretch out my hand and rid my people Israel
10 of him. Both shall be punished; the prophet and the man
11 who consults him alike are guilty. And never again will
the Israelites stray from their allegiance, never again defy
my will and bring pollution upon themselves; they will

[*a*] in my own person: *so Targ.; Heb.* through it.

become my people, and I will become their God. This is the very word of the Lord GOD.

✴ The situation, like that of 8: 1, is one in which representatives of the exiles come to seek guidance from the prophet. But here Ezekiel is instructed to deliver a prophecy concerning the deeds of the exiles themselves. Moreover, the message is one to end all prophecy, since it denies the right of idolaters to seek God's guidance through a prophet. It seems the exiles had adopted various objects of Babylonian worship. This was natural enough, for the God of Israel had apparently been overpowered in his own land and his people must have felt it wise to respect the gods of their conquerors. Certainly they had not rejected the God of their fathers altogether, as they were seeking his guidance through Ezekiel. But they were taking no chances by ignoring other powerful forces. Israel's God, however, demands unswerving loyalty to himself alone. The original prophecy is found in verses 4f. and 8. In verses 9f. Ezekiel appears to have added to the prophecy so as to deal with the case of a prophet who does give guidance to idolaters.

1. *elders of Israel*: not 'elders of Judah' as in 8: 1. Here it is emphasized again that the future of Israel lies with the exiles.

3. *set their hearts on their idols*: or 'set their idols in their hearts', so that their lives were governed by them. For *idols* see on 6: 3f., and for *sinful things that cause their downfall* see on 7: 19f.

4. The prophecy takes the form of priestly law in which a hypothetical case is described and a judgement concerning it is given (cp. Lev. 17: 3f., 8f., etc.). The judgement in this instance, that God will answer the idolater, does not contradict the refusal to give guidance which is implied by the rhetorical question in verse 3. The answer will be the idolater's exclusion from the community which lives under God's guidance (verse 8).

6f. The first of these additions (verse 6) specifies the purpose of verse 5, to bring about the people's repentance. The second (verse 7) largely repeats verse 4, but the case now includes a reference to *alien(s)*, as often in priestly law (e.g. Lev. 17: 10).

8. This verse originally continued and concluded the prophecy of verses 4f. The penalties are also borrowed from the priestly instruction of the sanctuaries. For God setting his face against a person, see Lev. 17: 10; for the transgressor as *an example and a byword*, see Deut. 28: 37; and for being literally 'cut off' from God's people, see again Lev. 17: 10. Such excommunication was extremely serious since it meant consignment to a living death, without the support or protection of God, in a world of hostile forces (see further on 18: 1–9 and 10–20).

9f. In this expansion of his earlier words Ezekiel is not concerned with false prophecy. Rather he deals with prophets persuaded or *seduced* to give guidance to idolaters, whether out of a desire to please, or even out of compassion for those who come to them. In view of what he has already said, Ezekiel can only conceive of a prophet obtaining guidance for idolaters if God intentionally misleads him. This seemingly callous explanation agrees with the thought of Deut. 13: 1–5, that prophets who encourage worship of other gods are sent by Israel's God to test his people, and such prophets should be put to death for their pains! Both Ezekiel and Deuteronomy affirm God's control of true prophetic inspiration. But their main concern is to prevent any later pronouncements being made, which might revoke their words against giving guidance to idolaters or encouraging false worship.

11. Like verse 6, this addition looks to the goal of the prophecy, envisaging an obedient nation no longer defiled by contact with idols. ✳

88

WHEN A COUNTRY SINS

These were the words of the LORD to me: Man, when a 12, 13
country sins by breaking faith with me, I will stretch out
my hand and cut short its daily bread.[a] I will send famine
upon it and destroy both men and cattle. Even if those 14
three men were living there, Noah, Danel[b] and Job,
they would save none but themselves by their righteousness. This is the very word of the Lord GOD. If I should 15
turn wild beasts loose in a country to destroy its inhabitants, until it became a waste through which no man
would pass for fear of the beasts, then, if those three men 16
were living there, as I live, says the Lord GOD, they would
not save even their own sons and daughters; they would
save themselves alone, and the country would become a
waste. Or if I should bring the sword upon that country 17
and command it to go through the land and should
destroy men and cattle, then, if those three men were 18
living there, as I live, says the Lord GOD, they could save
neither son nor daughter; they would save themselves
alone. Or if I should send pestilence on that land and pour 19
out my fury upon it in blood, to destroy men and cattle,
then, if Noah, Danel and Job were living there, as I live, 20
says the Lord GOD, they would save neither son nor
daughter; they would save themselves alone by their
righteousness.

These were the words of the Lord GOD: How much 21
less hope is there for Jerusalem when I inflict on her these
four punishments of mine, sword and famine, wild

---

[a] *Lit.* and break its stick of bread.
[b] *Or, as otherwise read,* Daniel.

beasts and pestilence, to destroy both men and cattle!
22 Some will be left in her, some survivors to be brought
out, both sons and daughters. Look at them as they come
out to you, and see how they have behaved and what they
have done. This will be some comfort to you for all the
harm I have done to Jerusalem and all I have inflicted
23 upon her. It will bring you comfort when you see how
they have behaved and what they have done; for you will
know that it was not without reason that I dealt thus with
her. This is the very word of the Lord GOD.

* The long legal discourse in verses 13–20 is followed in
verse 21 by a prophecy of the complete destruction of
Jerusalem's unrighteous inhabitants. Additions in the two
concluding verses acknowledge the existence of unrighteous
survivors, but the prophet's original intention was to show
the inevitability and justice of the city's impending doom.
No appeal to righteous individuals among the inhabitants of
Jerusalem could turn back divine punishment. Possibly
some other prophet had raised the exiles' hopes for Jerusalem,
interceding as Abraham had done for Sodom (Gen. 18:
22–33), asking for a repeal of judgement on account of a few
righteous men within it. Jeremiah himself had apparently
interceded for Jerusalem, but the response he received from
God to his plea was an unqualified 'No'. Not even if Moses
and Samuel together interceded would God relent and avert
the 'four kinds of doom' appointed for his people (Jer. 15:
1–3). Features of both the passages in Genesis and Jeremiah
are combined in these verses. Ezekiel supposes the existence
of three figures of exemplary virtue dwelling in a particular
country. Each time one of four kinds of punishment falls
upon the country it is affirmed that the three righteous men
alone will be saved. The verbal repetition implies the exhaus-
tion of every possibility of escape, as does the list of four

scourges (see on 5: 16f.). By swearing on his own life (verses 16, 18, 20) God stakes his honour on the execution of just punishment. The implication that God's authority extends to all countries and peoples is an important feature of the passage. The matter of the individual's own responsibility for his guilt or righteousness is dealt with in ch. 18.

13. *breaking faith*: the expression is common in priestly material and means the conscious breaking of religious laws (see also 15: 8 and elsewhere).

14. Noah was the one righteous man of his time (Gen. 7: 1) and his family was saved with him. Danel appears in ancient texts from north Syria (Ugarit) as a wise and righteous ruler; his proverbial wisdom is mentioned in Ezek. 28: 3 (see further *The Making of the Old Testament*, pp. 25ff., in this series). He has probably then become the hero of the book of Daniel, though the precise relationship is uncertain. The righteousness of Job is further attested in the Old Testament book of that name (Job 1: 1, 8), but it is clear that the author of the biblical Job was drawing on an old and popular tale, known also to Ezekiel.

21. If only the righteous escape from one type of punishment, how complete the destruction of the unrighteous will be when four kinds of punishment come upon Jerusalem.

22f. In verse 22*a* Ezekiel has revised the earlier judgement, acknowledging the existence of unrighteous survivors 'who bring out' sons and daughters. Their evil behaviour will show how richly they deserved punishment. Verse 23*b*, *for you will know . . .*, once concluded the judgement, confirming its justice. The remainder of these verses, *This will be some comfort . . . what they have done* (22*b*–23*a*), is a later addition, repeating part of verse 22*a*, but changing Ezekiel's own addition from an example and warning to the exiles into a word of comfort. ✳

FUEL FOR THE FIRE

15 These were the words of the Lord to me:

2   Man, how is the vine better than any other tree,
than a branch from a tree in the forest?

3   Is wood got from it
fit to make anything useful?
Can men make it into a peg
and hang things on it?

4   If it is put on the fire for fuel,
if its two ends are burnt by the fire
and the middle is charred,
is it fit for anything useful?

5   Nothing useful could be made of it even when
whole;
how much less, when it is burnt by the fire and
charred,
can it be made into anything useful!

6 So these are the words of the Lord God:

I treat the vine, as against forest-trees,
only as fuel for the fire,
even so I treat the people of Jerusalem;

7   I set my face against them.
Though they escape from the fire, fire shall burn
them up.
Thus you shall know that I am the Lord
when I set my face against them,

8   making the land a waste
because they have broken faith.
This is the very word of the Lord God.

✲ The allegory of the vine portrays the total destruction of
the people of Jerusalem because they are unproductive and
valueless. Earlier prophets likened God's people to a vine.
Isaiah (5: 1–7) has a comparison between Judah and a vineyard which produces 'wild grapes' in spite of all God's care,
and Jeremiah (2: 21) spoke of the people as 'true stock'which
became debased and worthless on account of their sin. Jesus
used the same figure for Israel (e.g. Mark 12: 1–9) and he
appears as the true vine himself in John 15: 1–6. But, as is
typical of Ezekiel, there is no reference here to the people's
former virtues and he ignores the importance of the vine to
the success of the grape harvest. He focuses directly on the
point of the vine wood's uselessness – except as firewood. The
figure of a vine is found again in ch. 17. This is the first
chapter of Ezekiel to be printed as poetry in the N.E.B.,
although it is not the first poem in the book (see on 7: 1–9).
Some scholars have regarded the poetry of the book as the
only words to have come from the prophet himself, but
among other things that assumes a more exact knowledge of
Hebrew poetry than we in fact have. A few of its characteristic features are mentioned in the notes on 7: 10–27 and 19: 1–9.
It is extremely difficult to render adequately in English the
similar or contrasting ideas, or the rhythm of the Hebrew,
particularly in a text as complex and irregular as Ezekiel's.

2. In comparing the vine and common forest trees the
prophet intends to correct the belief that Israel, as God's
people, had of right a favoured position over against other
nations.

4. *its two ends* were the northern kingdom of Israel, sacked
in 722 B.C., and the southern kingdom of Judah, conquered
in 597 B.C. Only Jerusalem remained in between, and that
was depleted or *charred* by the exile of its leaders.

7f. *Though they escape* may be read as 'though they have
escaped'. The subject is still the people of Jerusalem, who
escaped the first deportation but who will not escape the
second onslaught on the city. The allegory and its inter-

pretation originally concluded with the words, *I am the* LORD. The remaining words are a secondary description of the judgement and its cause, reinforcing the lesson of what ensued from *broken faith* after the disaster of 587 B.C. ✷

A FOUNDLING'S TALE

16 1,2 The word of the LORD came to me: Man, he said, make
3 Jerusalem see her abominable conduct. Tell her that these are the words of the Lord GOD to her: Canaan is the land of your ancestry and there you were born; an Amorite
4 was your father and a Hittite your mother. This is how you were treated at birth: when you were born, your navel-string was not tied,*a* you were not bathed in water ready for the rubbing, you were not salted as you should
5 have been nor wrapped in swaddling clothes. No one cared for you enough to do any of these things or, indeed, to have any pity for you; you were thrown out on the bare ground in your own filth on the day of your
6 birth. Then I came by and saw you kicking helplessly in your own blood; I spoke to you, there in your blood,
7 and bade you live.*b* I tended you like an evergreen plant, like something growing in the fields; you throve and grew. You came to full womanhood; your breasts became firm and your hair grew, but still you were naked and exposed.
8   Again I came by and saw that you were ripe for love. I spread the skirt of my robe over you and covered your naked body. Then I plighted my troth and entered into a covenant with you, says the Lord GOD, and you became

[a] *Prob. rdg., cp. one MS.; others* cut.
[b] I spoke. . .live: *so some MSS.; others repeat these words.*

mine. Then I bathed you in water and washed off the 9
blood and anointed you with oil. I gave you robes of 10
brocade and sandals of stout*a* hide; I fastened a linen girdle
round you and dressed you in lawn.*b* For jewellery I put 11
bracelets on your arms and a chain round your neck; I 12
gave you a nose-ring, I put pendants in your ears and a
beautiful coronet on your head. You had ornaments of 13
gold and silver, your dresses were of linen, lawn,*b* and
brocade. You had flour and honey and olive oil for food,
and you grew very beautiful, you grew into a queen.
The fame of your beauty went all over the world, for the 14
splendour with which I decked you made it perfect. This
is the very word of the Lord GOD.

✶ Both Hosea and Jeremiah described God's people as his
bride (Hos. 2; Jer. 2: 2); Ezekiel takes up that theme here
and in ch. 23, applying the figure of the bride to the capital
cities of Judah and Israel. But in the present chapter he also
adopts a common folk-tale of an abandoned infant, found and
cared for by a benevolent stranger whom she later marries.
The chapter is extremely complex. The prophecy originally
consisted of the tale told as a parable of Jerusalem's rejection
of her covenant responsibilities (verses 1–14), followed by a
brief declaration of overwhelming judgement in verses
39–41. Ezekiel himself appears to have turned the simple
parable into a detailed allegory, by the interpretation of
several features of the tale in verses 15–34. But in verses 44–58
his followers have combined with the prophet's words
features of ch. 23, charging Jerusalem with crimes worse
than those of her sister cities. Finally, a word of encouragement and future hope has been added (verses 59–63), based on
Ezekiel's later words concerning a new covenant. Verses

[*a*] *Lit.* sea-cow.   [*b*] *Mng. of Heb. word uncertain.*

1–14 describe the outcast infant's rise to good fortune. This emphasizes the extent of divine pity in caring for one so undesirable and of such poor parentage. The apparent harmony of the relationship between God and his young bride should be noted too (cp. Hos. 2: 15) for elsewhere Ezekiel portrays the relationship as one of unrelieved betrayal and rebellion on Jerusalem's part (see on 20: 1–7; 23: 3).

2f. The situation is that of a law court. Like a prosecuting counsel, Ezekiel is to declare to Jerusalem the crimes of which she stands accused, but the message is intended as much for the ears of the exiles, as for the city itself. Jerusalem was a Canaanite – or, more specifically, Jebusite – city, captured by David to serve as the capital of the united kingdoms of Israel and Judah (2 Sam. 5: 6–9). The words 'Canaanite' and 'Amorite' are often synonymous in the Old Testament and, although the Amorites were of the same Semitic stock as the Israelites, they were associated with the pagan ways of the pre-Israelite inhabitants of Palestine. The Hittites from Asia Minor were an Indo-European people, extremely influential during the second millennium B.C. Ezekiel's description underlines Jerusalem's alien ways.

4. Being of mixed race, and pagan races at that, the infant is treated in a pagan fashion. It was a widespread custom to leave unwanted children, especially girls, exposed to die. Otherwise infants were washed (anointed with oil), and rubbed with salt, according to the practice still followed in Palestine. Such cleansing may have been intended to ward off evil spirits. The baby would then have been bound tightly in strips of cloth for seven days, at which time the washing and anointing was repeated.

6. *in your own blood*: readily understood as the child's birth blood. But in the Hebrew the plural is used for *blood* and an implicit meaning is the defiling guilt of bloodshed, with which the city is elsewhere charged (22: 2; 24: 6). These words may be an element of later expansion. *live:* an imperative in the Hebrew. The command to 'Live!' comes like the

creative word of life in Gen. 1, making possible what is commanded.

7. *your hair grew*: that is, pubic hair. *naked and exposed*: the young woman had nothing to pride herself on but her natural beauty.

8. 'Spreading one's skirt' and 'covering a woman's naked-ness' were colloquial expressions for marriage and the protec-tion it conferred on the wife. For the former see Ruth 3: 9, and for marriage as a binding covenant see Mal. 2: 14.

10. Although some words here are obscure the overall meaning is clear. The very finest apparel was provided for the young bride.

13f. *you grew into a queen*: a late addition. It may have been assumed that the 'coronet' or 'crown' of verse 12 was a royal, rather than a bridal, crown. Jerusalem is not, however, portrayed elsewhere in this chapter as a royal city. Originally these verses may have read simply: *You had ornaments of gold and silver...and you grew very beautiful*. The remainder repeats part of verse 10 and reflects the widespread political notoriety attributed to Jerusalem in ch. 23. ✳

YOU PROSTITUTED YOURSELF

But you trusted to your beauty and prostituted your fame; 15 you committed fornication, offering yourself freely to any passer-by for your beauty to become his. You took 16 some of your clothes and decked a platform for yourself in gay colours and there you committed fornication; you had intercourse with him for your beauty to become his.[a] You took the splendid ornaments of gold and silver 17 which I had given you, and made for yourself male images with which you committed fornication. You 18 covered them with your robes of brocade and offered up

[a] you had intercourse... his: *prob. rdg.; Heb. obscure.*

19 my oil and my incense before them. You took the food I had given you, the flour, the oil, and the honey, with which I had fed you, and set it before them as an offering of soothing odour.[a] This is the very word of the Lord GOD.

20 You took the sons and daughters whom you had borne to me, and sacrificed them to these images for their food.
21 Was this of less account than your fornication? No! you slaughtered my children and handed them over, you
22 surrendered them to your images. With all your abominable fornication you forgot those early days when you lay naked and exposed, kicking helplessly in your own blood.
23 After all the evil you had done (Oh! the pity of it, says
24 the Lord GOD), you built yourself a couch and constructed
25 a high-stool in every open place. You built up your high-stools at the top of every street and disgraced your beauty, offering your body to any passer-by in countless
26 acts of fornication. You committed fornication with your gross neighbours, the Egyptians, and you provoked me to anger by your countless acts of fornication.

27 I stretched out my hand against you and cut down your portion. Then I gave you up to women who hated you, Philistine women, who were so disgusted by your lewd
28 ways. Not content with this, you committed fornication with the Assyrians, led them into fornication and still
29 were not content. You committed countless acts of fornication in Chaldaea, the land of commerce, and even with this you were not content.

30 How you anger me! says the Lord GOD. You have done
31 all this like the imperious whore you are. You have built

[a] *So Pesh.; Heb. adds* and it was.

98

your couch at the top of every street and constructed
your stool in every open place, but, unlike the common
prostitute, you have scorned a fee. An adulterous wife 32
who owes obedience to her husband takes a fee from*[a]*
strangers. The prostitute also takes her fee; but you give 33
presents to all your lovers, you bribe them to come
from all quarters to commit fornication with you. You 34
are the very opposite of other women in your fornication:
no one runs after you, you do not receive a fee, you give
it. You are the very opposite.

* The term 'to pass or come by' occurred twice in the
previous section (verses 6, 8). It was an expression of importance in the tradition known in Deuteronomy, Hosea and
Jeremiah, of God 'finding' Israel in the wilderness and there
entering into a special relationship with her. The same term
is found in verses 15 and 23–5 of the present section, which
originally described, in quite concise terms, the misdeeds
of the young bride. She offered her favours to any 'passer-by'.
Subsequently this misdeed has been elaborated, partly by
Ezekiel himself, into a detailed allegory in which the misuse
of each gift and the manner of fornication are explained.

15. *your fame*: or literally 'your name' as a woman of rare
beauty, an idea already elaborated in verse 14. *for your beauty
to become his:* the meaning of the Hebrew is obscure and the
words may represent the beginning of verse 23, repeated here
in error when verses 16–22 were inserted. The N.E.B.
rendering here has been repeated for the equally obscure words
at the end of verse 16.

16–22. Four accusations are introduced with the words
You took (verses 16, 17, 19, 20).

16. The first deals with the misuse of the clothes (verse 10).
The *platform* was literally a 'high-place' or country sanctuary.

[a] a fee from: *prob. rdg.; Heb. om.*

Both male and female prostitutes were attached to some country sanctuaries and apparently even to the temple (Hos. 4: 18; 2 Kings 23: 7). According to Canaanite belief, intercourse with them stimulated the procreative activities of the gods and so helped make fertile the crops and herds (see also on 8: 14). The young bride offered herself at a sanctuary of her own.

17. *male images*: probably phallic symbols, also used in fertility rites.

18. The verse should begin: 'and you took your robes of brocade and covered them', i.e. the male images. The remainder of the verse is a later addition. Incense is not mentioned among the divine gifts in the previous section.

19. This too is a later addition. The verse begins not with the words *You took*, but: 'and my bread (or food), which I gave you. . .you set before them . . .' The phrase *the flour, the oil, and the honey, with which I had fed you* are a still later insertion, based on verse 13.

20. The last and – judging by the sarcastic question at the end of the verse – most serious of the accusations is that of child sacrifice. This is reported of the reigns of Ahaz and Manasseh of Judah who allegedly sacrificed their own sons – the most valuable of offerings – in times of war (2 Kings 16: 3; 21: 6). Josiah attempted to eliminate the custom (2 Kings 23: 10), but the words of both Jeremiah (Jer. 7: 31) and Ezekiel suggest that the crises of 597 and 587 B.C. brought about its revival.

21f. The first of these verses expands on verse 20. *you surrendered them to your images*: the Hebrew here reflects the technical expression for human sacrifice, 'cause to pass through the fire' (2 Kings 23: 10). That meant the destruction of the victim by fire. The second verse is also an addition, charging the city with ingratitude for God's favours.

23. The original narrative resumes at this point, although the cry of distress (in brackets) is readily distinguishable as a later addition.

24f. *a couch and...a high-stool*: parallel expressions for raised couches on which sacred prostitutes offered themselves for acts of ritual intercourse. Not content with such acts at a single sanctuary (verse 16), places of prostitution were multiplied. The words, *built up your high-stools at the top of every street and*, are an addition further exaggerating the prophetic hyperbole. It remains an open question whether Ezekiel had in mind perversions of his own or former days. Certainly ritual prostitution is not mentioned in ch. 8. But the figure of prostitution may well be more appropriately understood as a symbol of unfaithfulness to God, manifest in a variety of religious practices, including those already portrayed around the temple.

26-9. The explanation of Jerusalem's unfaithfulness in terms of her political alliances diverges from the foregoing. Jerusalem has courted foreign powers in vain attempts to find security. The influence of ch. 23 is unmistakable and the significance of the allusions in verses 26 and 28f. is clear there. Chaldaea is also referred to as a *land of commerce* (verse 29) in 17: 4. Verse 27 is still later material in its present context and probably derives from Ezekiel's followers. It refers to an alliance with Egypt to revolt against Assyria. As a reprisal, Sennacherib made a gift of Judaean territory to the Philistines in 701 B.C. That should have been a warning against entering foreign alliances. The metaphor of Jerusalem as a young maiden is sustained by the reference to the Philistine cities as *women*.

30-4. The parable is carried to its ultimate absurdity in this addition, which is also from Ezekiel's followers. Not only has Jerusalem – *the imperious whore* – prostituted herself by her aspirations after political power, but she has given her lovers the gifts God gave to her. Here the authors have in mind tribute paid to foreign powers. Verse 32 interrupts the form of address, and its concern with adultery rather than prostitution distinguishes it as a later insertion. ✳

A PROSTITUTE'S END

35 Listen to the words of the LORD, whore that you are.
36 These are the words of the Lord GOD: You have been prodigal in your excesses, you have exposed your naked body in fornication with your lovers. In return for your abominable idols and for the slaughter of the children you
37 have given them, I will gather all those lovers to whom you made advances,*a* all whom you loved and all whom you hated. I will gather them in from all quarters against you; I will strip you naked before them, and they shall
38 see your whole body naked. I will put you on trial for adultery and murder, and I will charge you with*b* blood
39 shed in jealousy and fury. Then I will hand you over to them. They will demolish your couch and pull down your high-stool; they will strip your clothes off, take away your splendid ornaments, and leave you naked and
40 exposed. They will bring up the mob against you and stone you, they will hack you to pieces with their swords.
41 They will burn down your houses and execute judgement on you, and many women shall see it. I will put an end to your fornication, and you shall never again give a fee
42 to your lovers. Then I will abate my fury, and my jealousy will turn away from you. I will be calm and will
43*a* no longer be provoked to anger. For you had forgotten the days of your youth and exasperated me with all your doings: so I in my turn*c* brought retribution upon you for your deeds. This is the very word of the Lord GOD.

[*a*] to whom. . .advances: *or* whom you charmed.
[*b*] charge you with: *prob. mng.; Heb.* give you.
[*c*] *So Vulg.; Heb. adds* behold.

✻ The analysis of the previous section assists in distinguishing the original judgement against the city. Introduced by verse 35, it is found in the opening words of verse 37, 'I will gather all (your) lovers', and it then continues from verse 39 to the first half of verse 41. God will cause the lovers to destroy the prostitute's couches, strip her and have her slain.

36–8. Another reason for the judgement has been added in verse 36, introducing nakedness and idolatry to the previous list of accusations. In verse 37 there is additional commentary on the lovers, some of whom it now appears were loathed (cp. 23: 28). The remainder of the verse, and verse 38, speak of God himself executing judgement on the woman.

39–41*a*. Stripped of God's gifts, Jerusalem will be as she was before God betrothed her – *naked and exposed* (cp. verse 7). *the mob* (verse 40) is literally 'the assembly', a recognized judicial authority in cases of prostitution and adultery, and responsible too for the execution of the offenders by stoning according to Deut. 22: 21. The words with which the judgement originally concluded, *many women shall see it*, suggests that other cities will be warned by the example made of Jerusalem.

41*b*–43*a*. The judgement envisaging Jerusalem's complete destruction is now modified. God himself will put an end to the woman's waywardness (cp. 23: 27, 48) and satisfy his *fury* (cp. 5: 13). But the repentance and continued existence of Jerusalem is implied. Like verses 36–8, these verses represent several successive attempts by Ezekiel's followers to complete the prophecy, by recalling earlier parts of it and linking ideas in it with other words of the prophet. ✻

SINS WORSE THAN HER SISTERS'

Did you not commit these obscenities, as well as all your 43*b*
other abominations? Dealers in proverbs will say of you 44
'Like mother, like daughter.' You are a true daughter 45

of a mother who loathed her husband and children. You are a true sister of your sisters*a* who loathed their husbands and children. You are all daughters of a Hittite mother
46 and an Amorite father. Your elder sister was Samaria, who lived with her daughters to the north of you; your younger sister, who lived with her daughters to the south of
47 you, was Sodom. Did you not behave as they did and commit the same abominations? You came very near to
48 doing even worse than they. As I live, says the Lord GOD, your sister Sodom and her daughters never behaved as
49 you and your daughters have done. This was the iniquity of your sister Sodom: she and her daughters had pride of wealth and food in plenty, comfort and ease, and yet she
50 never helped the poor and wretched. They grew haughty and did deeds abominable in my sight, and I made
51 away with them, as you have seen. Samaria was never half the sinner you have been; you have committed more abominations than she, abominations which have
52 made your sister seem innocent. You must bear the humiliation which you thought your sisters*b* deserved. Your sins are so much more abominable than theirs that they appear innocent in comparison with you; and now you must bear your shame and humiliation and make your sisters*b* seem innocent.

53   But I will restore the fortunes of Sodom and her daughters and of Samaria and her daughters, and I will
54 restore*c* yours at the same time. Even though you bring them comfort, you will bear your shame, you will be
55 disgraced for all you have done; but when your sister

[a] *So Sept.; Heb.* sister.   [b] *So some MSS.; others* sister.
[c] I will restore: *so Sept.; Heb.* restoration.

Sodom and her daughters become what they were of old, and when your sister Samaria and her daughters become what they were of old, then you and your daughters will be restored. Did you not hear and talk much of your 56 sister Sodom in the days of your pride, before your 57 wickedness was exposed, in the days when the daughters of Aram with those about her were disgraced, and the daughters of the Philistines round about, who so despised you? Now you too must bear the consequences of your 58 lewd and abominable conduct. This is the very word of the LORD.

✣ This and the following section are supplements to the prophecy of the foundling child, from the period after 587 B.C. The example of ch. 23, in which Samaria is described as a sister of Jerusalem, may have contributed to the notion of Jerusalem having yet another sister, Sodom. That city was the epitome of evil and its punishment was complete obliteration (Gen. 19). So the assertion here of its comparative innocence was intended to intensify Jerusalem's guilt and justify beyond question the punishment that had fallen on it. There was no reference to any other children in the story of the foundling, so in introducing them the author recalls Ezekiel's account of Jerusalem's origins (verse 45). In verses 53 and 55 later additions anticipate the restoration of Jerusalem, along with her sister cities. But the remarkable words of hope for Samaria and Sodom were originally intended to contrast with Jerusalem's continuing ignominy (verses 52 and 58).

43*b*. An editorial addition necessitated by the later development of the prophecy.

44f. No mention was made by Ezekiel of the mother's behaviour. The inverse truth of the proverb has been assumed, for the mother's behaviour is described in terms of the daughter's actions in verses 15–20.

46f. *daughters*: satellite cities. In ch. 23 too Samaria is described as the *elder sister*. *You came very near to doing even worse than they*: the whole point of the supplement is that Jerusalem had done worse than her sisters. It therefore seems preferable to adopt an alternative rendering of these words: 'And soon you did even worse than they.'

49f. Since Sodom's sins are not mentioned elsewhere in Ezekiel they have been listed here, in what is probably a later addition. The list is surprising in view of Gen. 19, where sexual immorality appears as the foremost reason for Sodom's destruction. The intention of the author may have been to restate, though indirectly, the requirements of righteousness which Jerusalem should have strived to attain, rather than to focus on grosser crimes which might have allowed the people to plead their own comparative innocence.

52. *and now you must bear* . . .: this largely repeats the first half of the verse and may be just a different form of it. *and make your sisters seem innocent*: this suggests the sisters' innocence depends on Jerusalem bearing her punishment, rather than on her having committed worse sins. A better reading would be: 'for you have made your sisters seem innocent'.

53. *and I will restore yours at the same time*: with the deletion of these and similar words in verse 55, verses 53–8 become consistent with the emphasis of verses 44–52. The sisters, rendered innocent by Jerusalem's far worse crimes, will be restored, while Jerusalem continues to bear her shame. These encouraging words would have been added in the light of verses 59–63.

55. The verse should read: 'but your sister Sodom and her daughters will become what they were of old, and your sister Samaria and her daughters will become what they were of old'. The reason for deleting the last words has been given in the commentary on verse 53.

57. *in the days when the daughters of Aram with those about her were disgraced*: Hebrew manuscripts indicate that 'Edom' should be read for *Aram*. But it was Jerusalem whose disgrace-

ful acts were exposed. So we should probably read with the Septuagint: 'now you are like her (Sodom), an object of disgrace for the daughters of Edom and those about her'. The reference then is to the Ammonites, Moabites and Edomites, who would have observed the collapse of Jerusalem with great interest. In ch. 25, however, there are prophecies against those nations because of the delight they took in the event. *and the daughters of the Philistines round about*: an addition taking into account the Philistine's role in verse 27. ✻

THE COVENANT RE-ESTABLISHED

These are the words of the Lord GOD: I will treat you as 59 you have deserved, because you violated a covenant and made light of a solemn oath. But I will remember the 60 covenant I made with you when you were young, and I will establish with you a covenant which shall last for ever. And you will remember your past ways and feel ashamed 61 when you receive your sisters, the elder and the younger. For I will give them to you as daughters, and they shall not be outside your covenant.[a] Thus I will establish my 62 covenant with you, and you shall know that I am the LORD. You will remember, and will be so ashamed and 63 humiliated that you will never open your mouth again once I have accepted expiation for all you have done. This is the very word of the Lord GOD.

✻ The last major stage in the development of the chapter was the addition of these words to mitigate what had gone before. A disciple has – not unjustifiably – attempted to complete the prophecy by calling to mind Ezekiel's later words of encouragement and hope, without which the point

[a] and they...covenant: *or* though not on the ground of your covenant.

of continued striving, for those who retained a deep affection for Jerusalem, would have been lost. A number of words and phrases recall earlier parts of the chapter and the amazing breadth of concern with the sister cities, already seen in the previous section, is maintained in the anticipation of a renewed covenant relationship between Jerusalem and God.

59. *I will treat you.... .*: the impression is given that judgement has yet to fall. The *covenant* is the marriage agreement sealed by oaths.

60. For *a covenant which shall last for ever*, see 37: 26, but the phrase 'to establish a covenant', here and in verse 62, is characteristic of the Priestly school of writers. Ezekiel prefers an older expression, which rendered literally is 'to cut a covenant'. The word *remember*, repeated in verses 61 and 63, is also of significance. God's act of recalling the former covenant emphasizes the importance of history. The past is not forgotten but has relevance for continuing relationships. The recollection of the past on the part of God's people, however, amounts to an act of repentance (see on 6: 9).

61. *I will give them to you as daughters*: the land will be restored, from northern Israel to the wasted places of the Jordan valley (cp. 47: 8ff.), with Jerusalem as its capital. *and they shall not be outside your covenant*: the meaning of these words is unclear. An alternative rendering is given in the footnotes, suggesting that the gift of the daughter cities was not part of the covenant.

63. *once I have accepted expiation*: the putting right of the relationship between God and Jerusalem required that the latter be punished for violating the covenant. God's acceptance of the punishment as satisfying justice is evident from his gracious re-establishment of the covenant. The importance of such thought for later Christian theories of the atonement is self-evident, though the Christian response of joy is lacking here. Jerusalem's proud boasting of her own righteousness (verse 56) will be heard no more, but her shame and humiliation will be apparent. ✴

THE ALLEGORY OF THE EAGLES

These were the words of the LORD to me: Man, speak to **17**₁,₂
the Israelites in allegory and parable. Tell them that these ₃
are the words of the Lord GOD:

> A great eagle
> with broad wings and long pinions,
> in full plumage, richly patterned,
> > came to Lebanon.
> He took the very top of a cedar-tree,
> he plucked its highest twig;   4
> he carried it off to a land of commerce,
> > and planted it in a city of merchants.
> Then he took a native seed   5
> > and put it in nursery-ground;
> > he set it like a willow,
> a shoot beside abundant water.
> It sprouted and became a vine,   6
> > sprawling low along the ground
> and bending its trailing boughs towards him*a*
> with its roots growing beneath him.
> So it became a vine, it branched out
> > and put forth shoots.
> But there was another*b* great eagle   7
> with broad wings and thick plumage;
> and this vine gave its roots
> > a twist towards him;*a*
> it pushed out its trailing boughs towards him,
> seeking drink from the bed where it was planted,
> > though it had been set   8

[*a*] *Or* inwards.   [*b*] *So Sept.; Heb.* one.

in good ground beside abundant water
that it might bear shoots and be fruitful
and become a noble vine.

9 Tell them that these are the words of the Lord GOD:

Can such a vine flourish?
Will not its roots be broken off
and its fruit be stripped,
and all its fresh sprouting leaves wither,[a]
until it is uprooted and carried away
with little effort and few hands?

10 If it is transplanted, can it flourish?
Will it not be utterly shrivelled,
as though by the touch of the east wind,
on the bed where it ought to sprout?

* Zedekiah's wavering loyalty to Nebuchadrezzar, and its inevitable outcome, is described first in poetry.

2. *allegory and parable*: used as synonyms, since both words may refer to stories of which the real meanings lie beneath the surface. The narrative here is actually presented as a riddle in the form of a fable, in which animals and plants speak and act as humans.

3f. *A great eagle*: Nebuchadrezzar. The eagle was a symbol of power, representing the sun god in both Babylon and Egypt. The *cedar*, prized among trees, stands for the house of David, whose heir (or topmost branch) was Jehoiachin when Nebuchadrezzar came to Jerusalem (*Lebanon*) and, in 597 B.C., took the young king into exile.

5f. the *vine* is Zedekiah, the regent, established in favourable circumstances by Nebuchadrezzar and continuing in dependence on him (*its roots growing beneath him*).

7f. the second *great eagle* was either Pharaoh Psammetichus II

[a] *So Sept.; Heb. adds* it will wither.

(593–588 B.C.) or Pharaoh Hophra (588–569 B.C.). Zedekiah sought independence from Babylon by appealing to Egypt – the vine is depicted as turning towards the eagle – although in the event support came too late (Jer. 37: 5ff.).

9. The question implies the destruction of the vine.

10. The ideas of transplanting and destruction as though by the east wind are new elements in the fable, added later to reinforce verse 9 and specify the destroyer. *the east wind*: a hot, dry and dusty wind that could quickly lay waste all vegetation (Gen. 41: 6); a figure of Nebuchadrezzar (see also 19: 12). ✲

THE FIRST INTERPRETATIONS

These were the words of the LORD to me: Say to that 11,12 rebellious people, Do you not know what this means? The king of Babylon came to Jerusalem, took its king and its officers and had them brought to him at Babylon. He took a prince of the royal line and made a treaty with 13 him, putting him on his oath. He took away the chief men of the country, so that it should become a humble 14 kingdom unable to raise itself but ready to observe the treaty and keep it in force. But the prince rebelled against 15 him and sent messengers to Egypt, asking for horses and men in plenty. Can such a man prosper? Can he escape destruction if he acts in this way? Can he violate a covenant and escape? As I live, says the Lord GOD, I 16 swear that he shall die in the land of the king who put him on the throne; he made light of his oath and violated the covenant he made with him. He shall die in Babylon. Pharaoh will send no large army, no great host, to protect 17 him in battle; no siege-ramp will be raised, no watch-tower put up, nor will the lives of many men be lost. He 18 has violated a covenant and has made light of his oath.

He had submitted, and yet he did all these things; he shall not escape.

19 These then are the words of the Lord GOD: As I live, he has made light of the oath he took by me and has violated the covenant I made with him. I will bring 20 retribution upon him; I will cast my net over him, and he shall be caught in its meshes. I will carry him to Babylon and bring him to judgement there, because he 21 has broken faith with me. In all his squadrons every commander shall fall by the sword; those who are left will be scattered to the four winds. Thus you shall know that it is I, the LORD, who have spoken.

✲ The need for any interpretation of an allegory whose meaning would have been clear to its first hearers has been questioned. Also, within these verses there are two distinct interpretations, one in poetry (verses 11–15, 19) and one in prose (verses 16–18), while the following section (verses 22–4) develops the allegory in quite another way. These facts again indicate that the book of Ezekiel grew as the words of the prophet were repeated, explained, and reapplied, whether by the prophet himself or by his followers. The original allegory dates from the years of Zedekiah's revolt against Babylon (589–587 B.C.), and so too may the poetic interpretation in verses 11–15, which concludes with the prophecy of doom in verse 19 – 'I will bring retribution upon him.' But the prose interpretation (verses 16–18) reveals knowledge of the death of Zedekiah in Babylon and the failure of Egyptian support, so that it is to be dated after 587 B.C. Moreover, Zedekiah is literally said to have been 'made king' in verse 16. This is out of character with the prophet's avoidance of the title 'king' for Zedekiah elsewhere. Thus these verses appear to be later expansions of the poetic interpretation, like verses 20f., which are little different from 12: 13f.

12. *its king and its officers*: Jehoiachin and his ministers.

13. *a treaty...putting him on his oath*: Zedekiah was made to pledge loyalty to Nebuchadrezzar.

16. *who put him on the throne*: literally 'who made him king'.

17. *no siege-ramp will be raised...*: rather read, 'when a siege-ramp is raised, and watch-towers put up, to cut off the lives of many men'; a critical reflection on Pharaoh Hophra's belated and inadequate support for the besieged Jerusalem (see on verses 7f.).

19. *the oath he took by me*: Zedekiah would have sworn by the name of his God to keep the covenant and so God became the guardian of the agreement.

20f. See on 12: 13f. *bring him to judgement there*: that is, in Babylon. Zedekiah was in fact judged at Riblah (see on 12: 12). ✳

A NOBLE CEDAR

These are the words of the Lord GOD: 22

> I, too, will take a slip
>   from the lofty crown of the cedar
>   and set it in the soil;
> I will pluck a tender shoot from the topmost branch
>   and plant it.
> I will plant it high on a lofty mountain,   23
>   the highest mountain in Israel.
> It will put out branches, bear its fruit,
>   and become a noble cedar.
> Winged birds of every kind will roost under it,
>   they will roost in the shelter of its sweeping
>   boughs.
>   All the trees of the country-side will know   24
>   that it is I, the LORD,

who bring low the tall tree
and raise the low tree high,
who dry up the green tree
and make the dry tree put forth buds.
I, the LORD, have spoken and will do it.

✳ This second allegory is only loosely related to that of the two eagles, although it is intended to relieve the despairing note of the previous verses. It is God who plants the young shoot and there is no longer any concern with Zedekiah's behaviour. Instead there is taken up the figure of the 'highest twig' (verse 4), meaning now the royal line of David, a descendant of which will reign on Mount Zion ('the highest mountain in Israel') and bring peace for all mankind. Ezekiel himself anticipated an heir of David assuming rule in Jerusalem (see on 21: 25–7; 37: 21–3) and his thought has here been elaborated by his followers, probably some time after 587 B.C., to encourage the exiles with the hope of a legitimate new ruler arising among them.

22. *a tender shoot from the topmost branch*: the Messiah, a king of David's line, is referred to as a 'shoot' or 'branch' in a number of other prophecies (Isa. 11: 1; Jer. 23:5; Zech. 3: 8; 6: 12).

23. *a lofty mountain. . .*: cp. 40: 2; Isa. 2: 2. *Winged birds. . .*: read instead with the Septuagint 'every kind of beast will dwell under it, and every kind of bird will roost in the shelter . . .' The picture of a great tree, which gives protection to all creatures, is drawn from a common stock of ancient Near-Eastern imagery (see on 31: 1–18; and cp. Dan. 4: 10–12; Matt. 13: 32).

24. *All the trees of the country-side*: that is, other nations, who will realize God's part in human affairs, whether he humbles men or causes them to prosper. ✳

THE RIGHTEOUS SHALL LIVE

These were the words of the LORD to me: What do you **18**₁,₂
all mean by repeating this proverb in the land of Israel:

> 'The fathers have eaten sour grapes,
> and the children's teeth are set on edge'?

As I live, says the Lord GOD, this proverb shall never again 3
be used in Israel. Every living soul belongs to me; father 4
and son alike are mine. The soul that sins shall die.

Consider the man who is righteous and does what is 5
just and right. He never feasts at mountain-shrines, never 6
lifts his eyes to the idols of Israel, never dishonours
another man's wife, never approaches a woman during
her periods. He oppresses no man, he returns the debtor's 7
pledge,ᵃ he never robs. He gives bread to the hungry and
clothes to those who have none. He never lends either at 8
discount or at interest. He shuns injustice and deals fairly
between man and man. He conforms to my statutes and 9
loyally observes my laws. Such a man is righteous: he
shall live, says the Lord GOD.

✶ Ch. 18 contains the fullest explanation of the theme of
individual responsibility, the best-known element in Ezekiel's
teaching. As if in debate with his people, the prophet takes up
a number of their sayings as he argues that God has acted
toward them precisely as they have deserved. But he concludes that the repentance of any individual will ensure that
that person will nonetheless 'live'. Set between allegories of
Israel's princes in chs. 17 and 19, this chapter is intrusive in its
present context. So too are the related passages, 3: 16–21 and
33: 1–20. They deal with Ezekiel's appointment as a 'watch-

[a] the debtor's pledge: *so Sept.; Heb. unintelligible.*

man' or pastor of Israel, probably after 587 B.C., and the terms in which 'righteousness' and 'life' are to be proclaimed in the community.

The idea of men's individual responsibility before God should not be thought of as Ezekiel's own invention, nor even as having arisen in Ezekiel's period. The very early laws in the Book of the Covenant (Exod. 20: 22 – 23: 33) take for granted the principle of individual responsibility for wrong behaviour. But a saying which must have been current in the time of Jeremiah and Ezekiel is quoted by both prophets: 'the fathers have eaten sour grapes and the children's teeth are set on edge' (Jer. 31: 29; Ezek. 18: 2). It suggests that people had taken to heart the threat familiar to all Israelites from the so-called Ten Commandments, that God would punish the children for the sins of the fathers to the third and fourth generations (Exod. 20: 5; Deut. 5: 9). This may partly have been a means of shifting the blame for the tragedy of exile to the previous generation. But there was also a feeling abroad that the whole community was caught up in a web of guilt which was deadly and inescapable (33: 10).

In the face of resigned acceptance of inevitable punishment that could not be avoided by any means, both Jeremiah and Ezekiel struck new notes of hope. Jeremiah proclaimed the New Covenant (Jer. 31: 31–4) while Ezekiel stressed that it was still possible for each individual to fulfil the conditions of righteousness. And this Ezekiel did in terms already familiar to the people. For all who went to worship at the temple, or at other sanctuaries, had heard at some stage the conditions of righteousness such as are found in Pss. 15; 24: 3–6 and elsewhere. If the worshippers had observed the conditions (and they were not regarded as impossible to fulfil), then the priest declared them 'righteous'. They were thus included in the worshipping community whose 'life' was from God. 'Life' in this sense was not merely continued physical existence, nor some kind of future existence. Life for the Israelite meant good health and material prosperity, which were only to be found in obedience to, and fellowship with, God. For the exiles, far from the temple and familiar patterns of worship, the possibility of such life in a renewed relationship with God must have seemed beyond imagining.

2. *set on edge*: literally 'blunt'. Whatever the original meaning of the image, it adequately conveys the sense that the deeds of the fathers affected their children.

4. *soul*: as used here the word means the whole person, every living being, each equally the possession of God.

5–9. Fifteen laws, governing both worship and relations between people, are given here as examples of right living.

6. For *mountain-shrines* and *idols* see on 6: 3f. To eat at such shrines meant sharing in sacrificial meals, while 'lifting up the eyes' meant to worship. Adultery was prohibited in the Ten Commandments, while intercourse during a woman's menstruation was forbidden in the Holiness Code (Lev. 18: 19; 20: 18); it was believed to be a source of impurity.

7. The Book of the Covenant outlawed oppression of strangers (Exod. 22: 21) and the Holiness Code made the same prohibition explicit in the case of neighbours (Lev. 19: 13). The same verse in Leviticus outlaws robbery, while the return of a debtor's pledge is required in Exod. 22: 26. The giving of food and clothing to the poor follows from general commands to care for the needy (cp. Deut. 15: 7).

8. *discount. . .interest*: both are forms of interest on loans. The distinction is explained in Lev. 25: 36: 'You shall not charge him interest on a loan, either by deducting it in advance from the capital sum, or by adding it on repayment.' A literal rendering of *discount* is 'something bitten off'. This prohibition against exploiting poorer members of the community reflects Exod. 22: 25; Lev. 25: 36f.; Deut. 23: 20. The shunning of *injustice*, etc., follows such instructions as Lev. 19: 15.

9. The two final requirements, of observing the statutes and laws of God, summarize the keeping of instructions in both Deuteronomy and the Holiness Code (Deut. 7: 11;

Lev. 25: 18). The declaration of 'righteousness' and 'life' conclude this example of the behaviour of a just man. ✶

THE SOUL THAT SINS SHALL DIE

10 He may have a son who is a man of violence and a cut-
11 throat who turns his back on these rules.*a* He obeys
none of them, he feasts at mountain-shrines, he dis-
12 honours another man's wife, he oppresses the unfortunate
and the poor, he is a robber, he does not return the
debtor's pledge, he lifts his eyes to idols and joins in abom-
13 inable rites; he lends both at discount and at interest. Such
a man shall not live. Because he has committed all these
abominations he shall die, and his blood will be on his
own head.

14 This man in turn may have a son who sees all his
15 father's sins; he sees, but he commits none of them. He
never feasts at mountain-shrines, never lifts his eyes to the
16 idols of Israel, never dishonours another man's wife. He
oppresses no man, takes no pledge, does not rob. He
gives bread to the hungry and clothes to those who have
17 none. He shuns injustice,*b* he never lends either at discount or at interest. He keeps my laws and conforms to
my statutes. Such a man shall not die for his father's
wrongdoing; he shall live.

18 His father may have been guilty of oppression and
robbery*c* and may have lived an evil life among his
19 kinsfolk, and so has died because of his iniquity. You may
ask, 'Why is the son not punished for his father's iniquity?'

[a] who turns. . .rules: *prob. rdg.; Heb. unintelligible.*
[b] injustice: *so Sept.; Heb.* the unfortunate.
[c] *So Sept.; Heb.* robbery of a brother.

Because he has always done what is just and right and has
been careful to obey all my laws, therefore he shall live.
It is the soul that sins, and no other, that shall die; a son 20
shall not share a father's guilt, nor a father his son's. The
righteous man shall reap the fruit of his own righteousness, and the wicked man the fruit of his own wickedness.

✷ The example of behaviour within a single family continues. A wicked son of the righteous man is condemned (verses
10–13), while his son in turn, by obeying the law, finds life
(verses 14–17). The last point is strongly reinforced in the
summary of verses 18–20.

10–13. Only eight of the laws mentioned in verses 6–9
are said to have been broken. They occur in a different order
and the prohibition against idolatry now includes participation
in *abominable rites* (verse 12). Characterized as 'violent' and
'a shedder of blood' (verse 10), the son is excluded from the
community of the faithful. For this sense of the word 'death',
see on 14: 8. The formula *he shall die* (verse 13) corresponds
precisely to the phrase 'he shall live' in verse 9. There is no
advantage gained from his father's righteousness. The son is
responsible for himself. *his blood will be on his own head*:
that is, he could be put to death without any blood-guilt (see
on 22: 3) falling on his executioners (cp. Lev. 20: 9, 11, 12,
etc.).

14–17. Two of the laws mentioned in verses 6–9 are not
referred to here and the order of the laws differs too. So there
was apparently no necessity to test a man's behaviour minutely
against a standard list of laws. By exchanging his father's
manner of life for behaviour in general accord with God's
laws, the son of a wicked man could find life.

18–20. In the summary of the argument at this point there
are also rejected the possibilities of a father suffering for sins
of his son, and indeed of any person (or *soul*) suffering for the
sins of another (verse 20). ✷

TURN FROM YOUR OFFENCES

21 It may be that a wicked man gives up his sinful ways and keeps all my laws, doing what is just and right. That man
22 shall live; he shall not die. None of the offences he has committed shall be remembered against him; he shall
23 live because of his righteous deeds. Have I any desire, says the Lord GOD, for the death of a wicked man? Would I not rather that he should mend his ways and live?

24   It may be that a righteous man turns back from his righteous ways and commits every kind of abomination that the wicked practise; shall he do this and live? No, none of his former righteousness will be remembered in his favour; he has broken his faith, he has sinned, and he
25 shall die. You say that the Lord acts without principle? Listen, you Israelites, it is you who act without principle,
26 not I. If a righteous man turns from his righteousness, takes to evil ways and dies,*a* it is because of these evil
27 ways that he dies. Again, if a wicked man turns from his wicked ways and does what is just and right, he will save
28 his life. If he sees his offences as they are and turns his back on them all, then he shall live; he shall not die.

29   'The Lord acts without principle', say the Israelites. No, Israelites, it is you who act without principle, not I.
30 Therefore, Israelites, says the Lord GOD, I will judge every man of you on his deeds. Turn, turn from your offences,
31 or your iniquity will be your downfall. Throw off the load of your past misdeeds; get yourselves a new heart

[a] *Prob. rdg.; Heb. adds* because of them.

and a new spirit. Why should you die, you men of Israel?
I have no desire for any man's death. This is the very word 32
of the Lord GOD.[a]

✻ Verses 21–5 carry the argument a stage further. It is a most
important development, associated with a protest from the
people against God's injustice. Verses 26–9 are a doublet,
treating the cases in the reverse order and putting the objection
of the Israelites in the form of an indirect quotation. By the
charge of acting without principle (verses 25 and 29), the
Israelites accused God of punishing the innocent along with
the guilty. Implicit in his rejection of the charge is Ezekiel's
belief that all deserved the punishment that had come upon
the nation. But the opportunity for each generation to live
or die according to its own behaviour is now extended to
each individual within his life-time. The possibility of the
righteous dying because they turn to sin may seem harsh. But
the opportunity for the wicked to leave past guilt behind is
all the more significant for Ezekiel's sweeping condemnation
of Israel elsewhere. The oracle of verses 30–2 is the climax of
the chapter, commanding response to the possibility of
attaining life that had just been declared.

31. In contrast to the earlier promise of the people's
spontaneous renewal by God (11: 19), they are now told:
get yourselves a new heart and a new spirit. But a contrast
between exhortations to repentance and belief in the necessity
of divine action to make repentance possible can be seen in
words of other prophets (Hos. 14: 1–3; cp. 5: 4; Jer. 3: 19 –
4: 4, cp. 24: 7; 31: 31–4). The command here emphasizes
the need for men to accept the new God-given possibility of
renewal. For the significance of the human heart and spirit,
see on 11: 19f. ✻

[a] *So Sept.; Heb. adds* and bring back and live.

A LAMENT OVER THE PRINCES OF ISRAEL

19₁, ₂ Raise a lament over the princes of Israel and say:

> Your mother was a lioness
>> among the lions!
> She made her lair among the young lions
>> and many were the cubs she bore.

3
> One of her cubs she raised,
>> and he grew into a young lion.
> He learnt to tear his prey,
>> he devoured men.

4
> Then the nations shouted at[a] him
>> and he was caught in their pit,
> and they dragged him with hooks to the land of
>> Egypt.

5
> His case, she saw, was desperate, her hope was lost;
>> so she took another[b] of her cubs
>> and made him a young lion.

6
> He prowled among the lions
>> and acted like a young lion.
> He learnt to tear his prey,
>> he devoured men;

7
> he broke down their palaces,[c] laid their cities in ruins.
>> The land and all that was in it
>> was aghast at the noise of his roaring.

8
> From the provinces all round
>> the nations raised the hue and cry;
> they cast their net over him
>> and he was caught in their pit.

---

[a] shouted at: *or* heard a report about.   [b] *So Sept.; Heb.* one.
[c] he broke ... palaces: *so Targ.; Heb.* he knew his widows.

> With hooks they drew him into a cage   9
>   and brought him to the king of Babylon,
>   who flung him into prison,
>   that his voice might never again be heard
>   on the mountains of Israel.

* In many parts of the ancient world the dead were honoured by the chanting of laments or dirges, recalling their virtues and accomplishments. Professional mourners were employed to sing the laments, which often had a regular halting rhythm (the second half-verse shorter than the first) intended to convey a sense of grief (so the book of Lamentations). In such settings laments naturally told of past events. But Israel's prophets adopted this style of poetry to foretell events that would bring mourning in the future, when God's judgement would fall on the wayward. The present chapter is associated with the allegory of the eagles in ch. 17, although now separated from it by ch. 18. The subject is again, in part, the fate of Zedekiah, who, like his brother Jehoahaz, is pictured as a young lion, hunted and taken into captivity (verses 6–9). The prophecy predates 587 B.C.

1. *Your mother was a lioness among the lions*: the figure of the kings of Judah as lions probably derives from Gen. 49: 9 'Judah, you lion's whelp'. The lioness, and mother of the two 'young lions' referred to later in the poem, was Hamutal, the wife of King Josiah. As queen and later as queen mother, Hamutal's power in the court was second only to that of the king.

3f. When Josiah was killed by Pharaoh Necho in 609 B.C., Jehoahaz was anointed king of Judah rather than his elder half-brother Jehoiakim. Jehoahaz reigned only three months before Necho deposed him in favour of Jehoiakim, presumably because the pharaoh believed Jehoiakim would be more loyal to him. Jehoahaz for his part was removed captive to Egypt (2 Kings 23: 29–35). The allusion to the vigour of

Jehoahaz's brief reign – *He learnt to tear his prey...* (verse 3) – cannot be substantiated from other sources. The allusion is repeated in verse 6 and it has been supposed that Ezekiel has based this prophecy on a popular folk tale about a lion which was so destructive and notorious that men set out to capture and destroy it. The imagery should not be too closely related to the actual manner of rule or accomplishments of either king.

5. Hamutal's personal influence in the anointing of another of her sons as king is explicit here.

9. *With hooks*: rings through the lip or nose. The words here are an addition repeated from verse 4. *they drew him into a cage*: rather read 'they put him in a wooden neck stock'. ✶

THERE IS NO STRONG BRANCH

10   Your mother was a vine in a vineyard[a]
      planted by the waterside.
  It grew fruitful and luxuriant,
      for there was water in plenty.

11   It had stout branches,
      fit to make sceptres for those who bear rule.
  It grew tall, finding its way through the foliage,
  and conspicuous for its height and many trailing
      boughs.

12   But it was torn up in anger and thrown to the ground;
      the east wind blighted it,
        its fruit was blown off,
        its strong branches were blighted,
      and fire burnt it.

13   Now it is replanted in the wilderness,
      in a dry and thirsty land;

      [a] in a vineyard: *prob. rdg.; Heb. obscure in context.*

124

and fire bursts forth from its own branches   14
and burns up its shoots.[a]
It has no strong branch any more
to make a sceptre for those who bear rule.

This is the lament and as a lament it passed into use.

* Once more Ezekiel resorts to the image of a vine, used this
time as a figure of the queen mother, Hamutal. In the previous
section she was spoken of as a lioness, rearing two cubs.
Although the present section also belongs to the period before
587 B.C., it is clearly not a continuation of the earlier verses of
the chapter. Hamutal is again the subject at the beginning
but her offspring as a whole are rejected as being unfit to rule
Israel.

10f. *a vine*: in 17: 5–8 Zedekiah was likened to a vine. Now
the image is applied to his mother. The verses reflect her
favoured position in the court and her considerable influence
there. *It had stout branches*: some versions read the singular
here, assuming a reference to Zedekiah. For the significance
of the word 'branch', see on 17: 22.

12. *the east wind*: Nebuchadrezzar (see on 17: 10).

13–14a. Confusion over the subject of the prophecy is
compounded by these verses, added by a later hand. From
the reference to replanting in the wilderness, the versions
have assumed the subject of the original prophecy to be
Zedekiah alone, rather than the princes of whom Hamutal
was the mother or grandmother. The fire springing from
within the branches refers to Zedekiah's rebellion (see on
17: 7f.). But that the verses are an inappropriate revision of
the original is evident from the fact that fire has already
consumed the vine (verse 12).

14b. *It has no strong branch. . .*: the execution of the sons of
Zedekiah is recorded in 2 Kings 25: 7. *This is the lament . . .*:

[a] *Prob. rdg.; Heb. adds* its fruit.

the prophetic lament in anticipation of disaster became a lament recalling the event and acknowledging the truth of the prophet's word (cp. 32: 16). ✻

A NEW INQUIRY

20 On the tenth day of the fifth month in the seventh year, some of the elders of Israel came to consult the LORD and
2 were sitting with me. Then this word came to me from
3 the LORD: Man, say to the elders of Israel, This is the word of the Lord GOD: Do you come to consult me? As I live, I will not be consulted by you. This is the very word of the Lord GOD.
4   Will you judge them? Will you judge them, O man?
5 Then tell them of the abominations of their forefathers and say to them, These are the words of the Lord GOD: When I chose Israel, with uplifted hand I bound myself by oath to the race of Jacob and revealed myself to them in Egypt; I lifted up my hand and declared: I am the
6 LORD your God. On that day I swore with hand uplifted that I would bring them out of Egypt into the land I had sought out for them, a land flowing with milk and honey,
7 fairest of all lands. I told them, every one, to cast away the loathsome things on which they feasted their eyes and not to defile themselves with the idols of Egypt. I am the LORD your God, I said.

✻ Once more the elders come to inquire of God through the prophet (cp. 8: 1; 14: 1). This time their request for guidance is refused, but not before a kind of sermon has been delivered to them on Israel's whole evil history. The significance of the occasion is emphasized by the date in verse 1. The revision which the chapter (ending at verse 44 in the Hebrew text) has undergone complicates any explanation of it. After the long discourse on Israel's past misdeeds, however, verse 31 concludes the reply to the elders' inquiry. A feature of the discourse is its picture of unrelieved rebellion against God. In contrast to ch. 16 (see on verses 1–14) and to earlier prophets (cp. Hos. 2: 14f.), Ezekiel now denies that there was ever a time of harmony between God and his people, despite God's patience for the sake of 'his name'. Verses 32–44 are from a later period and envisage a penitent and hopeful future. Verses 1–7 introduce this unique history.

1. The date is July–August 591 B.C., eleven months after the last date given in 8: 1. Mention of the elders here is little more than a device, setting the passage in the context of an address to the exiles. The outcome of the inquiry was not an answer to the matters troubling the elders, but God's case against his people.

4. The repeated *Will you judge them?* has the force of a command, as in 22: 2.

5. *I chose Israel*: Deuteronomy's emphasis on God's election or choice of his people is reflected here, though it does not appear so explicitly elsewhere in Ezekiel. No reason is given for God's choice of Israel: he acts simply because he is God. It is also of interest that Ezekiel dates the election from the period in Egypt, not from the time of the patriarchs whom he completely ignores (cp. Deut. 4: 37; 10: 15). *with uplifted hand*: in token of an oath solemnly entered into (cp. Gen. 14: 22). *the race of Jacob*: a term including the tribes of the former northern kingdom of Israel. Because Ezekiel sometimes uses the name 'Israel' of the people of Judah alone, here he specifies the involvement of the whole people. *and revealed myself to them*: just as two of the narrative strands composing the Pentateuch have God reveal his name at a certain point of time (Exod. 3: 13–15; 6: 2–8), so too with Ezekiel, although here the revelation takes place in Egypt rather than during the wilderness wanderings.

6f. A number of the phrases are paralleled in the Pentateuch. But again only Ezekiel refers to commandments given in Egypt. *loathsome things*: idols in general. *the idols of Egypt*: a tradition of Israelite idolatry in Egypt, also reflected in Josh. 24: 14, but not mentioned in Exodus. It is part of the Jewish Passover service, and has been for centuries, to recall that Israel's forefathers 'worshipped other gods' (Josh. 24: 2–4), even before they were tempted by the idols of Egypt. ✷

REBELLION BEGINS IN EGYPT

8 But they rebelled against me, they refused to listen to me, and not one of them cast away the loathsome things on which he feasted his eyes or forsook the idols of Egypt. I had thought to pour out my wrath and exhaust my 9 anger on them in Egypt. I acted for the honour of my name, that it might not be profaned in the sight of the nations among whom Israel was living: I revealed myself 10 to them by bringing Israel out of Egypt. I brought them 11 out of Egypt and led them into the wilderness. There I gave my statutes to them and taught them my laws, so 12 that by keeping them men might have life. Further, I gave them my sabbaths as a sign between us, so that they should know that I, the LORD, was hallowing them for 13 myself. But the Israelites rebelled against me in the wilderness; they did not conform to my statutes, they rejected my laws, though by keeping them men might have life, and they utterly desecrated my sabbaths. So again I thought to pour out my wrath on them in the wilderness 14 to destroy them. I acted for the honour of my name, that it might not be profaned in the sight of the nations who had seen me bring them out.

Further, I swore to them in the wilderness with uplifted 15
hand that I would not bring them into the land I had given
them, that land flowing with milk and honey, fairest of
all lands. For they had rejected my laws, they would not 16
conform to my statutes and they desecrated my sabbaths,
because they loved to follow idols of their own. Yet I 17
pitied them too much to destroy them and did not make
an end of them in the wilderness. I commanded their sons 18
in the wilderness not to conform to their fathers' statutes,
nor observe their laws, nor defile themselves with their
idols. I said, I am the LORD your God, you must conform 19
to my statutes; you must observe my laws and act
according to them. You must keep my sabbaths holy, and 20
they will become a sign between us; so you will know that
I am the LORD your God.

✡ 9. God's reluctance to punish his people *for the honour of (his) name*, or 'for (his) name's sake', is the recurrent theme of this chapter. For the Israelite, a man's name represented what the person was in himself. So by God's *name* was meant all that he represented in terms of faithfulness and power. To prevent the misconception of God being limited to a given earthly locality, the stream of thought represented by Deuteronomy personified the name of God as the form of his presence in the Jerusalem temple. God dwells in heaven (Deut. 26: 15), but he causes his name to dwell at his chosen sanctuary (12: 5 and 11). Once God had revealed his name to Israel, respect for him among the nations was linked with the fate of his chosen people. The appropriate punishment for their idolatry – leaving them in Egypt – would have shown him in the eyes of the nations to be fickle and powerless. But his name would thus have been profaned. For Ezekiel's hearers and readers, the name 'Babylon' would have come to mind in place of Egypt.

11. The allusion here is to the law given at Sinai. On the possibility of obtaining life by obedience to the law, cp. 18: 9.

12. Although the origin of the custom is obscure, the sabbath day had long been kept as a day of rest and religious observance in Israel (see e.g. Exod. 23: 12; Amos 8: 5). But it did not, at any earlier period, have the significance attributed to it in this chapter. In verses 12f., 16, 20f. and 24, failure to keep the sabbath is held, along with disobeying the law, to jeopardize the whole covenant relationship. The sabbath certainly came to have great importance for the exiles as one means of preserving their religious identity in a foreign land. Death was to be the punishment for those who profaned it according to the late Priestly author of Exod. 31: 12–17. But such an attitude as we find in the first part of ch. 20 is nowhere else in evidence in Ezekiel. Desecration of the sabbath is one feature of a general failure of religious observance according to 22: 8, 26; 23: 37–9, but sabbath observance goes unmentioned in the requirements of ch. 18 and in the description of acceptable worship later in ch. 20. The references to the sabbath in verses 12f., 16, 20f. and 24 are therefore to be regarded as the contribution of a Priestly editor. The sabbath was intended as a sign of a continuing alliance between God and Israel.

13f. The pattern of disobedience and action for the sake of God's name, which was established in Egypt, is repeated.

15–17. This recalls the tradition of the older generation of Israelites dying in the wilderness (cp. Deut. 1: 34–9). ✳

THE SONS TOO REBELLED

21 But the sons too rebelled against me. They did not conform to my statutes or observe my laws, though any who had done so would have had life through them, and they desecrated my sabbaths. Again I thought to pour out my

wrath and exhaust my anger on them in the wilderness.[a]
I acted for the honour of my name, that it might not be 22
profaned in the sight of the nations who had seen me
bring them out. Yes, and in the wilderness I swore to them 23
with uplifted hand that I would disperse them among the
nations and scatter them abroad, because they had dis- 24
obeyed my laws, rejected my statutes, desecrated my
sabbaths, and turned longing eyes toward the idols of
their forefathers. I did more; I imposed on them statutes 25
that were not good statutes, and laws by which they could
not win life. I let them defile themselves with gifts to 26
idols; I made them surrender their eldest sons to them so
that I might fill them with horror. Thus they would
know that I am the LORD.

Speak then, O man, to the Israelites and say to them, 27
These are the words of the Lord GOD: Once again your
forefathers insulted me and broke faith with me: when I 28
brought them into the land which I had sworn with
uplifted hand to give them, they marked down every hill-
top and every leafy tree, and there they offered their
sacrifices, they made the gifts which roused my anger, they
set out their offerings of soothing odour and poured out
their drink-offerings. I asked them, What is this hill- 29
shrine to which you are going up? And 'hill-shrine' has
been its name ever since.

So tell the Israelites, These are the words of the Lord 30
GOD: Are you defiling yourselves as your forefathers
did? Are you wantonly giving yourselves to their
loathsome gods? When you bring your gifts, when you 31
pass your sons through the fire, you are still defiling

[a] *So Sept.; Heb. adds* and then withdraw my hand.

131

yourselves in the service of your crowd of idols. How can I let you consult me, men of Israel? As I live, says the Lord GOD, I will not be consulted by you.

✶ Verses 21–6 mark the end of God's plan of salvation for his people and the beginning of a plan of destruction. The first of the two concluding oracles (verses 27–9) is an addition from a disciple who wished to include some specific reference to sins committed after settlement in Canaan. But the previous verses make it plain that the nation's guilt was completed by God's proclamation of evil laws. Verses 30f. are the original conclusion to the recital of Israel's misdeeds.

21–3. The younger generation also showed themselves to be rebellious, and although, for the sake of his *name*, God brought them to the land promised to their fathers, it was only with a view to their eventual exile. Like other prophets, Ezekiel regarded misfortune not as the work of some other divine power working against the God of Israel, but as that same God punishing his own wayward people.

25f. There is something quite new here. Other Old Testament passages speak of God purposely misleading people (2 Sam. 24: 1; 1 Kings 22: 17–23) and Isa. 6: 9f. implies that God refused to let Israel understand how to find healing. But now in response to their continuing disobedience (verse 24), Ezekiel claims that laws were given by God with the express intention of leading Israel to despair and death.

Obedience to these 'evil laws' (*not good statutes*) will lead to *horror*, a profound inward revulsion and sense of desolation. A similar point is developed by Paul in Rom. 1: 28–32. The words at the end of verse 26, *Thus they would know that I am the LORD*, have been added by a later hand (they are not in the Septuagint), but they serve to express the positive outcome of this terrible experience.

The extent of these laws is not clear, but among them was the command to sacrifice eldest sons (verse 26). The prophet may here be interpreting literally the instruction of Exod.

22: 29: 'You shall give me your first-born sons.' There is evidence that human sacrifice was occasionally practised in Israel, as among other peoples (see on 16: 20), but as an alien custom and not in response to the law of the first-born. For in Israel there were explicit instructions that humans, unlike first-born animals, were to be redeemed or bought back by the exchange of some other offering once they had been symbolically presented to God (Exod. 13: 13; 34: 20; cp. Gen. 22: 1–18). Jeremiah opposed the suggestion that God required human sacrifices (Jer. 7: 31) and Ezekiel regarded the practice as a source of defilement (cp. Ezek. 16: 21; 20: 31). But in his concern to affirm God's control of his people, even in the evil they did, Ezekiel boldly reinterpreted the purpose of the law.

29. There is a play on the word for *hill-shrine* (*bāmāh*), suggesting fancifully that the meaning is 'a place to which people come' (the Hebrew word for 'come' is *bā'*).

30. The questions are rhetorical. That the exiles were defiled went without saying and their punishment included God's refusal to answer their inquiries through the prophet (cp. 14: 1–11).

31. It is unlikely that the exiles practised child sacrifice. The first sentence of the verse is probably an addition specifying the charges of defilement and idolatry already made. ✳

A NEW EXODUS

When you say to yourselves, 'Let us become like the 32 nations and tribes of other lands and worship wood and stone', you are thinking of something that can never be. As I live, says the Lord GOD, I will reign over you with a 33 strong hand, with arm outstretched and wrath outpoured. I will bring you out from the peoples and gather you 34 from the lands over which you have been scattered by my strong hand, my outstretched arm and outpoured wrath.

35 I will bring you into the wilderness of the peoples; there
will I confront you, and there will I state my case against
36 you. Even as I did in the wilderness of Egypt against your
forefathers, so will I state my case against you. This is the
very word of the Lord GOD.

37   I will pass you under the rod and bring you within the
38 bond[a] of the covenant. I will rid you of those who revolt
and rebel against me. I will take them out of the land
where they are now living, but they shall not set foot
on the soil of Israel. Thus shall you know that I am the
LORD.

39   Now, men of Israel, these are the words of the Lord
GOD: Go, sweep away[b] your idols, every man of you.
So in days to come you will never be disobedient to me
or desecrate my holy name with your gifts and your
40 idolatries. But on my holy hill, the lofty hill of Israel,
says the Lord GOD, there shall the Israelites serve me in the
land, every one of them. There will I receive them with
favour; there will I demand your contribution and the
best of your offerings, with all your consecrated gifts.
41 I will receive your offerings of soothing odour, when I
have brought you out from the peoples and gathered
you from the lands where you have been scattered. I, and
only I, will have your worship, for all the nations to see.
42   You will know that I am the LORD, when I bring you
home to the soil of Israel, to the land which I swore with
43 uplifted hand to give your forefathers. There you will
remember your past ways and all the wanton deeds with
which you have defiled yourselves, and will loathe your-

[a] *Or* muster.
[b] sweep away: *so Sept.; Heb.* serve.

selves for all the evils you have done. You will know that
I am the LORD, when I have dealt with you, O men of
Israel, not as your wicked ways and your vicious deeds 44
deserve but for the honour of my name. This is the very
word of the Lord GOD.

* The remainder of the passage dates from after the fall of
Jerusalem. Addressing himself to the despairing exiles, the
prophet resumes the theme of wilderness wandering and
expands his earlier prophecy with words of hope for Israel's
restoration. God will not allow Israel's waywardness to end
in final abandonment. Hosea had prophesied a time of renewal
in a return to the wilderness (2: 14; 12: 9). But the second
period in the wilderness is here seen as a time of severe judgement, not of deliverance or consolation. And the rebellious
will not share in the restoration of Israel's fortunes.

Verses 39–44 represent successive expansions of verses
1–38. The defilement of the past is erased and the future state
of restoration is described with words that foreshadow the
vision of the new temple in chs. 40–8. Emphasis lies on right
worship characterizing the restored community. This is
typical of the Priestly point of view. But in the concluding
verses the memory of past misdeeds is also recalled, for right
worship assumes penitence. The honour of God's name remains the motive for his gracious actions.

32f. *Let us become like the nations*: the verse reflects the
exiles' feeling of abandonment by their God. They think they
must seek alternative objects of worship. *I will reign over you*:
the words may have been intended to recall Israel's earlier
words of rebellion, 'we will have a king over us; then we
shall be like other nations' (1 Sam. 8: 20; cp. on 34: 17–31).
with a strong hand...: in this chapter the strong hand and
outstretched arm of God are symbols of judgement against
Israel, rather than symbols of protection for Israel and judgement against her enemies as in Deuteronomy.

35. *the wilderness of the peoples*: not simply the wilderness of Sinai (cp. verses 15 and 36). Since all Israel's exiles are referred to, from Assyria and Egypt as well as Babylon, this is a general term with no specific location intended.

37. *I will pass you under the rod*: a figure of a shepherd's care, when he sorts and counts his sheep at the door of the fold. *within the bond of the covenant*: read with the Septuagint, 'in by number' (cp. footnote 'muster'). The word for 'covenant' has been added in error here, because the first word of the next verse is very similar in the Hebrew.

39. The Hebrew is difficult. As the footnote indicates, it may be understood as an ironic command to the exiles to 'serve' idols if they wish. The punishment that would follow such idolatry was declared in the previous verse. But God's name was no longer to be dishonoured by worship of him being associated with worship of idols.

40. *my holy hill*: Jerusalem or Zion, where the people's worship would be acceptable. *there will I demand. . .*: a new stage of expansion is marked at this point by the second person address to the exiles. *contribution*: possibly a compulsory gift. *offerings*: another technical term, possibly voluntary gifts. *consecrated gifts*: things dedicated, perhaps by a vow, as offerings.

41. *soothing odour*: the odour of sacrifices, originally thought of as pleasing the gods, but used as a technical term in the Old Testament for an acceptable offering. ✶

AGAINST THE FOREST OF THE SOUTH

45,[a] 46 These were the words of the LORD to me: Man, turn and face towards Teman[b] and pour out your words to the
47 south; prophesy to the rough country of the Negeb. Say to it, Listen to the words of the LORD. These are the

[a] *21: 1 in Heb.*
[b] *Or* face southward.

words of the Lord GOD: I will set fire to you, and the
fire will consume all the wood, green and dry alike. Its
fiery flame shall not be put out, but from the Negeb
northwards every face will be scorched by it. All men 48
will see that it is I, the LORD, who have set it ablaze; it
shall not be put out. 'Ah no! O Lord GOD,' I cried; 'they 49
say of me, "He deals only in parables."'

These were the words of the LORD to me: Man, turn **21**1, 2
and face towards Jerusalem, and pour out your words
against her sanctuary;[a] prophesy against the land of
Israel. Say to the land of Israel, These are the words of 3
the LORD: I am against you; I will draw my sword from the
scabbard and cut off from you both righteous and wicked.
It is because I would cut off your righteous and your 4
wicked equally that my sword will be drawn from the
scabbard against all men, from the Negeb northwards.
All men shall know that I the LORD have drawn my 5
sword; it shall never again be sheathed. Groan in their 6
presence, man, groan bitterly until your lungs are bursting.
When they ask you why you are groaning, say to them, 7
'I groan at the thing I have heard; when it comes, all
hearts melt, all courage fails, all hands fall limp, all men's
knees run with urine. It is coming. It is here.' This is the
very word of the Lord GOD.

✷ As the Hebrew text indicates (see footnote verse 45), the
last verses of ch. 20 belong with ch. 21 since they are part of a
series of sayings in which the catchword 'sword' occurs.
Ezekiel is instructed to prophesy, in an allegory (parable),
against the forest of the south. When he protests that people

[a] her sanctuary: *prob. rdg.; Heb.* sanctuaries.

complain of this means of prophecy (20: 49), he is given an interpretation of the allegory to proclaim. So in unmistakable terms the destruction of Jerusalem and the execution of both righteous and wicked are described. The sword of the LORD (verse 5) is Babylon. Verses 6f. are a separate saying, similar in content to 12: 17–20 but directed to the exiles. This brief acted prophecy has been included here to stress the horror and immediacy of Jerusalem's destruction.

46. *Teman . . . Negeb*: both words are used here in a general sense to indicate 'the south', meaning the direction of Jerusalem. Although Babylon lay to the east of Jerusalem (see map, p. 169), the actual line of approach for travellers was from north to south (cp. 26: 7, where it is implied that Babylon is 'north' of Palestine). The word *Teman* is also found in 47: 19 and 48: 28, where it is correctly rendered as 'south'. The *Negeb* proper was the barren region south of Judah. For *the rough country*, read 'the forest' with the Hebrew. The allegory depends on the figure of a wood or forest.

49. *parables*: see on 17: 2. The apparent granting of permission to interpret the allegory is not surprising since elsewhere allegories are followed by their interpretations (e.g. chs. 15, 17). The question is a rhetorical device, intended to stress the personal responsibility of the prophet's audience. They could not excuse themselves by claiming to have misunderstood the prophet's message.

21: 3. *both righteous and wicked*: the phrase parallels 'green and dry alike' in verse 47. All were to be included in the disaster. The judgement is repeated in the following verse in such a way as to affirm again the execution of the righteous (cp. Ezekiel's reaction to prophecies of extermination in 9: 8; 11: 13, and the preservation of the righteous in 14: 12–23). ✳

THE SONG OF THE SWORD

These were the words of the LORD to me: Prophesy, man, 8, 9
and say, This is the word of the Lord:

> A sword, a sword is sharpened and burnished,
>> sharpened to kill and kill again;   10
>> burnished to flash*a* like lightning.
> Ah! the club is brandished, my son,
>> to defy all wooden idols!*b*
> The sword is given to be burnished   11
>> ready for the hand to grasp.
> The sword – it is sharpened,
>> it is burnished,
> ready to be put into the slayer's hand.

Cry, man, and howl; for all this falls on my people, it 12
falls on Israel's princes who are delivered over to the
sword and are slain with my people. Therefore beat your
breast*c* in remorse, for it is the test – and what if it is not 13
in truth the club of defiance? This is the very word of
the Lord GOD.

> But you, man, prophesy and clap your hands   14
>> together;
>> swing the sword twice, thrice:
>> it is the sword of slaughter,
> the great sword of slaughter whirling about them.
> That their hearts may be troubled and many stumble 15
>> and fall,
> I have set the threat of the sword at all their gates,

[a] to flash: *prob. rdg.; Heb. unintelligible.*
[b] wooden idols: *lit.* wood.   [c] *Lit.* thigh.

the threat of the sword*a* made to flash like
  lightning
and drawn to kill.

16   Be sharpened,*b* turn right; be unsheathed, turn left,
wherever your point is aimed.

17   I, too, will clap my hands together and abate my anger. I,
the LORD, have spoken.

⁂ These verses have been called 'the song of the sword' and
it is possible that the song is based on a traditional poem
associated with the 'whirling and flashing' sword of the
garden of Eden (Gen. 3 : 24). The poem is badly preserved and
is interrupted by later additions, but it portrays most vividly
the vigour with which divine judgement will be executed
and the prophet's involvement in the judgement. In the latter
part of the poem the sword almost assumes an existence of its
own, 'whirling about' the objects of attack (verse 14). And the
repetition of words and symbolic actions suggest that an element of magic-making also lies in the background, as in the
story of Elisha, when repeated blows with arrows assured
success in war (2 Kings 13 : 14–19).

10. *Ah! the club is brandished* . . .: the text is very difficult.
The suggestion offered in the N.E.B. is that the sword is
brandished like a *club* (literally 'staff' or 'rod') to destroy
wooden idols, but '(weapons of) wood' (cp. footnote) may be
the object of the sword's attack.

12. The prophet's speech is interrupted by a command of
God, but the note of grief is intrusive in the context of the
poem's sustained savagery. This verse and the following one
have been added to the original poem.

13. *for it is the test*. . .: another obscure verse. The Hebrew
implies that there has been reflection on the appropriateness

[a] the threat of the sword: *prob. rdg.; Heb. obscure in context.*
[b] *So Targ.; Heb.* Unify yourself.

of punishment or testing: 'and why, if you despise the rod (or *club* that destroys "idols", verse 10) should it not take place?'

14. *clap your hands together*: perhaps suggesting the sound of sword blows, but also indicating an intense fury of activity until anger is exhausted (cp. verse 17).

16f. The sword is now addressed and told to cut where directed. And God confirms that it is he in fact who wields the sword of judgement. ✻

THE SWORD OF THE KING OF BABYLON

These were the words of the LORD to me: Man, trace out 18, 19 two roads by which the sword of the king of Babylon may come, starting both of them from the same land. Then carve a signpost, carve it at the point where the highway forks. Mark out a road for the sword to come 20 to*a* the Ammonite city of Rabbah, to*a* Judah, and to Jerusalem at the heart of it. For the king of Babylon halts to 21 take the omens at the parting of the ways, where the road divides. He casts lots with arrows, consults teraphim*b* and inspects the livers of beasts. The augur's arrow marked 22 'Jerusalem' falls at his right hand: here, then,*c* he must raise a shout*d* and sound the battle-cry, set battering-rams against the gates, pile siege-ramps and build watch-towers. It may well seem to the people that the auguries 23 are false,*e* whereas they will put me in mind of their wrongdoing, and they will fall into the enemies' hand. These therefore are the words of the Lord GOD: Because 24

[a] *So Sept.; Heb.* with.   [b] *Or* household gods.
[c] *Prob. rdg.; Heb. adds* he must set battering-rams.
[d] raise a shout: *so Sept.; Heb.* open his mouth in slaughter.
[e] *So Sept.; Heb. adds an unintelligible phrase.*

you have kept me mindful of your wrongdoing by your open rebellion, and your sins have been revealed in all your acts, because you have kept yourselves in my mind, you will fall into the enemies' hand by force.

✻ According to this acted prophecy the sword of Nebuchadrezzar is to be God's instrument of justice. The king chooses, by the ancient means of divination or augury, which of two ways to go, and the lot falls to Jerusalem. The year was 589 B.C., after an alliance of Judah and other neighbouring states, including Ammon, had plotted to revolt against Babylon (see further on 25: 1–7).

19. *from the same land*: Babylon itself may have been in mind, or Syria, where Nebuchadrezzar had his camp at Riblah. The drawing may have been done on the ground or on a tile as in 4: 1.

20. *Rabbah*: the capital of Ammon, east of the Jordan, the modern Amman. *to Judah, and to Jerusalem at the heart of it*: the Hebrew implies a single sign, 'and to Judah, whose fortress is Jerusalem'.

21f. *He casts lots with arrows*: once a popular means among the Arabs of determining an appropriate course of action. Arrows were marked with alternative choices and then shaken in a quiver. The first to fall or be drawn out indicated the divine intention, in this case that Jerusalem should be attacked first. For *falls at his right hand* read 'is in his right hand'. This method of casting lots has an analogy in the Urim and Thummim of the Old Testament (1 Sam. 14: 41). *consults teraphim*: teraphim were household gods, mentioned in the stories of Jacob (Gen. 31: 34), and of David (1 Sam. 19: 13). Their use in divination is sometimes referred to in disapproving ways (1 Sam. 15: 23 – see N.E.B. footnote; Zech. 10: 2), but it is not known how they were consulted. *inspects the livers of beasts*: animals were sacrificed and their livers examined in the belief that the future could be told by reading signs known to diviners. It was a popular means of obtaining guidance among Babylonians and many clay models for instruction in this type of divination have been preserved. Nebuchadrezzar is portrayed as conscientious in seeking, by every possible means, to perform the will of his god. The fact that the lot coincides with the will of Israel's God, though incidental to the narrative indicates God's control even of pagan divinatory procedures. A similar point is made in the Chronicler's account of Josiah's death (2 Chron. 35: 21f.). *

AGAINST ISRAEL'S IMPIOUS PRINCE

You, too, you impious and wicked prince of Israel, your 25 fate has come upon you in the hour of final punishment. These are the words of the Lord GOD: Put off your 26 diadem, lay aside your crown. All is changed; raise the low and bring down the high. Ruin! Ruin! I will bring 27 about such ruin as never was before, until the rightful sovereign comes. Then I will give him all.

* This brief passage, appended here on account of its links with the rebellion against Babylon and the doom of Jerusalem, raises a difficult problem. The 'wicked prince' (verse 25) is Zedekiah, who broke his sacred oath (see on 17: 19) of allegiance to Nebuchadrezzar and therefore is called 'impious'. But is the promise of 'the rightful sovereign' (verse 27) a promise of hope or of judgement? Some see it as a prophecy of the Messiah (see on 17: 22), others as an allusion to Nebuchadrezzar, translating the Hebrew less freely as 'he is coming to whom judgement belongs'. But against the latter view, it may be understood that judgement had already been executed and Nebuchadrezzar is elsewhere referred to quite explicitly. The guarded language as just rendered is reminiscent of the description of the ruler of Judah in Gen. 49: 10 (reading with N.E.B. footnote, 'until he comes to [whom it belongs]'). This

suggests that Jehoiachin was in fact the one in mind. He was regarded by Ezekiel as still the rightful king, but before 587 B.C. words encouraging thought of restoration would naturally have been guarded, and prefaced, as here, with the certainty of judgement for Jerusalem. For Ezekiel's later expectations for the monarchy, see on 34: 23f.

26. *diadem*: or 'turban', originally a royal head-dress (cp. Isa. 62: 3) but part of the high-priest's apparel in the post-exilic period (Exod. 28: 4). ✳

AGAINST AMMON AND THE SWORD

28 Man, prophesy and say, These are the words of the Lord
GOD to the Ammonites and to their shameful god:

A sword, a sword drawn for slaughter,
    burnished for destruction,*a*
    to flash like lightning!
29 Your visions are false, your auguries a lie,
    which bid you bring it*b* down
    upon the necks of impious and wicked men,
        whose fate has come upon them
        in the hour of final punishment.
30   Sheathe it again.
    I will judge you in the place where you were born,
        the land of your origin.
31   I will pour out my rage upon you;
    I will breathe out my blazing wrath over you.
        I will hand you over to brutal men,
            skilled in destruction.
32   You shall become fuel for fire,

[a] for destruction: *prob. rdg.; Heb. obscure.*
[b] *Prob. rdg.; Heb.* you.

your blood shall be shed within the land
    and you shall leave no memory behind.

For I, the LORD, have spoken.

✳ Ezekiel's followers have added verses 28f. in response to the assertion that Ammon too deserved punishment (verse 20). Ezekiel's own prophecy against Ammon follows in ch. 25. The remaining verses (30–2) also derive from the prophet's disciples and are a prophecy against Babylon. The sword that was once God's instrument of judgement is itself judged, and then destroyed by brutal men. A number of phrases from the sword song and other prophecies are drawn upon in this attempt to tidy up what were thought to be loose strands of Ezekiel's work.

28f. *to the Ammonites and to their shameful god*: this rendering understands the words as a judgement on people and deity alike, the alien deity being described in a characteristically derogatory fashion. But it is better to translate: 'concerning the Ammonites and their reproach'. 'their reproach' was the Ammonites' implied rebuke of Judah for the wrong-doing which led to its overthrow (see 36: 15 and on 36: 13–15). The poem is best understood as addressed to Nebuchadrezzar's sword, not to the Ammonites. So read 'O sword, sword, drawn for slaughter, burnished for destruction, to flash like lightning, to be brought down – while they (the Ammonites) see false visions and lying auguries about you – upon the necks of impious and wicked men . . .' Ammonite diviners had misled their people into thinking they would escape punishment, but that was not to be.

30–2. The interpretation of these verses is much debated. But the opening words, *Sheathe it again*, may be taken as an instruction to the wielder of the sword, Nebuchadrezzar, to cease his activities. The sword is then addressed again, but this time as a figure of Nebuchadrezzar himself. (The pronoun *you* is feminine throughout, as is the Hebrew word for sword.)

Once Babylon had served its purpose as God's instrument of punishment, it was, like Assyria (Isa. 10: 12), to be consigned to destruction.

32. *you shall leave no memory behind*: the worst of all punishments. ✳

THE BLOODY CITY

22₁,₂ These were the words of the LORD to me: Man, will you judge her, will you judge the murderous city and bring
3 home to her all her abominable deeds? Say to her, These are the words of the Lord GOD: Alas for*ᵃ* the city that sheds blood within her walls and brings her fate upon herself, the city that makes herself idols and is defiled thereby!
4 The guilt is yours for the blood you have shed, the pollution is on you for the idols you have made. You have shortened your days by this and brought the end of your years nearer. This is why I exposed you to the contempt
5 of the nations and the mockery of every country. Lands far and near will taunt you with your infamy and gross
6 disorder. In you the princes of Israel, one and all, have
7 used their power to shed blood; men have treated their fathers and mothers with contempt, they have oppressed
8 the alien and ill-treated the orphan and the widow. You have disdained what is sacred to me and desecrated my
9 sabbaths. In you, Jerusalem, informers have worked to procure bloodshed; in you are men who have feasted
10 at mountain-shrines and have committed lewdness. In you men have*ᵇ* exposed their fathers' nakedness; they
11 have violated women during their periods; they have committed an outrage with their neighbours' wives and

[a] Alas for: *so Sept.; Heb. om.*   [b] *So Sept.; Heb.* he has.

have lewdly defiled their daughters-in-law; they have
ravished their sisters, their own fathers' daughters. In 12
you men have accepted bribes to shed blood, and they*ᵃ*
have exacted discount and interest on their loans. You
have oppressed your fellows for gain, and you have
forgotten me. This is the very word of the Lord GOD.

See, I strike with my clenched fist in anger at your ill- 13
gotten gains and at the bloodshed within your walls.
Will your strength or courage stand when I deal with you? 14
I, the LORD, have spoken and I will act. I will disperse 15
you among the nations and scatter you abroad; thus will
I rid you altogether of your defilement. I will sift you*ᵇ* in 16
the sight of the nations, and you will know that I am the
LORD.

✷ The charge of 'bloodshed' is the theme of this section, as
the prophet calls attention both to wrong actions between men
and to faults of religious observance. Verses 3–5 describe the
violence and idolatry of Jerusalem in general terms and
conclude with the original judgement against the city.
Verses 6–12 give a more specific list of crimes, dealing in
turn largely with social, sexual and commercial sins. Two
additional judgements follow. The first (verses 13f.) takes up
the charges of extortion and bloodshed, the second (verses
15f.) makes the earlier judgements more concrete in terms of
impending exile.

2. The double question implies a command, as in 20: 4.

3. The shedding of human blood demanded vengeance
(Gen. 9: 6), except in cases of self-defence and the execution
of criminals. The bloodguilt of homicide lay on the entire
community (Deut. 21: 8), and if the guilty individual was not

[a] *So Sept.; Heb.* you.
[b] I will sift you: *or* You will be profaned.

punished or expiation made for the death of an innocent man, God took upon himself the duty of avenger (Gen. 9: 5).

4b–5. The judgement begins: *This is why...* Those nations which taunted Jerusalem at her fall were later to become subjects of judgement themselves (chs. 25ff.).

7. Respect for parents was essential according to Israelite law. It was numbered among the so-called Ten Commandments (Exod. 20: 12) and failure to show respect was a dire matter, punishable even by death (Exod. 21: 17; Lev. 20: 9; cp. Deut. 21: 18–21). The rights of the alien, the orphan and the widow were also upheld in Israel's law (Exod. 22: 21–4). Oppression or extortion practised against foreigners living in Israel and abiding by its laws was a breach of hospitality, a serious matter in the east. The orphan and widow represented the under-privileged of society and the prophets constantly recalled Israel to its responsibility for them (e.g. Isa. 1: 17; Jer. 22: 3).

8. The close relationship between Ezekiel's thought and that of the author of the Holiness Code, Lev. 17–26 (see on p. 7), is well illustrated in this section. The words here for example describe conduct almost exactly the opposite of that laid down in Lev. 19: 30: 'You shall keep my sabbaths, and revere my sanctuary.' *what is sacred to me* appears for 'my sanctuary', providing wider grounds for the accusation (see further on 22: 26). For *my sabbaths* see on 20: 12.

9. *informers*: or 'slanderers'. Slander is forbidden in Lev. 19: 16.

10f. The *lewdness* referred to in verse 9 is explained here in terms of sexual immorality. Prohibitions against such acts are to be found in Lev. 18: 6–20 and analogous passages. To 'expose a father's nakedness' was for a son to have intercourse with his mother or step-mother. This is the most serious of the sexual sins mentioned here (cp. Deut. 27: 20).

12. Bribery was widespread in the east and is condemned in Exod. 23: 8 as leading to injustice. For lending at *discount* or *interest* see on 18: 8.

13. Striking of the hand or *fist* is here a sign of extreme displeasure.

16. *I will sift you...*: an alternative rendering of these words is, 'I will let myself be profaned in the sight of the nations.' In contrast to God's earlier concern that his name should not be brought into disrepute (cp. 20: 9), he is now prepared to allow even this so that Jerusalem might bring upon itself an appropriate punishment. ✶

ISRAEL IS DROSS

These were the words of the LORD to me: Man, to me all 17, 18 Israelites are an alloy, their silver alloyed with copper, tin, iron, and lead.[a] Therefore, these are the words of the 19 Lord GOD: Because you have all become alloyed, I will gather you together into Jerusalem, as a mass of silver, 20 copper, iron, lead, and tin is gathered into a crucible for the fire to be blown to full heat to melt them. So will I gather you in my anger and wrath, set you there and melt you; I will collect you and blow up the fire of my 21 anger until you are melted within it. You will be melted 22 as silver is melted in a crucible, and you will know that I, the LORD, have poured out my anger upon you.

✶ Ezekiel's prophecy of Jerusalem serving as a crucible is uncompromising, rejecting Israel in its entirety. Isaiah had spoken of God refining his people as silver was refined from base metals (1: 22, 25). Jeremiah, on the other hand, found it impossible to separate the silver from the dross or slag and therefore justified God's rejection of his people (6: 27-30). Similarly with Ezekiel, the people cannot be refined because they are simply dross, without so much as a trace of silver

[a] their silver ... lead: *prob. rdg.*; *Heb.* copper, tin, iron, and lead inside a crucible; they are an alloy, silver.

(verse 18; the N.E.B. obscures this point). They will be destroyed ('melted') when God's anger is displayed against Jerusalem.

18f. As the footnote indicates, the Hebrew has the word 'silver' at the end of the verse. There is no question of Israel being an alloy of silver and other metals. Read, 'Man, to me all Israelites have become dross, copper, tin, iron and lead. They have become dross from silver.' And read 'dross' for 'alloyed' in verse 19.

20. *silver, copper, iron*. . .: the silver ore, which goes into the crucible to be purified. The essential feature of the judgement is that by firing the crucible the molten impurities can be removed. ✲

WORTHLESS LEADERS

23, 24 These were the words of the LORD to me: Man, say to Jerusalem, You are like a land on which no rain has fallen;*a* no shower has come down upon you*b* in the days of
25 indignation. The princes within her are*c* like lions growling as they tear their prey. They have devoured men, and seized their treasure and all their wealth; they
26 have widowed many women within her walls. Her priests have done violence to my law*d* and profaned what is sacred to me. They make no distinction between sacred and common, and lead men to see no difference between clean and unclean. They have disregarded my sabbaths,
27 and I am dishonoured among them. Her officers within her are like wolves tearing their prey, shedding blood
28 and destroying men's lives to acquire ill-gotten gain. Her

[a] on which. . . fallen: *so Sept.; Heb.* which has not been cleansed.
[b] *Prob. rdg.; Heb.* it.
[c] The princes. . . are: *so Sept.; Heb.* The conspiracy of her prophets within her is.   [d] *Or* instruction.

prophets use whitewash instead of plaster;[a] their vision is false and their divination a lie. They say, 'This is the word of the Lord GOD', when the LORD has not spoken. The common people are bullies and robbers; they ill- 29 treat the unfortunate and the poor, they are unjust and cruel to the alien. I looked for a man among them who 30 could build up a barricade, who could stand before me in the breach to defend the land from ruin; but I found no such man. I poured out my indignation upon them and 31 utterly destroyed them in the fire of my wrath. Thus I brought on them the punishment they had deserved. This is the very word of the Lord GOD.

* Zeph. 3: 1–4 and 8 is the basis of this justification of God's judgement on Jerusalem, which derives from Ezekiel's followers. The four kinds of leaders in the city – princes, priests, officers and prophets – were corrupt, as were the common people, so destruction was inevitable. The passage is a sermon rather than a prophecy, instructing people how they should behave by describing wrong behaviour. The fall of Jerusalem is presupposed.

24. Rainfall is essential to life, but as her punishment Jerusalem was denied such essentials. *the days of indignation*: the days when God's indignation was expressed by Jerusalem's overthrow (see verse 31).

26. The priests are accused among other things of mishandling the law, perhaps by giving false instruction in return for bribes as Mic. 3: 11 charges. *sacred and common*: sacred or holy things were those set apart from profane or common use for the service of God. Priests were responsible on the one hand for protecting sacred things from common use, and on the other for protecting people from the danger of unguarded contact with the holy (see on 42: 13f.). Much of the Priestly

[a] Cp. 13: 8–16.

material of the Pentateuch preserves teaching to this end. *clean and unclean*: that which was common could be either clean or unclean. Consumption of, or contact with, unclean things – certain foods, bodily discharges, dead bodies (see Lev. 11–15) – rendered a person unclean and unfit to approach God, the source of holiness, in worship. Such persons were unable to share the sacredness of God's people (Lev. 19: 2), until cleansed in various stipulated ways (see again Lev. 11–15 and 16). The responsibility of priests for teaching people to distinguish between the sacred and profane, the clean and unclean, is reinforced in Ezek. 44: 23. For the importance of the *sabbaths* see on 20: 12.

27. *officers*: nobles, heads of important families.

30. No man of the classes mentioned could do what was the duty of a prophet according to 13: 5, namely to renew the nation's spiritual defences by encouraging reform. ✻

THE TWO SISTERS

231,2 The word of the LORD came to me: Man, he said, there were once two women, daughters of the same mother.

3 They played the whore in Egypt, played the whore while they were still girls; for there they let their breasts be

4 fondled and their virgin bosoms pressed. The elder was named Oholah, her sister Oholibah. They became mine and bore me sons and daughters. 'Oholah' is Samaria,

5 'Oholibah' Jerusalem. While she owed me obedience Oholah played the whore and was infatuated with her

6 Assyrian lovers, staff officers in blue,[a] viceroys and governors, handsome young cavaliers all of them, riding

7 on horseback. She played the whore with all of them, the flower of the Assyrian youth; and she let herself be

8 defiled with all their idols, wherever her lust led her. She

[a] Or violet.

never gave up the whorish ways she had learnt in Egypt, where men had lain with her when young, had pressed her virgin bosom and overwhelmed her with their fornication. So I abandoned her to her lovers, the Assyrians, with whom she was infatuated. They ravished her, they took her sons and daughters, and they killed her with the sword. She became a byword among women, and judgement was passed upon her.

✶ The theme of this chapter is the political alliances of Samaria and Jerusalem. The portrayal of both cities as prostitutes emphasizes the arbitrary way they sought to satisfy their own immediate desires and interests, irrespective of the allegiance they owed to God. Ezekiel, like Isaiah before him, condemned all alliances with foreign powers as a symptom of a basic mistrust of God. In ch. 16 Jerusalem was character- ized as a whore on account of her apostasy. The two themes, apostasy and foreign alliances, come to be interwoven; relationships with other nations, as Deuteronomy in particular emphasizes, inevitably bring about alien religious practices, though it is by no means clear that ancient conquerors such as the Assyrians imposed their own gods on their subjects. The evil rests in lack of trust in God and in the risk of contam- ination. The idea of Samaria and Jerusalem as adulterous sisters derives from Jer. 3: 6–11. Indeed, Ezekiel has attempted to give substance to Jeremiah's words in this extended allegory. The present verses introduce the theme and deal with Samaria in her relations with Assyria.

2. For Jerusalem, Samaria and Sodom as sisters see 16: 45f.

3. *played the whore*: entered into a political alliance. It is not clear what alliances Ezekiel could have been thinking of here. He wanted to affirm the sisters' wantonness from their youth and the verse may be a general reflection on the time when the Israelite tribes dwelt in Egypt on friendly terms (cp. Gen. 47: 1–6).

4. *Oholah*: traditionally understood to mean '(she who has) her own tent', referring to the northern kingdom of Israel with its own shrines, while *Oholibah*, 'my tent (is) in her', refers to the southern kingdom with the legitimate sanctuary of God at Jerusalem. *'ōhel* ('tent') was a name for the sanctuary in the wilderness (Exod. 33: 7). This is not an altogether satisfactory explanation, but the similarity of the names at least suggests the sisters' common origin, guilt and fate. *They became mine and bore me sons and daughters*: Hos. 1: 2 gave a precedent for the idea of God marrying an already wanton woman. Explicit identification of the sisters was unnecessary and the last sentence of the verse has been added later to the allegory.

5. For Samaria's relations with Assyria see 2 Kings 15: 19f. Menahem of Israel paid tribute to Assyria to consolidate his rule in Samaria.

9f. The judgement relates to the Assyrian exile and the fall of Samaria (2 Kings 17: 6). ✽

OHOLIBAH ALSO INFATUATED

11 Oholibah, her sister, had watched her, and she gave herself up to lust and played the whore worse than her
12 sister. She, too, was infatuated with Assyrians, viceroys, governors and staff officers, all handsome young cavaliers,
13 in full dress, riding on horseback. I found that she too had let herself be defiled; both had gone the same way;
14 but she carried her fornication to greater lengths: she saw male figures carved on the wall, sculptured forms of
15 Chaldaeans, picked out in vermilion. Belts were round their waists, and on their heads turbans with dangling ends. All seemed to be high officers and looked like
16 Babylonians, natives of Chaldaea. As she looked she was infatuated with them, so she sent messengers to Chaldaea

for them. And the Babylonians came to her to share her 17
bed, and defiled her with fornication; she was defiled
by them until she was filled with revulsion. She made no 18
secret that she was a whore but let herself be ravished until
I was filled with revulsion against her as I was against her
sister. She played the whore again and again, remem- 19
bering how in her youth she had played the whore in
Egypt. She was infatuated with their male prostitutes, 20
whose members were like those of asses and whose seed
came in floods like that of horses. So, Oholibah, you 21
relived the lewdness of your girlhood in Egypt when you
let your bosom be pressed and your breasts fondled.[a]

❋ The addition in verses 12–14a, which partly repeat verses
5f., recalls Judah's dealings with Assyria in the days of King
Ahaz (2 Kings 16: 7–20). But Ezekiel saw Judah's greater
whoredom lying in her advances to Babylon and Egypt.

11. *Oholibah, her sister, had watched her*: cp. Jer. 3: 7, 'her
sister Judah, saw it all'.

14b–15. *she saw male figures carved on the wall...*: the
precise circumstance Ezekiel has in mind is unknown, but as
evidence of cultural interchange there is Jeremiah's reference
to an attempt to decorate the Jerusalem palace with vermilion
panels (Jer. 22: 14). Presumably there were wall reliefs in
Babylon, as there were in Assyria, impressive in their display of
military might. *sculptured forms of Chaldaeans*: Ezekiel distinguished between the terms 'Chaldaean' and 'Babylonian'
(see verse 23). Only later did 'Chaldaean' become a general
term for both the Babylonians and the Aramaic-speaking
Chaldaeans. Since verse 15 indicates that Babylonians were
portrayed on the wall, these words are secondary.

16f. The wall reliefs were appealing inasmuch as they
suggested Babylonian power might offer Judah escape from

[a] fondled: *prob. rdg.; Heb. unintelligible.*

155

Assyrian domination. As Assyrian power declined toward the end of the seventh century B.C., Josiah allied Judah with the cause of Nabopolassar of Babylon by trying to cut off Egyptian aid to Assyria. Josiah was killed in the confrontation with Pharaoh Necho at Megiddo and his son Jehoahaz was deposed by Necho after a very short reign (see on 19: 3f.), presumably because he continued to oppose Egypt and by implication courted the favour of Babylon. His successor, Jehoiakim, though enthroned at the instigation of Necho, may also have conspired with Babylon against Egypt. Certainly he became for a time the vassal of Babylon when Nebuchadrezzar defeated Egypt in 605 B.C. (2 Kings 24: 1). *she was defiled by them until she was filled with revulsion*: independence was no nearer under Babylon than it had been under Assyria and Jehoiakim eventually rebelled against Nebuchadrezzar, so bringing about the exile of 597 B.C.

19f. Both Jehoiakim and Zedekiah sought Egypt's help against Babylon. The scathing denunciation of the Egyptians here (cp. 16: 26) reflects a widespread belief that they were a lustful people (cp. Gen. 12: 11–20; 39: 7–18). ✶

HER LOVERS WILL JUDGE HER

22 Therefore these are the words of the Lord GOD: I will rouse them against you, Oholibah, those lovers of yours who have filled you with revulsion, and bring them upon
23 you from every side, the Babylonians and all those Chaldaeans, men of Pekod, Shoa, and Koa, and all the Assyrians with them. Handsome young men they are, viceroys and governors, commanders and staff officers,[a]
24 riding on horseback. They will come against you with war-horses,[b] with chariots and wagons, with a host

[a] staff officers: *prob. rdg., cp. verses 5 and 12; Heb. obscure.*
[b] *So some MSS.; others have an unknown word.*

drawn from the nations, armed with shield, buckler, and
helmet; they will beset you on every side. I will give them
authority to judge, and they will use that authority to
judge you. I will turn my jealous wrath loose on you, 25
and they will make you feel their fury. They will cut
off your nose and your ears, and in the end you*a* will fall
by the sword.*b* They will strip you of your clothes and 26
take away all your finery. So I will put a stop to your 27
lewdness and the way in which you learnt to play the
whore in Egypt. You will never cast longing eyes on such
things again, never remember Egypt any more.

* The judgement was that God would entrust the punishment of Jerusalem to Babylon and its allies. So mutilated
would Jerusalem then be that she would never again presume
to play the seductress, never again enter into foreign alliances
to gain her own immediate satisfactions.

23. *Babylonians. . .Chaldaeans*: these terms serve respectively to distinguish the city-dwellers from the tribal groups
east and south of Babylon. *Pekod* was a powerful Chaldaean
tribe dwelling near the mouth of the river Tigris. The other
two tribes have not been clearly identified. *and all the Assyrians
. . .Handsome young men. . .*: like verse 12 these words are an
addition based on verses 5f.

25. *cut off your nose*: recorded in contemporary documents
as the punishment for an adulteress in Egypt and Assyria.

27. Egypt's corrupting influence is again stressed (cp. 20:
7f.). *

[*a*] in the end you: *or* your successors.
[*b*] *Prob. rdg.; Heb. adds* They will take your sons and daughters, and
in the end you will be burnt.

A FATE LIKE SAMARIA'S

28 These are the words of the Lord GOD: I am handing you over to those whom you hate, those who have filled you
29 with revulsion; and they will make you feel their hatred. They will take all you have earned and leave you naked and exposed; that body with which you have played the whore will be ravished. It is your lewdness and your fornication
30 that have brought this upon you, it is because you have followed alien peoples and played the whore and have
31 allowed yourself to be defiled with their idols. You have followed in your sister's footsteps, and I will put her cup into your hand.

32   These are the words of the Lord GOD:

> You shall drink from your sister's cup,
>   a cup deep and wide,
> charged with mockery and scorn,
>   more than ever cup can hold.

33   It*a* will be full of drunkenness and grief,
>   a cup of ruin and desolation,
> the cup of your sister Samaria;

34   and you shall drink it to the dregs.
> Then you will chew*b* it in pieces
>   and tear out your breasts.
> This is my verdict, says the Lord GOD.

35   Therefore, these are the words of the Lord GOD: Because you have forgotten me and flung me behind your back, you must bear the guilt of your lewdness and your fornication.

[a] *Prob. rdg.; Heb.* You.   [b] *Or* dash.

✻ To the original allegory have been added a number of related passages. Three separate judgements are found first. In verses 28–30 the Babylonians are not called Jerusalem's 'lovers' but 'those whom you hate', and idolatry is included as a reason for the judgement. The theme of a cup of judgement, in the poem of verses 31–4, is used by other prophets, including Jeremiah (Jer. 25: 15f.). Although the identification of the sister as Samaria (verse 33) is secondary, the poem may well be Ezekiel's own, applying the symbol of divine wrath, expressed in Samaria's case by the exile of 722 B.C., to Jerusalem.

29. *naked and exposed*: a return to the state described in 16: 7 and 39. It is interesting too to notice that 16: 39 was reflected in the stripping off of clothes and jewels in verse 26, illustrating the elaboration of the one chapter by the other.

32. *charged with mockery and scorn*: these words are intrusive. The second half of the verse originally read: 'for it contains much'.

34. *chew it in pieces*: so as to get the very last drop. *and tear out your breasts* is omitted in the Septuagint, but indicates that Jerusalem will suffer such anguish that she will mutilate herself and so remove her one remaining source of physical attractiveness. ✻

FURTHER INTERPRETATIONS

The LORD said to me, Man, will you judge Oholah and 36
Oholibah? Then tax them with their vile offences. They 37
have committed adultery, and there is blood on their
hands. They have committed adultery with their idols
and offered my children to them for food, the children
they had borne me. This too they have done to me: they 38
have polluted my sanctuary*a* and desecrated my sabbaths.
They came into my sanctuary and desecrated it*a* by 39

[a] *So Sept.; Heb. adds* on that day.

slaughtering their sons as an offering to their idols; this
40 they did in my own house. They would send for men
from a far-off country; and the men came at the messenger's bidding. You bathed your body for these men, you
41 painted your eyes, decked yourself in your finery, you
sat yourself upon a bed of state and had a table put ready
before it and laid my own incense and my own oil on it.
42 Loud were the voices of the light-hearted crowd; and
besides ordinary folk Sabaeans were there, brought from
the wilderness; they put bracelets on the women's hands
43 and beautiful garlands on their heads. I thought: Ah that
woman, grown old in adultery! Now they will commit
44 fornication with her – with her of all women[a]! They[b]
resorted to her as a prostitute; they resorted to Oholah
45 and Oholibah, those lewd women. Upright men will
condemn them for their adultery and bloodshed; for
adulterous they are, and blood is on their hands.

46   These are the words of the Lord GOD: Summon the
47 invading host; abandon them to terror and rapine. Let
the host stone them and hack them to pieces with their
swords, kill their sons and daughters and burn down their
48 houses. Thus I will put an end to lewdness in the land, and
other women shall be taught not to be as lewd as they.[c]
49 You shall pay the penalty for your lewd conduct and be
punished for your idolatries, and you will know that I
am the Lord GOD.

[a] with her of all women: *lit.* and her.
[b] *So one MS.; others* He.   [c] *So Sept.; Heb.* you.

✻ These verses retell the allegory of Oholah and Oholibah, drawing together elements of chs. 16, 20 and 23 and describing the simultaneous fate of the sisters. The verses are clearly secondary and from more than one author. But though they are in places disconnected and obscure, they illustrate again the application and reinterpretation of the prophet's words in later periods. The first faults of the sisters are adultery and bloodshed, explained in terms of idol worship and human sacrifice (verses 37–9). Adultery in terms of foreign alliances is then dealt with (verses 40–4), but sometimes one and sometimes two women are referred to. Upright men are to be the judges of the sisters (verse 45) and the judgement (verses 46–9) is to be executed by the community. The allegory thus becomes, in verse 48, a warning against adultery in general, a warning to individuals rather than to nations (cp. on 22: 23–31).

40. *They would send for men*: an allusion to verse 16 seems intended here. But the second half of the verse (*You bathed your body* . . .) and the following verse describe the preparations of only one woman.

42. The picture is of a festive occasion which many lovers attend. *and besides ordinary folk Sabaeans were there, brought from the wilderness*: for these words read, 'of men brought from the wilderness'. The word for 'brought' has been read twice in the Hebrew and understood the second time as a reference to a particular people – the cultured Sabaeans of south-west Arabia.

43. *Ah that woman* . . . : note the reference to only one woman through to the second half of the following verse.

46f. *the invading host*: literally 'an assembly', not a foreign army but, as in 16: 40, a community of Israelites assembled for the purpose of executing judgement. Punishment by death was prescribed for crimes of adultery in both Deuteronomy (22: 22) and the Holiness Code (Lev. 20: 10). ✻

THE ALLEGORY OF THE CAULDRON

24 These were the words of the LORD, spoken to me on the
2 tenth day of the tenth month in the ninth year: Man,
write down a name for this day, this very day: This is the
3 day the king of Babylon invested Jerusalem. Sing a song
of derision to this people of rebels; say to them, These are
the words of the Lord GOD:

> Set a cauldron on the fire,
>   set it on and pour water into it.
4   Into it collect the pieces,
>   all the choice pieces,
>   cram it with leg and shoulder and the best of the
>   bones;
5   take the best of the flock.
>   Pack the logs[a] round it underneath;
>   seethe the stew
>   and boil the bones in it.
>
6   O city running with blood,
>   O pot green with corrosion,
>   corrosion that will never be clean!

Therefore these are the words of the Lord GOD:

> Empty it, piece after piece,
>   though no lot is cast for any of them.
7   The city had blood in her midst
>   and she poured it out on the gleaming rock,
>   not on the ground: she did not pour it there
>   for the dust to cover it.

[a] *Prob. rdg., cp. verse 10; Heb.* bones.

But I too have spilt blood on the gleaming white   8
  rock
    so that it cannot be covered,
to make anger flare up and to call down vengeance.

Therefore these are the words of the Lord GOD: 9

    O city running with blood,
  I too will make a great fire-pit.
Fill it with logs, light the fire;   10
    make an end of the meat,
pour out all the broth*a* and the bones with it.*b*
  Then set the pot empty on the coals   11
so that its copper may be heated red-hot,
    and then the impurities in it may be melted
    and its corrosion burnt off.
    Try as you may,*c*   12
the corrosion is so deep that it will not come off;
    only fire will rid it of corrosion for you.
Even so, when I cleansed you in your filthy lewdness,   13
    you did not become clean from it,
      and therefore you shall never again be clean
    until I have satisfied my anger against you.

I, the LORD, have spoken; the time is coming, I will act.   14
I will not refrain nor pity nor relent; I*d* will judge you for
your conduct and for all that you have done. This is the
very word of the Lord GOD.

[a] pour . . . broth: *prob. rdg.; Heb.* mix ointment.
[b] with it: *prob. rdg.; Heb.* will be scorched.
[c] Try as you may: *prob. rdg.; Heb. obscure.*
[d] *So Sept.; Heb.* they.

✻ The instruction to record the date when Nebuchadrezzar began laying siege to Jerusalem emphasizes the importance of the day. But whether in fact the prophet knew the precise date, by some premonition or act of clairvoyancy, we cannot tell. The unusual way the date is expressed in Hebrew suggests it has been supplied from 2 Kings 25: 1. An editor may have made Ezekiel's date conform to the accepted one. Nonetheless there is confirmation here of how deeply Ezekiel felt himself to be aware of events in his distant homeland.

In 11: 1–13 the figure of a cauldron was used of Jerusalem. Ezekiel is now instructed to deliver a brief allegorical poem of a boiling cauldron filled with fine meat (verses 3–5). But this time the cauldron is a vessel of siege and destruction, not a symbol of protection. The meat is the populace, seethed within the city. The interpretation of the poem is to be found in verses 9f. The remaining verses (6–8 and 11), which liken Jerusalem to a corroded pot that must be purified by fire, may belong to the same period. They have become intertwined with the poem and its interpretation because of the common figure of the heated pot. The pot is again Jerusalem, but the inhabitants of the city are now described as the corrosion on it. Verses 12–14 are later additions.

1. The date, which was later observed as one of the times of fasting (Zech. 8: 19), was in December 589–January 588 B.C.

3. *Sing a song of derision*: literally 'utter a parable (or allegory)'.

6. In the Hebrew the verse begins, *Therefore these are the words...*, marking the start of the allegory of the corroded pot. *that will never be clean!*: this rendering may assume that verses 12f. were originally part of this second allegory. But verse 11 affirms the possibility of cleansing, so read here: 'that has not come clean'. *Empty it, piece after piece...*: these words belong with verses 3–5. They are an addition emphasizing that all the inhabitants of Jerusalem will suffer equally. Possibly the choice of those to be taken into exile in 597 B.C. was made by casting lots.

7f. Uncovered blood was said to 'cry from the ground' for God to take vengeance (Gen. 4: 10; Job 16: 18). So blood of the victims of injustice in Jerusalem, which was brazenly spilled on rock that could not absorb it, required God to act against the city. Verse 8 is an addition attributing the spilling of blood on rock to God himself, so that punishment might come (cp. on 22: 16).

12–14. These verses represent later attempts to press the imagery further and affirm the closeness of judgement. The Hebrew of verse 12 may be taken to imply that even fire cannot cleanse the pot: 'its deep corrosion will not come off by fire'. Verse 13 interprets the corrosion as lewdness. ✶

DO NOT MOURN

These were the words of the LORD to me: Man, I am tak- 15,16
ing from you at one blow the dearest thing you have, but
you must not wail or weep or give way to tears. Keep in 17
good heart; be quiet, and make no mourning for the
dead; cover your head as usual and put sandals on your
feet. You shall not cover your upper lip in mourning nor
eat the bread of despair.

I spoke to the people in the morning; and that very 18
evening my wife died. Next morning I did as I was told.
The people asked me to say what meaning my behaviour 19
had for them. I answered, These were the words of the 20
LORD to me: Tell the Israelites, This is the word of the 21
Lord GOD: I will desecrate my sanctuary, which has been
the pride of your strength, the delight of your eyes and
your heart's desire; and the sons and daughters whom you
have left behind shall fall by the sword. But, I said, you 22
shall do as I have done: you shall not cover your upper
lip in mourning nor eat the bread of despair. You shall 23

cover your head and put sandals on your feet; you shall not wail nor weep. Because of your wickedness you will
24 pine away and will lament to[a] one another. The LORD says, Ezekiel will be a sign to warn you, and when it happens you will do as he has done, and you will know that I am the Lord GOD.

�֎ This moving passage has sometimes been taken to indicate the prophet's heartlessness in turning personal grief into an act of prophecy. In fact the depth of his personal feeling is quite evident. And although Ezekiel was prepared to subject his own feelings to his prophetic task, this narrative of his wife's death is presented as the climax of his first period of activity, recording his last words before news of Jerusalem's fall reached the exiles. Jeremiah was instructed not to share in mourning rites as a sign that the national disaster which lay ahead would be overwhelming. All feelings would be numb. The dead would not be honoured by the living and the living would find none to comfort them in sorrow (Jer. 16: 5–9). In assessing the meaning of his wife's death, Ezekiel appears to have adopted this idea of his contemporary's, adding to it a new dimension of his own. For apart from the prophecy of devastating, imminent disaster for the temple and for families still in Jerusalem, the meaning of the prophecy is that grief for what is lost is not to dominate the future (cp. 2 Sam. 12: 22f.). Desire for former relationships and old securities, however deep, is not to bring the exiles themselves to the grave in mourning. Despite the bitterness of their loss, the people are, like Ezekiel, to be prepared for a future of new activity. Thus there is implicit here the beginning of a fresh hope, even as the old one was about to be finally shattered. God's nature would be vindicated as just, and though the people's 'dearest things' were to be taken from them, they would be free to share a new future, recognizing him as Lord.

[a] *Or* for.

16. *the dearest thing you have*: literally 'the delight of your eyes', suggesting a real depth of attachment (cp. 'his delight', Lam. 2: 4; 'the dearest offspring', Hos. 9: 16). The cause of death is not indicated, though the Hebrew for *at one blow* may mean a sudden and unexpected illness (cp. Num. 14: 37).

17. *Keep in good heart*: the Hebrew reads 'groan' or 'sigh'. Some suppressed expression of grief such as 'sigh (but not aloud)' may have been permitted the prophet. The first part of the verse could thus be rendered, 'Keep your sorrow to yourself' *and make no mourning. . .*; the latter part goes on to refer to the traditional outward signs of mourning. The moustache was a symbol of proud manhood and *the bread of despair* (literally 'the bread of men') was food brought by friends to mourners, since food could not be prepared in the house of the dead.

18. *I spoke to the people in the morning*: according to the following verse the prophet explains his actions in response to the people's question. These words may represent what was originally a command, 'you shall speak to the people in the morning'.

22f. An addition which interrupts the divine address and in the second part of verse 23 introduces the idea of the people mourning.

24. Only here and in 1: 3 is Ezekiel's name mentioned. ✼

A FUGITIVE WILL COME

And now, man, a word for you: I am taking from them 25 that fortress whose beauty so gladdened them, the delight of their eyes, their heart's desire; I am taking their sons and their daughters. Soon fugitives will come and tell 26 you their news by word of mouth. At once you will 27 recover the power of speech and speak with the fugitives; you will no longer be dumb. So will you be a portent to them, and they shall know that I am the LORD.

✣ An editorial link between 24: 15–24 and 33: 21f. When those passages were separated by the insertion of chs. 25–32, an editor added this prophecy of Ezekiel's recovery from dumbness when news of Jerusalem's fall reached him. Verse 25 draws on verse 21 and verses 26f. use the words of 33: 21f.

25. *that fortress whose beauty so gladdened them*: the equivalent of 'my sanctuary, which has been the pride of your strength' in verse 21; that is, the temple.

26f. The N.E.B. has smoothed out one of the difficulties of these verses by rendering the Hebrew 'on that day' by *Soon* in verse 26. The Hebrew implies that a fugitive arrived in Babylon the same day Jerusalem fell, whereas 33: 21 indicates that his journey took six months. Also the N.E.B. has understood the Hebrew for 'the fugitive' as a collective noun: *fugitives*. Ezekiel elsewhere uses the plural when speaking of more than one fugitive and the article in the Hebrew suggests that a particular individual, one designated by God to convey a message to the prophet, was meant by the prophet in 33: 21. ✣

Prophecies against foreign nations

✣ Chs. 25–32 make up the second main section of the book of Ezekiel. Most of the prophecies date from the period around the time of Jerusalem's fall in 587 B.C., although 29: 17 gives the latest date in the book, 571 B.C. There are three subsections. The first comprises prophecies against the nations which were Judah's neighbours; these presuppose Jerusalem's destruction (ch. 25). The second is directed mainly against Tyre (chs. 26–8) and the third against Egypt (chs. 29–32).

Each of these sub-sections represents a collection of prophecies originating from Ezekiel himself. But the section as a whole has been influenced by the example of other collections of prophecies against the nations, particularly Amos 1–2. The

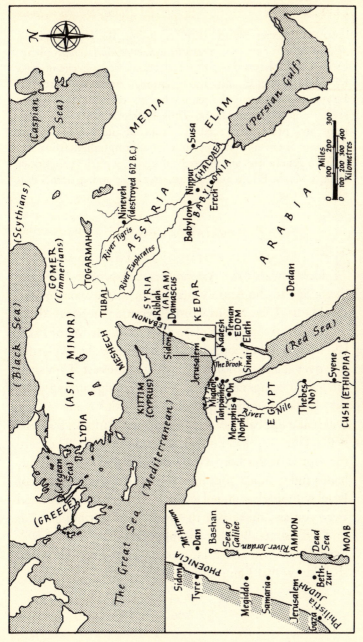

I. The main locations referred to in Ezekiel.

169

seven prophecies found there (excluding the late prophecy against Judah) exercised a strong influence on later prophetic groups, and what was at first a collection of prophecies uttered by Ezekiel against only three nations, Ammon, Tyre and Egypt, has been supplemented by his disciples to provide seven subjects of prophecy. Thus Ezekiel's concrete accusations and precisely described means of judgement against Ammon, Tyre and Egypt may be distinguished from the relative generalities and borrowed imagery of the prophecies against Moab, Edom and Philistia in ch. 25 and against Sidon in ch. 28. ✶

AGAINST AMMON

251, 2 THESE WERE THE WORDS OF THE LORD TO ME: Man, look towards the Ammonites and prophesy against
3 them. Say to the Ammonites, Listen to the word of the Lord GOD. These are his words: Because you cried 'Aha!' when you saw my holy place desecrated, the soil of Israel
4 laid waste and the people of Judah sent into exile, I will hand you over as a possession to the tribes of the east. They shall pitch their camps and put up their dwellings among you;
5 they shall eat your crops; they shall drink your milk. I will make Rabbah a camel-pasture and Ammon a sheep-
6 walk. Thus you shall know that I am the LORD. These are the words of the Lord GOD: Because you clapped your hands and stamped your feet, and exulted over the land of
7 Israel with single-minded scorn, I will stretch out my hand over you and make you the prey of the nations and cut you off from all other peoples; in every land I will exterminate you and bring you to utter ruin. Thus you shall know that I am the LORD.

✻ Ezekiel, or the editor of his prophecies, begins with the denunciation of the people to the north-east of Judah. The Ammonites had, at the turn of the sixth century B.C., supported Babylon against Judah (2 Kings 24: 1f.). But they later encouraged Zedekiah to revolt against Babylon (Jer. 27: 1-11), and then conspired against Gedaliah, the governor of Judah appointed by Nebuchadrezzar (Jer. 40: 14). The prophet is concerned not with the Ammonites' political treachery but with their belief that the destruction of Jerusalem would mean the end of God's influence through his temple, land and people. Even as they rejoiced that Israel's God had been shown ineffectual, that same God was proclaiming Ammon's doom.

To the first prophecy against Ammon (verses 1-5) has been added one which has the marks of later composition (verses 6f.). With the intention of reinforcing the punishment, the disciples of Ezekiel have added a more general threat of extermination in terms such as Ezekiel uses elsewhere against Israel.

2. *look towards the Ammonites*: see on 4: 13. There is a strong sense of God's power, active to judge, in such looking.

3. *Aha!*: a cry of malicious glee.

4f. *the tribes of the east*: wandering Bedouin, who would consume the corn and milk of the settled inhabitants, leaving their land fit only for the grazing of the nomads' animals. *Rabbah*: the capital city of Ammon. *Thus you shall know . . .*: by the fulfilment of these prophecies foreign nations would acknowledge the God of Israel to be the LORD. ✻

AGAINST MOAB

These are the words of the Lord GOD: Because Moab*a*   8
said, 'Judah is like all the rest', I will expose the flank of   9
Moab and lay open its cities,*b* from one end to the other –

[a] *So Sept.; Heb. adds* and Seir.
[b] *and lay. . . cities: prob. rdg.; Heb.* from the cities, from its cities.

the fairest of its cities: Beth-jeshimoth, Baal-meon and
10 Kiriathaim. I will hand over Moab and Ammon together
to the tribes of the east to be their possession, so that the
Ammonites shall not be remembered among the nations,
11 and so that I may execute judgement upon Moab. Thus
they shall know that I am the LORD.

✻ Moab, to the east of Judah, had been involved in the same
political circumstances as Ammon, at first supporting Babylon
against Judah and then encouraging Zedekiah's revolt. But
this prophecy, like the two that follow against Edom and the
Philistines, is not introduced by mention of the word of God
coming to the prophet and the command to him to prophesy
(cp. 25: 1f.). Nor are the nations directly addressed. These
facts confirm what was said in introducing this section of
prophecies, namely that these have been composed by Ezekiel's
disciples to round out his words against Judah's enemies.

8. *Judah is like all the rest*: implicit in these words is scorn
for Israel's God, who was unable to protect his people from a
fate like that of other nations.

9. *the flank of Moab*: the high tableland north of the
country, defended by the three cities mentioned.

10. *Moab and Ammon*: both reported, by the Jewish his-
torian Josephus (see p. ix), to have been conquered by
Nebuchadrezzar in 582 B.C. Such a link between the two nations
is found also in the prophecies of Jeremiah (e.g. Jer. 27: 3)
and Zephaniah (2: 8f.). ✻

AGAINST EDOM

12 These are the words of the Lord GOD: Because Edom took
deliberate revenge on Judah and by so doing incurred
13 lasting guilt, I will stretch my hand out over Edom, says
the Lord GOD, and destroy both man and beast in it,
laying waste the land from Teman as far as Dedan; they

shall fall by the sword. I will wreak my vengeance upon 14
Edom through my people Israel. They will deal with
Edom as my anger and fury demand, and it shall feel my
vengeance. This is the very word of the Lord GOD.

* Edom lay to the south-east of Judah and relations between
the two states were often marked by extreme hostility.
Although Edom joined with Judah, Ammon and Moab in the
revolt planned against Babylon in 594–593 B.C., on the
destruction of Jerusalem Edomites gradually occupied the
Judaean hill-country south of Beth-zur, giving rise to the
accusation made here. Edom apparently escaped destruction
from Babylon and the extraordinary prophecy is made that
Israel will exact punishment for all she has suffered at Edom's
hand (see too on ch. 35 and 36: 1–15, and the harsh words
against Edom in the book of Obadiah).

13. *from Teman as far as Dedan*: from north to south,
although Dedan in fact lay well south of Edom's border.

14. *through my people Israel*: the idea that Israel will execute
vengeance on God's behalf belongs not to Ezekiel, but to
his followers. *

AGAINST THE PHILISTINES

These are the words of the Lord GOD: Because the 15
Philistines have taken deliberate revenge and have
avenged themselves with single-minded scorn, giving
vent to their age-long enmity in destruction, I will 16
stretch out my hand over the Philistines, says the Lord
GOD, I will wipe out the Kerethites and destroy all the
rest of the dwellers by the sea. I will take fearful vengeance 17
upon them and punish them in my fury. When I take my
vengeance, they shall know that I am the LORD.

✻ The Philistines to the west are the next subject of prophecy. The Philistines had suffered the deportation of their leaders in 605 B.C. after a revolt against Babylon, but they were later given a portion of Judaean territory by Nebuchadrezzar as punishment of Judah. Although they had once been hated enemies of Israel, the Philistines had come to be treated with a measure of respect and goodwill and the intense enmity reflected here is unexpected.

16. *wipe out the Kerethites*: there is a play on words here, for the Hebrew letters of the words rendered *wipe out* (or 'cut off', *krt*) are the same as those of the name *Kerethites*, a Philistine tribe presumably originating in Crete (*crt* or *krt*). David's personal guard had been composed of Kerethites and Pelethites (2 Sam. 8: 18). The latter name was probably a form of the word 'Philistines'. ✻

THE FIRST ORACLE AGAINST TYRE

26 These were the words of the LORD to me on the first day
2 of the first*[a]* month in the eleventh year: Man, Tyre has said of Jerusalem,

> Aha! she that was the gateway of the nations
> > is broken,
> her gates swing open to me;
> I grow rich, she lies in ruins.*[b]*

3 Therefore these are the words of the Lord GOD:

> I am against you, Tyre,
> and will bring up many nations against you
> > as the sea brings up its waves;
4 > they will destroy the walls of Tyre and pull down her
> > towers.

[a] first: *so Sept.; Heb. om.*
[b] I . . . ruins: *or, with Sept.*, she that was rich lies in ruins.

I will scrape the soil off her
and make her a gleaming rock,
she shall be an islet where men spread their nets;   5
    I have spoken, says the Lord GOD.
  She shall become the prey of nations,
and her daughters[a] shall be slain by the sword in the   6
    open country.
Thus they shall know that I am the LORD.

✳ These verses begin three chapters almost wholly devoted
to the fate of Tyre. As one of the major conspirators in the
revolt planned in 594–593 B.C., Tyre held a heavy burden of
responsibility for encouraging Jerusalem's rebellion and
eventual destruction. Also as a major power opposing
Nebuchadrezzar, whom Ezekiel saw as God's instrument of
punishment, Tyre dominated the prophet's concern with
Judah's neighbours. Located on a rocky island, Tyre seemed
impregnable. It was the chief city of Phoenicia. It was an
important commercial centre, and its culture – including its
worship of Baal – had influenced Judah as well as Israel,
despite opposition from the prophets. After the destruction of
Jerusalem, Nebuchadrezzar began a thirteen-year siege of
Tyre. The prophecies date from this period.
  Ch. 26 follows the pattern of the previous chapter, with the
first prophecy fully introduced and dated while subsequent
prophecies begin with a brief introductory formula. Also
verses 1–6 contain a prophecy which is very likely to derive
from Ezekiel himself, but the following three prophecies are
of more doubtful authenticity. The executor of judgement is
stated in general terms to be 'many nations' (verse 3), but the
threat itself is most appropriate for the island city. Those who
come to her at first will do so not to court her for her influential status as successor to Jerusalem, but to destroy her like
mighty waves and strip her of hope for the future. And those

[a] *Or* daughter-towns.

175

who come to her in the end will be fishermen using her desolate shores only to spread their nets.

1. *the first month in the eleventh year*: the number of the month is missing from the Hebrew and has been supplied from the Septuagint. But the date must be understood in relation to 33: 21, according to the corrected text of which Ezekiel received news of the fall of Jerusalem in the tenth month of the eleventh year. Since this prophecy against Tyre presupposes Jerusalem's fall, the 'eleventh' or 'twelfth' month should be read, that is January–February or February–March 586 B.C.

2. The malicious joy, such as Ammon also expressed at the fall of Jerusalem, was prompted on Tyre's part by the removal of the city as a political and commercial centre on the route between Asia Minor and Mesopotamia to the north, and Egypt and Arabia to the south. No longer would there be competition between Tyre and Jerusalem for political and economic influence. *I grow rich*: it is difficult to see in what ways Tyre would have profited materially from Jerusalem's destruction. The Septuagint alternative, 'She that was rich lies in ruins', should be noted.

5f. *She shall become the prey of nations* . . .: these are additional threats of plundering and of the destruction of Tyre's neighbouring mainland cities (see the footnote). They are intended to complete the picture of destruction. ✱

NEBUCHADREZZAR AGAINST TYRE

7 These are the words of the Lord GOD: I am bringing against Tyre from the north Nebuchadrezzar king of Babylon, king of kings. He will come with horses and chariots, with cavalry and a great army.

8   Your daughters in the open country
        he will put to the sword.
     He will set up watch-towers against you,

    pile up siege-ramps against you
    and raise against you a screen of shields.
He will launch his battering-rams on your walls   9
    and break down your towers with his axes.
He will cover you with dust from the thousands of   10
       his cavalry;
    at the thunder of his horses
    and of his chariot-wheels
your walls will quake when he enters your gates
    as men enter a city that is breached.
He will trample all your streets   11
    with the hooves of his horses
and put your people to the sword,
and your strong pillars will fall to the ground.
    Your wealth will become spoil,   12
       your merchandise will be plundered,
       your walls levelled,
    your pleasant houses pulled down;
    your stones, your timber and your rubble
       will be dumped into the sea.*a*
So I will silence the clamour of your songs,   13
and the sound of your harps shall be heard no more.
    I will make you a gleaming rock,   14
    a place for fishermen to spread their nets,
       and you*b* shall never be rebuilt.
    I, the LORD, have spoken.
       This is the very word of the Lord GOD.

       [a] *Lit.* water.
       [b] *So Sept.; Heb.* she.

* These verses reinforce the previous prophecy, enlarging on the scene of destruction and quoting from both verses 1–6 and other prophecies. The date, as with the two following passages, cannot be later than the twenty-seventh year of Jehoiachin's exile, for in 29: 17ff. it is acknowledged that the things prophesied against Tyre had not been fulfilled at that time. There is evidence here then of the exposition of Ezekiel's words by his disciples even before the last dated prophecy.

7. The general description of the avenger as 'many nations' (verse 3) is here specified as the *king of kings* and his *great army*. *from the north*: traditionally regarded as the area from which legendary forces of destruction would come. The idea was common to Jeremiah, who after 605 B.C. identified the people from the north as the Babylonians. *Nebuchadrezzar*: the name intrudes awkwardly in the Hebrew text and has probably been added later. *king of kings*: a title used by Assyrian kings and later by the kings of Persia. It is not used of Nebuchadrezzar elsewhere.

8. *Your daughters...*: as the footnote to verse 6 indicates, neighbouring mainland cities are referred to here. They would be the first objects of attack in order that Tyre might be isolated. *watch-towers*: or 'siege walls' – words parallel in meaning to *siege-ramps*. These and the other figures of war are traditional and there is some dependence on Ezekiel's description of the attack to be mounted against Jerusalem in 4: 2. The use of conventional means of siege against an island city may be supported by the attacks from the mainland against Tyre of two Assyrian kings in the seventh century B.C. and the successful attack by Alexander the Great, who built a causeway from the mainland in 332 B.C. But these verses present a mundane picture of destruction beside the concise and forceful imagery of nations sweeping over Tyre like waves in verses 3f.

11. *strong pillars*: pillars, usually in pairs, were commonly found in temples of the time though their significance is not

clear (cp. 40: 49; 1 Kings 7: 15–22). The reference is probably to the destruction of places of worship and refuge.

13f. The concluding verses draw on the prophecy of Amos 5: 23 and Ezekiel's own portrayal of Tyre's abandonment in 26: 4*b*–5*a*. ✶

THE LAMENT OF THE SEA-KINGS

These are the words of the Lord GOD to Tyre: How the 15 coasts and islands will shake at the sound of your downfall, while the wounded groan, and the slaughter goes on*a* in your midst! Then all the sea-kings will come down 16 from their thrones, and lay aside their cloaks, and strip off their brocaded robes. They will wear coarse loincloths; they will sit on the ground, shuddering at every moment, horror-struck at your fate. Then they will 17 raise this dirge over you:

How you are undone, swept*b* from the sea,
    O famous city!
You whose strength lay in the sea,
    you and your inhabitants,
    who spread their terror throughout the mainland.*c*
Now the coast-lands tremble on the day of your   18
        downfall,
and the isles of the sea are appalled at your passing.

✶ The lament is closely related to the concluding verses of ch. 27, and may be original there. The fall of Tyre brings no malicious joy to her neighbours, but trembling at the destruc-

[*a*] and ... goes on: *or, with slight change,* when he who is struck is bowed down.
[*b*] swept: *so Sept.; Heb.* inhabited.
[*c*] the mainland: *prob. rdg.; Heb.* her inhabitants.

tion of one so great and fear lest Tyre's fate should become theirs. The prophecy is reflected in Rev. 18: 9f.

16. *the sea-kings*: or 'princes', rulers of the nations with which Tyre traded by ship. *lay aside their cloaks . . .*: as signs of mourning (cp. Job 2: 12f.; Jonah 3: 5f.).

17. *who spread their terror throughout the mainland*: the text of the verse is complicated by a number of additions. These words may once have alluded to Tyre's power among coastal and island peoples. In their present form they suggest that Tyre rivalled Egypt in her power on the mainland, but that was not the case (cp. 32: 17–32, where Egypt is ranked among those who 'spread their terror' in the land of the living). *

DOWN TO THE ABYSS

19 For these are the words of the Lord GOD: When I make you a desolate city, like a city where no man can live, when I bring up the primeval ocean against you and the
20 great waters cover you, I will thrust you down with those that descend to the abyss, to the dead of all the ages. I will make you dwell in the underworld as in places long desolate, with those that go down to the abyss. So you will never again be inhabited or take your place[a] in the
21 land of the living. I will bring you to a fearful end, and you shall be no more; men may look for you but will never find you again. This is the very word of the Lord GOD.

* Again there are parallels with other prophecies, in particular with those concerning Egypt in 31: 14–18 and 32: 17–32. The destruction of Tyre is now portrayed in terms of a cosmic convulsion.

[a] or. . .place: *so Sept.; Heb.* I will give beauty.

19. *the primeval ocean*: the 'waves' of verse 3 are now the primeval waters (cp. Gen. 1: 6–9), a symbol of terrifying disorder, controlled by God at the creation but now released to engulf Tyre.

20. *the abyss*: or underworld. A new image is introduced of Tyre dwelling in the half-world of the dead. Death, for the Israelite, did not mean annihilation but a loss of life force or vitality. See further on 32: 17–32. ✣

A DIRGE OVER THE SHIP OF TYRE

These were the words of the LORD to me: Man, raise a **27** 1, 2 dirge over Tyre and say, Tyre, throned above your 3 harbours, you who carry the trade of the nations to many coasts and islands, these are the words of the Lord GOD:

O Tyre, you said,
  'I am perfect in beauty.'
Your frontiers are on the high seas,   4
your builders made your beauty perfect;
they fashioned all your timbers   5
    of pine from Senir;
they took a cedar from Lebanon
to raise up a mast over you.
They made your oars of oaks from Bashan;   6
  they made your deck strong*a* with box-wood
      from the coasts of Kittim.
    Your canvas was linen,   7
  patterned linen from Egypt
  to make your sails;
your awnings were violet and purple
    from the coasts of Elishah.

[a] strong: *prob. rdg.; Heb.* ivory.

8   Men of Sidon and Arvad became your oarsmen;
        you had skilled men within you, O Tyre,
            who served as your helmsmen.
9   You had skilled veterans from Gebal
        caulking your seams.
     You had all sea-going ships and their sailors
        to market your wares;
10   men of Pharas,*a* Lud,*b* and Put, served
        as warriors in your army;
        they hung shield and helmet around you,
        and it was they who gave you your glory.
11   Men of Arvad and Cilicia manned all your walls,
        men of Gammad were posted on your towers
        and hung their shields around your battlements;
     it was they who made your beauty perfect.

✳ This chapter contains one of Ezekiel's finest poems. Tyre is pictured as a great ship which founders at sea with the loss of all on board. There are some minor additions in the poem and the lament is interrupted by one substantial prose passage (verses 12–24).

3. *you who carry . . . islands*: an addition preparing the way for the prose passage detailing Tyre's commercial transactions. *O Tyre, you said, 'I am perfect in beauty'*: the Hebrew word for *I am* has probably been misunderstood by scribes and should read 'ship', thus: 'Tyre, you are a ship, perfect in beauty'. The following verses go on to describe the ship.

4. *Your frontiers are on the high seas*: rather, with the emendation of one Hebrew word, 'they have made you great in the midst of the sea'. Tyre, the island city, was surrounded by sea.

5–7. The ship was constructed of materials from places renowned for their fine timbers. *Senir* was a part of Mount

[*a*] *Or* Persia.   [*b*] *Or* Lydia.

Hermon; *Bashan* lay east and north-east of Galilee; *Kittim* was originally a town in Cyprus which came to give its name to the whole south coast of Cyprus; *Elishah* may have been a city of Cyprus, on its east coast. *your awnings were violet and purple*: only one of the two colours ('blue-purple' and 'red-purple' in the Hebrew) is original. The purple awning adds a touch of regal splendour.

8–9*a*. Neighbouring Phoenician towns, all lying north of Tyre, provided the crew. For *you had skilled men within you, O Tyre*, read 'skilled men of Zemer were in you'.

9*b*. *You had all sea-going ships...*: the figure suddenly changes. Tyre is no longer pictured as a ship but as a city of trade whose wares are taken by ships to various destinations. Nonetheless, this half-verse may once have belonged to the original poem and referred to that part of the crew which engaged in trade. That would explain the insertion of the trade list of verses 12–24.

10f. Tyre's defences are now described, but as those of a city not a ship. These verses are likely to have been added to the poem later than the trade list and may have led to the change of imagery in verse 9*b*. *Pharas, Lud, and Put*: not the lands suggested in the footnotes, but probably north African tribes, the reference to them serving to emphasize the extent of Tyre's influence by her ability to hire men of such distant lands as mercenary soldiers. *Gammad* may have been in northern Syria. ✳

THE TRADE OF TYRE

Tarshish was a source of your commerce, from its 12 abundant resources offering silver and iron, tin and lead, as your staple wares. Javan,[a] Tubal, and Meshech dealt 13 with you, offering slaves and vessels of bronze as your imports. Men from Togarmah offered horses, mares, and 14 mules as your staple wares. Rhodians[b] dealt with you, 15

[a] Or Ionia.   [b] So Sept.; Heb. Dedanites.

great islands were a source of your commerce, paying
16 what was due to you in ivory and ebony. Edom[a] was a
source of your commerce, so many were your undertakings, and offered purple garnets, brocade and fine
linen, black coral and red jasper,[b] for your staple wares.
17 Judah and Israel dealt with you, offering wheat from
Minnith, and meal, syrup, oil, and balsam, as your
18 imports. Damascus was a source of your commerce, so
many were your undertakings, from its abundant re-
19 sources offering wine of Helbon and wool of Suhar, and
casks of wine from Izalla,[c] for your staple wares; wrought
iron, cassia, and sweet cane were among your imports.
20 Dedan dealt with you in coarse woollens for saddle-
21 cloths. Arabia and all the chiefs of Kedar were the source
of your commerce in lambs, rams, and he-goats; this was
22 your trade with them. Dealers from Sheba and Raamah
dealt with you, offering the choicest spices, every kind of
23 precious stone and gold, as your staple wares. Harran,
Kanneh, and Eden,[d] dealers from Asshur and all Media,[e]
24 dealt with you; they were your dealers in gorgeous
stuffs, violet cloths and brocades, in stores of coloured
fabric rolled up and tied with cords; your dealings with
them were in these.

☆ Although quite intrusive here, and certainly not from the
hand of Ezekiel, these verses are of interest as a sixth-century
B.C. trade list. The principal products of each place are given
and contemporary commercial terminology is evident in the

[a] *So some MSS.; others* Aram.   [b] *Or* and carbuncles.
[c] casks . . . Izalla: *prob. rdg.; Heb. obscure.*
[d] *So Sept.; Heb. adds* Sheba.
[e] all Media: *prob. rdg., cp. Targ.; Heb.* Kilmad.

repeated phrases. The list of places proceeds eastwards from Tarshish in Spain through Ionia (Javan) to north-west Asia Minor (Tubal, Meshech and Togarmah), taking in also the Aegean islands (verses 12–15). Then places from south to north through Palestine and Syria are mentioned (verses 16–18). The Arabian region is then dealt with (verses 19–22) and finally some Mesopotamian cities are mentioned. The object of including the list in the dirge may have been to establish Tyre as a great trader, whose downfall would be lamented by all the trading partners named.

17. *and Israel*: although Israel ceased to exist as an independent political entity in 722 B.C. its former territory was still referred to by name despite its division into provinces of Assyria. *wheat from Minnith*: literally 'wheat of Minnith'. Minnith was east of the Jordan and what is intended here is evidently a reference to the quality of the wheat, not to its source. ✳

THE DIRGE CONTINUES

Ships of Tarshish were the caravans for your imports;   25
   you were deeply laden with full cargoes
      on the high seas.
Your oarsmen brought you into many waters,   26
   but on the high seas an east wind wrecked you.
   Your wealth, your staple wares, your imports,   27
     your sailors and your helmsmen,
your caulkers, your merchants, and your warriors,
   all your ship's company,
     all who were with you,
were flung into the sea on the day of your disaster;
at the cries of your helmsmen the troubled waters   28
    tossed.
When all the rowers disembark from their ships,   29

when the sailors, the helmsmen all together, go
    ashore,
30   they exclaim over your fate,
        they cry out bitterly;
    they throw dust on their heads
        and sprinkle themselves with ashes.
31   They tear out their hair at your plight
        and put on sackcloth;
    they weep bitterly over you,
        bitterly wailing.
32 In their lamentation they raise a dirge over you,
        and this is their dirge:
    Who was like Tyre,
    with her buildings piled[a] off shore?
33   When your wares were unloaded off the sea
    you met the needs of many nations;
        with your vast resources and your imports
        you enriched the kings of the earth.
34   Now you are broken by the sea
        in deep water;
  your wares and all your company are gone
        overboard.
35   All who dwell on the coasts and islands
        are aghast at your fate;
    horror is written on the faces of their kings
        and their hair stands on end.
36 Among the nations the merchants jeer in derision at
        you;
  you have come to a fearful end and shall be no more
        for ever.

[a] with her buildings piled: *prob. rdg.; Heb. obscure.*

✳ The second half of verse 25 takes up again, from verse 9, the picture of Tyre as a ship. Verse 25*a* is a link between the trade list and the dirge. No direct mention is made of divine intervention. But implicit in the lament is the idea of the east wind (verse 26) as God's instrument, by which the splendid and prosperous vessel was brought to a humble end.

26. *many waters*: simply a parallel to 'high seas' (verse 25).

27. *and your warriors*: much of the verse may be a prosaic addition. Certainly the poem has been expanded to take account of the soldiers referred to in verses 10f.

28. *the troubled waters tossed*: the Hebrew word here rendered *troubled waters* is elsewhere rendered 'pastures'. Although the meaning is uncertain the verse may allude to the shaking of the coastlands at the sound of distress (cp. 26: 15), for the following verses go on to describe the anguish of the mariners of the coastlands.

32. *with her buildings piled off shore*: an alternative is to read simply 'in the midst of the sea'.

36. After all that has been said of the general horror at Tyre's fate, it is surprising to find derision as the reaction of the merchants. The verse appears to be an editorial addition duplicating parts of 26: 21 and 28: 19. ✳

AGAINST THE RULER OF TYRE

These were the words of the LORD to me: Man, say to the **28** 1, 2
prince of Tyre, This is the word of the Lord GOD:

> In your arrogance you say,
> 'I am a god;
> I sit throned like a god on the high seas.'
> Though you are a man and no god,
> you try to think the thoughts of a god.
> What? are you wiser than Danel[a]?   3
> Is no secret too dark for you?

[a] *Or, as otherwise read,* Daniel; *cp. 14: 14, 20.*

4   Clever and shrewd as you are,
    you have amassed wealth for yourself,
  you have amassed gold and silver in your treasuries;
5   by great cleverness in your trading
    you have heaped up riches,
  and with your riches your arrogance has grown.

6 Therefore these are the words of the Lord GOD:

Because you try to think the thoughts of a god
7   I will bring strangers against you,
    the most ruthless of nations,
  who will draw their swords against your fine wisdom
    and lay your pride in the dust,
8   sending you down to the pit[a] to die
    a death of disgrace on the high seas.
9   Will you dare to say that you are a god
    when you face your assailants,
  though you are a man and no god
    in the hands of those who lay you low?
10   You will die strengthless
    at the hands of strangers.

For I have spoken. This is the very word of the Lord GOD.

* This chapter contains both an oracle of doom against Tyre's king (verses 1–10) and a lament for him (verses 11–19). The passages were originally independent and both have been expanded considerably. But neither was directed against a particular monarch. In speaking of their king, Ezekiel could speak of the people as a whole, since the king was their representative. The reason for the oracle of doom is stated in verse 2 and the oracle itself is found in verses 6–10. Between the two there is a secondary explanation of the king's arrogance.

[a] *Or* to destruction.

In a number of ancient Eastern cultures kings were regarded as in some sense divine. In Israel the king, on his enthronement, was held to be God's son, as a representative of God's earthly presence, though only by virtue of God's election or adoption of him (Ps. 2: 7). In other places, such as Egypt, the monarch was so closely identified with divine beings that he was thought literally to embody the gods from his birth. Something of these beliefs are reflected in the king of Tyre's claim to be 'a god'. The claim would be shown false by the king's death at the hands of human avengers.

2. *the prince*: or 'ruler'. The term 'king' is used in verse 12. *on the high seas*: that is, in Tyre. *you try to think the thoughts of a god*: literally 'you have made your heart like the heart of a god'. The heart is the seat of intellectual activity (see on 11: 19f.).

3–5. The ruler's arrogance is here related to wisdom and the material possessions he has obtained by astute trading. *What? are you wiser than Danel? Is no secret too dark for you?*: the Hebrew is difficult. It may be read as a statement rather than as a question. The N.E.B. rendering suggests that the ruler has attempted to probe forbidden wisdom. A link between knowledge and human desire to be 'like gods' is familiar from the Genesis story of Eden (Gen. 3: 5). For Danel as an ancient hero, wise and righteous see on 14: 14.

7f. The *strangers* were the Babylonians. For *the pit* see on 26: 20, where a different word is used.

10. *strengthless*: literally 'the death of the uncircumcised'. The Phoenicians, like the Egyptians and Israelites, practised circumcision. But Ezekiel apparently used this phrase to signify an ignominious and shameful death. See also on 32: 19. *

ON GOD'S HOLY HILL

These were the words of the LORD to me: Man, raise 11, 12 this dirge over the king of Tyre, and say to him, This is the word of the Lord GOD:

189

You set the seal on perfection;
full of wisdom you were and altogether beautiful.

13 You were in an Eden, a garden of God,
adorned with gems of every kind:
sardin and chrysolite and jade,
topaz, cornelian and green jasper,
lapis lazuli,[a] purple garnet and green felspar.
Your jingling beads were of gold,
and the spangles you wore were made for you
on the day of your birth.

14 I set you with a towering cherub[b] as guardian;
you were on God's holy hill
and you walked proudly among stones that flashed
with fire.

15 You were blameless in all your ways
from the day of your birth
until your iniquity came to light.

16 Your commerce grew so great,
lawlessness filled your heart and you went wrong,
so I brought you down in disgrace from the mountain
of God,
and the guardian cherub banished you[c]
from among the stones that flashed like fire.

17 Your beauty made you arrogant,
you misused your wisdom to increase your dignity.
I flung you to the ground,
I left you there, a sight for kings to see.

18 So great was your sin in your wicked trading

[a] *Or* sapphire.
[b] I set . . . cherub: *prob. rdg.; Heb.* You were a towering cherub whom
I set.
[c] and the. . .you: *or* and I parted you, O guardian cherub, . . .

that you desecrated your sanctuaries.
So I kindled a fire within you,
   and it devoured you.
I left you as ashes on the ground
   for all to see.
All among the nations who knew you were aghast: 19
you came to a fearful end and shall be no more for
      ever.

✻ This interesting passage is a variant of the Eden story known
so well from Gen. 2–3. The king of Tyre is portrayed as the
first man, living 'blameless' in Eden until sin brings his
expulsion and ruin. Like the story of original man in Genesis,
this is the story of every man, for the king of Tyre, like Adam,
plays a representative role. The fate of all Tyre's inhabitants
is anticipated in these verses. A second idea reflected here, and
one which may be the reason for the growth of this alternative
story, is that the king was the guardian of God's sanctuary. So
he appears as a guardian of Eden (verses 14 and 16, footnotes)
robed like a priest. Such ideas may have been associated with
Solomon's temple, itself built by Tyrian craftsmen.

12f. *You set the seal on perfection*: the Hebrew is difficult,
although a change in the vowel signs would give the reading
'you were a seal (or signet-ring) of perfection' (cp. Jer. 22: 24
and Hag. 2: 23). The meaning is plain enough, that the king
was a perfect creature. Unlike the naked Adam of Genesis he
was apparently clothed and his clothes were adorned with
precious stones and some sort of gold ornaments. The list of
nine stones is an addition from the list of stones in the high
priest's breast-plate (Exod. 28: 17–20).

14. Again the text presents difficulties. The word for
towering may be read as 'anointed' and *guardian* (cp. Gen. 3:
24) both here and in verse 16 probably derived from the
description of the 'covering' wings of the cherubim of the
Ark (Exod. 25: 20; 1 Kings 8: 7). The Septuagint has neither

word in this verse. *God's holy hill*: here identified as the site of the garden of God. Belief that the gods dwelt on a far northern mountain was widespread in the ancient East (cp. Isa. 14: 13). *stones that flashed with fire*: literally 'stones of fire'. Ezekiel may be borrowing from Phoenician mythology here, in which case stars – thought of as divine beings – are intended.

16f. Originally the iniquity of the king was not stated until verse 17*a*. One later expansion of the text (which can be seen by the change from first to second person style in the Hebrew) identifies the sin as that of trading: *Your commerce grew so great, lawlessness filled your heart*(verse 16*a*). Another expansion, on the basis of verse 7, identifies the sin as the king's pride in his wisdom: *you misused your wisdom to increase your dignity* (verse 17*b*; so too in verse 12, 'full of wisdom you were'). But in the first place the punishment of God was banishment from the mountain because *Your beauty made you arrogant*. One can assume that the expression of this arrogance was the king's claim to divinity, as dealt with in the preceding oracle.

18f. Both verses elaborate the original dirge. The sin of trading is now associated with the defilement of sanctuaries, presumably through the offering of goods gained by dishonesty or lawlessness (verse 16), and the relevance of the dirge to the whole people of Tyre is emphasized by reference to a fire within the city. For the editorial verse 19, cp. 26: 21; 27: 35f. Those who transmitted Ezekiel's prophecies were much concerned with the evils of commerce. It was well known that unscrupulous trading could lead to injustice and violence, and from the time of Amos prophets had warned Israel of its guilt in such matters. Most trading by Israelites was directly between producers and consumers and only after the exile did a merchant class arise. But even then trading was regarded with suspicion since dishonesty so easily 'squeezes in between selling and buying' (cp. Ecclus. 26: 29 – 27: 2). ✳

AGAINST SIDON

These were the words of the LORD to me: Man, look 20, 21
towards Sidon and prophesy against her. These are the 22
words of the Lord GOD:

> Sidon, I am against you
>> and I will show my glory in your midst.

> Men will know that I am the LORD
> when I execute judgement upon her
>> and thereby prove my holiness.
> I will let loose pestilence upon her   23
>> and bloodshed in her streets;
> the slain will fall in her streets,
> beset on all sides by the sword;
> then men will know that I am the LORD.

✻ Sidon lay on the Mediterranean coast 25 miles (40 km)
north of Tyre. It had once been more prominent than Tyre
and after the siege of the latter it came to prominence again.
Involvement in the conspiracy against Babylon in 594–593
B.C., as well as the common association of Tyre and Sidon
in other prophetic writings, may be the reason for the
addition here, producing prophecies against a total of seven
foreign nations. No reason is given for the judgement against
the city and though a number of phrases are familiar from
other parts of the book the prophecy is not from Ezekiel. The
author is nonetheless true to Ezekiel's thought in associating
the proof of God's holiness with his execution of judgement. ✻

CONCLUDING SUMMARIES

24 No longer shall the Israelites suffer from the scorn of their neighbours, the pricking of briars and scratching of thorns, and they shall know that I am the Lord GOD.

25 These are the words of the Lord GOD: When I gather the Israelites from the peoples among whom they are scattered, I shall thereby prove my holiness in the sight

26 of all nations. They shall live on their native soil, which I gave to my servant Jacob. They shall live there in peace of mind, build houses and plant vineyards; they shall live there in peace of mind when I execute judgement on all their scornful neighbours. Thus they shall know that I am the LORD their God.

✴ First verse 24 and then verses 25f. were added by the editors of the book as concluding summaries to the prophecies against Israel's neighbours. The essential theme is that by reason of their judgement Israel would find peace and prosperity. Ezekiel's own view of the purpose of the prophecies against the nations and his prospects for the future are less dominated by nationalism and expectations of material well-being.

24. *briars. . .thorns*: Israel's enemies are described in similar terms in Num. 33: 55 and Josh. 23: 13.

25. *Jacob*: denotes the whole people, as in 20: 5. ✴

THE FIRST ORACLE AGAINST EGYPT

29 These were the words of the LORD to me on the twelfth

2 day of the tenth month in the tenth year: Man, look towards Pharaoh king of Egypt and prophesy against him

3 and all his country. Say, These are the words of the Lord GOD:

I am against you,
    Pharaoh king of Egypt,
    you great monster,*a*
lurking in the streams of the Nile.
You have said, 'My Nile is my own;
    it was I who made it.'*b*
I will put hooks in your jaws   4
and make them cling*c* to your scales.
I will hoist you out of its streams
with all its fish clinging to your scales.

    I will fling you into the wilderness,   5
you and all the fish in your streams;
you will fall on the bare ground
with none to pick you up and bury*d* you;
    I will make you food
    for beasts and for birds.
So all who live in Egypt will know   6
    that I am the LORD,
for the support that you*e* gave to the Israelites
    was no better than a reed,
which splintered in the hand when they grasped you,   7
    and tore their armpits;
when they leaned upon you, you snapped
and their limbs gave way.

This therefore is the word of the Lord GOD: I am bring- 8
ing a sword upon you to destroy both man and beast.
The land of Egypt shall become a desolate waste, and they 9

[a] monster: *so some MSS.; others* jackals.
[b] it was. . .it: *so Pesh., cp. verse 9; Heb.* I even made myself.
[c] make them cling: *prob. rdg.; Heb.* make the fish of your streams cling.
[d] bury: *so some MSS.; others* gather.
[e] *So Sept.; Heb.* they.

shall know that I am the LORD, because you[a] said, 'The
10 Nile is mine; it was I who made it.' I am against you
therefore, you and your Nile, and I will make Egypt
desolate, wasted by drought, from Migdol to Syene and
11 up to the very frontier of Cush. No foot of man shall
pass through it, no foot of beast; it shall lie uninhabited
12 for forty years. I will make the land of Egypt the most
desolate of desolate lands; her cities shall lie derelict among
the ruined cities. For forty years shall they lie derelict, and I
will scatter the Egyptians among the nations and disperse
them among the lands.

13   These are the words of the Lord GOD: At the end of
forty years I will gather the Egyptians from the peoples
14 among whom they are scattered. I will turn the fortunes
of Egypt and bring them back to Pathros, the land of
their origin, where they shall become a petty kingdom.
15 She shall be the most paltry of kingdoms and never again
exalt herself over the nations, for I will make the Egyp-
16 tians too few to rule over them. The Israelites will never
trust Egypt again; this will be a reminder to them of their
sin in turning to Egypt for help. They shall know that I
am the Lord GOD.

* This is the first of seven prophecies concerning Egypt, all
but one of which is dated, and all but one of the dated passages
fall within a matter of months before or after the destruction
of Jerusalem. Egypt had long involved herself in the political
affairs of Judah. After the death of King Josiah at the hands of
Pharaoh Necho (609 B.C.) that pharaoh enthroned Jehoiakim,
a king of his own choice, in Jerusalem and reduced Judah to a
dependent state. Soon after 605 B.C., however, Palestine

[a] *So Sept.; Heb.* he.

passed into the control of Nebuchadrezzar as a result of Babylonian expansion, and Egypt then proceeded to encourage Judah to revolt against Babylon with the promise of military support. Both Jeremiah (Jer. 2: 16–19; 46) and Ezekiel (Ezek. 17) warned against reliance on Egyptian support, seeing in such hopes rebellion against God, whom they believed was justly punishing his people by bringing them under Babylonian rule. And insofar as Egypt opposed Babylonian power it too opposed God. Egyptian influence in Judah at the time of Jerusalem's destruction provides the background to chs. 17 and 19. The pharaoh of the time was Hophra, grandson of Pharaoh Necho, and he ruled from 588 to 569 B.C.

The prophecy of 29: 1–16 is actually a collection of four oracles. Only the first (verses 1–6*a*) can be attributed with confidence to Ezekiel. The remainder appear to be attempts by his followers to elaborate his words.

1–6*a*. The oracle originally portrayed Pharaoh as a Nile crocodile which God drew out of the river and left for animals and birds to eat. Expansion is evident in the references of verses 4–5 to the fish of the stream which cling to the crocodile's scales. The intention was specifically to include the people of Egypt in the judgement.

1. The date is December 588–January 587 B.C., about six months before Jerusalem's destruction. This is therefore the earliest of the prophecies against foreign nations.

2. *and all his country*: probably an addition from those responsible for enlarging the original oracle.

3. *monster*: the use of this word associated with the crocodile the idea of the sea monster, believed to represent at the time of creation all the powers hostile to God (cp. Ps. 74: 13). *it was I who made it*: arrogance is the reason for the judgement against Pharaoh.

5. *I will make you food for beasts. . .*: a particularly terrible fate for an Egyptian, whose well-being in the after-life depended on a proper burial.

6*b*–9*a*. *for the support that you gave to the Israelites was no* *better than a reed. . .I am the LORD*: this oracle condemns Egypt for its failure to support Israel in the events of 587 B.C. It is no longer Pharaoh's arrogance in assuming creative powers rightly ascribed to God alone that constitutes the reason for the prophecy. The figure of Egypt as a reed staff which pierced the hand of the man seeking its support is also found in Isa. 36: 6. The judgement of verses 8–9a consists of stock phrases.

7. *armpits*: or 'shoulders', but the word for 'hand' should probably be read with the Septuagint and Peshitta.

9b–12. Here the accusation made against Pharaoh in verse 3 is taken up and a fresh judgement added. Egypt will suffer a fate like Judah's, her cities abandoned and her people exiled for forty years (cp. 4: 6). The prophecy was not fulfilled.

10. *from Migdol to Syene*: from north to south, i.e. the whole land. *Syene* was the modern Aswan; *Cush* was Ethiopia lying further to the south.

13–16. A further oracle is introduced, continuing the parallel between the fates of Judah and Egypt. The restoration of the Egyptians is striking confirmation that God was not concerned only for Israel. The final verse has a note of instruction as it reinforces the lesson of the past.

14. *Pathros*: 'the south land', i.e. Upper Egypt, excluding the Delta region. *

EGYPT FOR NEBUCHADREZZAR

17 These were the words of the LORD to me on the first
18 day of the first month in the twenty-seventh year: Man, long did Nebuchadrezzar king of Babylon keep his army in the field against Tyre, until every head was rubbed bare and every shoulder chafed. But neither he nor his army gained anything from Tyre for their long service
19 against her. This, therefore, is the word of the Lord GOD: I am giving the land of Egypt to Nebuchadrezzar king of

Babylon. He shall carry off its wealth, he shall spoil and plunder it, and so his army will be paid. I have given him 20 the land of Egypt as the wages for his service because they have disregarded me. This is the very word of the Lord GOD.

At that time I will make Israel put out fresh shoots,[a] 21 and give you back the power to speak among them, and they will know that I am the LORD.

* This is the latest dated prophecy, occurring on New Year's Day, March–April 571 B.C. The precise outcome of Nebuchadrezzar's thirteen-year siege of Tyre is unclear. The siege had been lifted a year or more before this prophecy and there is evidence in Babylonian documents that Nebuchadrezzar had left a commissioner in the city to act with the king in affairs of state. Thus Tyre was subject to some degree of Babylonian authority, and probably paid tribute. But wholesale destruction and looting, such as Ezekiel earlier anticipated, do not seem to have happened. Ezekiel had evidently regarded the spoil of Tyre as the due reward of Nebuchadrezzar and his army for executing divine punishment on the city. They are now to be compensated by the capture and sack of Egypt.

The preservation of this passage is remarkable for its frank acknowledgement of unfulfilled prophecies, especially in view of Ezekiel's own concern to authenticate his words (see on 1: 3). It gives reason to respect the prophet's integrity and to affirm his awareness of the actual historical situation. It is also important for the assessment of the book as a whole, that Ezekiel's followers were prepared to retain this evidence of error. Clearly the question of the literal fulfilment of prophecy was not as crucial for the prophet as it has become for some people who hold that the truth and value of the Bible hangs upon it. Ezekiel's faith in God's control of the affairs of men remained intact as he declared Egypt's imminent downfall.

[a] fresh shoots: *lit*. a horn.

18. *every head was rubbed bare. . .*: by the carrying of loads on the head and shoulders, possibly in the course of erecting siegeworks.

21. An addition to the oracle. *fresh shoots* or 'a horn' (Ps. 132: 17, footnote) were symbols of new vitality and strength, and allude also to a new Davidic monarch. The verse envisages hope for Israel at the time of Egypt's ruin. Nebuchadrezzar did invade Egypt in 568 B.C. although the extent of his victory is uncertain. But long before this time Ezekiel had regained his power of speech (see on 33: 21) and the reference to this in the present verse may be taken to imply that Egypt's defeat would bring renewed recognition among the people of the truth of the prophet's words. ✷

THE DAY OF THE LORD AGAINST EGYPT

301, 2 These were the words of the LORD to me: Man, prophesy and say, These are the words of the Lord GOD:

> Woe, woe for the day!
>
> 3   for a day is near,
>
> a day of the LORD is near,
>
> a day of cloud, a day of reckoning for the nations.
>
> 4   Then a sword will come upon Egypt,
>
> and there will be anguish in Cush,
>
> when the slain fall in Egypt,
>
> when its wealth is taken and its foundations are torn
>
> up.
>
> 5   Cush and Put and Lud,*a*
>
> all the Arabs and Libyans*b* and the peoples of
>
> allied lands,
>
> shall fall with them by the sword.

6 These are the words of the LORD:

[a] Or Lydia.   [b] So Sept.; Heb. Kub.

All who support Egypt shall fall
and her boasted might be brought low;
from Migdol to Syene men shall fall by the sword.
This is the very word of the Lord GOD.

They shall be the most desolate of desolate lands, and 7
their*a* cities shall lie derelict among the ruined cities.
When I set Egypt on fire and all her helpers are broken, 8
they will know that I am the LORD. When that time comes 9
messengers shall go out in haste*b* from my presence to
alarm Cush, still without a care, and anguish shall come
upon her in Egypt's hour. Even now it is on the way.
These are the words of the Lord GOD: 10

I will make an end of Egypt's hordes
by the hands of Nebuchadrezzar king of Babylon.
He and his people with him, the most ruthless of   11
nations,
will be brought to ravage the land.
They will draw their swords against Egypt
and fill the land with the slain.
I will make the streams of the Nile dry land   12
and sell Egypt to evil men;
I will lay waste the land and everything in it by
foreign hands.
I, the LORD, have spoken.

These are the words of the Lord GOD: 13

I will make an end of the lordlings*c*
and wipe out the princelings*d* of Noph;
and never again shall a prince arise in Egypt.

[a] *Prob. rdg., cp. Sept.; Heb.* his.
[b] in haste: *so Sept.; Heb.* in ships.
[c] *Or* idols.   [d] *Or* false gods.

Then I will put fear in that land,

14 I will lay Pathros waste and set fire to Zoan
      and execute judgement on No.

15 I will pour out my rage upon Sin,
          the bastion of Egypt,
      and destroy the horde of Noph.*a*

16 I will set Egypt on fire,
      and Syene*b* shall writhe in anguish;
      the walls of No shall be breached
          and flood-waters shall burst into it.*c*

17 The young men of On and Pi-beseth*d* shall fall by
          the sword
      and the cities themselves go into captivity.

18 Daylight shall fail in Tahpanhes
      when I break the yoke of Egypt there;
      then her boasted might shall be subdued;
      a cloud shall cover her,
      and her daughters*e* shall go into captivity.

19 Thus I will execute judgement on Egypt,
      and they shall know that I am the LORD.

✴ This is the only undated prophecy against Egypt. Like
29: 1–16, the first oracle has been expanded by successive
interpretations. But the parallels with other prophecies make
it doubtful whether any part of this prophecy is from Ezekiel
himself.

1–9. In ch. 7 the 'day of the LORD' against the land of
Israel was prophesied. Here it is portrayed as a day of anguish
for Egypt and her neighbours, which the prophet proceeds
to lament.

[a] *So Sept.; Heb.* No.   [b] *So Sept.; Heb.* Sin.
[c] flood-waters. . .it: *prob. rdg., cp. Sept.; Heb. obscure.*
[d] *Or* Bubastis.   [e] *Or* daughter-towns.

3. For the *day of the LORD* as *a day of cloud*, see Joel 2: 2; Zeph. 1: 15.

4. *Cush*: Ethiopia, often linked with Egypt, since Egypt was ruled by Ethiopia between 715 and 663 B.C.

5. The verse is a prose addition explaining 'All who support Egypt' in verse 6. For *Put* and *Lud* see on 27: 10. The Hebrew which is rendered *Libyans* is of uncertain meaning.

6. *Migdol to Syene*: see on 29: 10.

7–9. For verse 7, cp. 29: 12, and for the imagery of burning and breaking in verse 8, see Amos 1: 4f. Verse 9 is an interesting example of expansion of a prophecy by the application of another older prophecy. The words concerning Ethiopia (Cush) in verse 4 have been elaborated in terms of Isa. 18: 1–7, which tells of messengers, sent from Ethiopia to Jerusalem, crossing the Nile by ship (see the footnote to Ezek. 30: 9) and returning with a message of doom from Isaiah.

10–12. These verses presuppose the prophecy of Nebuchadrezzar turning against Egypt (29: 17–21), though a date before his actual attack in 568 B.C. is indicated by verse 10. The drying up of the Nile would cause famine (cp. 29: 9*b*–12). For Babylon as *the most ruthless of nations*, see 28: 7.

13–19. The combination of natural disasters and the onslaught of God's avengers, the Babylonians, is to be directed against Egypt's greatest cities. There is no apparent order to the list and some cities are mentioned more than once, suggesting that two or more existing lists of Egyptian cities have been combined by someone unsure of Egyptian geography. But at least there is conveyed the belief that destruction of the cities and their leaders will be complete.

13. *princelings*: the N.E.B. rightly follows the Septuagint in understanding this word as a parallel expression to 'prince' in the following line. A similar word meaning 'false gods' (see N.E.B. footnote) has been read in error in the Hebrew text and that has led to the addition of the preceding phrase, *make an end of the lordlings* (literally 'idols') *and*, dependent on the reference to 'the idols of Egypt' in 20: 7. *Noph* or

Memphis, just south of Cairo and the ancient capital of Lower Egypt.

14. For *Pathros* see on 29: 14. *Zoan*: on the eastern part of the Delta. *No* or Thebes in Greek, the most important city during Egypt's New Kingdom (1580–950 B.C.) and subsequently a priestly city, located in Upper Egypt.

15. *Sin*: a fortress on Egypt's north-eastern frontier.

16. For *Syene* see on 29: 10.

17. *On*, or Heliopolis, and *Pi-beseth* were both north-east of Memphis. The former was a famous centre of sun-worship, hence it is called Beth-shemesh ('house of the sun') in Jer. 43: 13.

18. *Tahpanhes*: also in the eastern Delta region, it was a frontier fortress close to the caravan route from Syria. It was a refuge for those who fled Jerusalem after the murder of Gedaliah, the administrator appointed by Nebuchadrezzar (Jer. 43: 7) and the scene of one of Jeremiah's prophecies against Egypt (43: 8–13). *Daylight shall fail*: darkness will come as it did when Moses brought the plagues on Egypt (Exod. 10: 21). *when I break the yoke of Egypt there*: the choice of Tahpanhes as the site where Egyptian power would be broken may have been influenced by the prophecy of Jeremiah just mentioned. ✵

THE BROKEN ARM OF PHARAOH

20 This was the word of the LORD to me on the seventh day
21 of the first month in the eleventh year: Man, I have broken the arm of Pharaoh king of Egypt. See, it has not been bound up with dressings and bandage[a] to give it
22 strength to wield a sword. These, therefore, are the words of the Lord GOD: I am against Pharaoh king of Egypt; I will break both his arms, the sound and the broken, and

[a] *So Sept.; Heb. adds* to bind it up.

make the sword drop from his hand. I will scatter the 23
Egyptians among the nations and disperse them over
many lands. Then I will strengthen the arms of the king 24
of Babylon and put my sword in his hand; but I will
break Pharaoh's arms, and he shall lie wounded and
groaning before him. I will give strength to the arms of the 25
king of Babylon, but the arms of Pharaoh will fall. Men
will know that I am the LORD, when I put my sword in
the hand of the king of Babylon, and he stretches it out
over the land of Egypt. I will scatter the Egyptians among 26
the nations and disperse them over many lands, and they
shall know that I am the LORD.

✻ Two separate oracles are combined here. The first consists
of verses 20 and 21, the second of verses 22 and 24, with the
remaining verses composed of expansions and doublets.

The date in verse 20 is March–April 587 B.C., three months
after the date in 29: 1 and three months before the fall of
Jerusalem. Thus verse 21, in which God reports having
broken Pharaoh's arm, refers to the defeat of Pharaoh
Hophra's forces when they came to the aid of Jerusalem. The
Babylonians left off the siege for a time to repulse the Egyptians (Jer. 37: 5). The implicit meaning is that Egypt was not
to be a source of hope among the exiles for Jerusalem's
deliverance. In verse 22 an oracle from a later period has been
added on account of the common subject, the arm or arms of
Pharaoh. In this oracle both arms of Pharaoh are to be
broken ('the sound and the broken' has been added to provide
the link with verse 21). And the arms or forces of Nebuchadrezzar are to be strengthened to execute judgement against
Egypt with God's own sword (verse 24). The oracle may date
from the same time as 29: 17–21.

23. Stock phrases which are repeated in verse 26.
25. A repetition of verse 24. ✻

AN ALLEGORY CONCERNING PHARAOH

31 On the first day of the third month in the eleventh year
2 this word came to me from the LORD: Man, say to
Pharaoh king of Egypt and all his horde:

What are you like in your greatness?

3 Look at Assyria: it was a cedar in Lebanon,
  whose fair branches overshadowed the forest,
  towering high with its crown finding a way through
    the foliage.
4 Springs nourished it, underground waters gave it
    height,
  their streams washed the soil all round it
  and sent forth their rills to every tree in the
    country.
5 So it grew taller than every other tree.
  Its boughs were many, its branches spread far;
  for water was abundant in the channels.
6 In its boughs all the birds of the air had their nests,
  under its branches all wild creatures bore their
    young,
  and in its shadow all great nations made their home.
7 A splendid great tree it was, with its long
    spreading boughs,
  for its roots were beside abundant waters.
8 No cedar in God's garden overshadowed it,
  no fir could compare with its boughs,
  and no plane-tree had such branches;
    not a tree in God's garden
  could rival its beauty.

I, the LORD, gave it beauty   9
  with its mass of spreading boughs,
the envy of all the trees in Eden,
  the garden of God.

Therefore these are the words of the Lord GOD: 10
Because it[a] grew so high and pushed its crown up through
the foliage, and its pride mounted as it grew, therefore   11
I handed it over to a prince of the nations to deal with it;
I made an example of it as its wickedness deserved.
Strangers from the most ruthless of nations hewed it   12
down and flung it away. Its sweeping boughs fell on the
mountains and in all the valleys, and its branches lay
broken beside all the streams in the land. All nations of the
earth came out from under its shade and left it. All the   13
birds of the air settled on its fallen trunk; the wild creatures all stood by its branches. Never again, therefore,   14
shall the well-watered trees grow so high or push their
crowns up through the foliage. Nor shall the strongest of
them, well watered though they be, stand erect in their
full height; for all have been given over to death, to the
world below, to share the common doom and go down
to the abyss.

These are the words of the Lord GOD: When he went   15
down to Sheol, I closed the deep over him as a gate, I
dammed its rivers, the great waters were held back. I
put Lebanon in mourning for him, and all the trees of the
country-side wilted. I made nations shake with the crash   16
of his fall, when I brought him down to Sheol with those
who go down to the abyss. From this all the trees of
Eden, all the choicest and best of Lebanon, all the well-

[a] *So Pesh.; Heb.* you.

17 watered trees, drew comfort in the world below. They too like him had gone down to Sheol, to those slain with the sword; and those who had lived in his shadow were
18 scattered among the nations. Which among the trees of Eden was like you in glory and greatness? Yet you will be brought down with the trees of Eden to the world below; you will lie with those who have been slain by the sword, in the company of the strengthless dead. This stands for Pharaoh and all his horde. This is the very word of the Lord GOD.

✶ Ezekiel has used a contemporary poem of a great tree (verses 3–9) as the basis of a further prophecy against Pharaoh (verses 10–13). Widespread beliefs about the world and its origins are reflected in the poem, not the least being that about the great tree itself, connecting heaven and earth and providing shelter for all creatures (cp. the tree of life, Gen. 3: 22–4). The poem should not be pressed to yield a picture of Pharaoh's world role. Ezekiel's purpose in using it, with its obvious tone of admiration for the great tree, was to throw into stark contrast the downfall of its subject. The imagery of the poem and its interpretation have been taken up in a secondary prophecy (verses 15–18) applying the judgement against Pharaoh to the leaders of world powers in general. A further development of this passage is to be found in Dan. 4: 10–18.

1f. The date is May–June 587 B.C., toward the end of the siege of Jerusalem. *and all his horde*: not the people of Egypt so much as the ostentatious wealth and ceremony of the pharaoh (cp. verse 10). The word for *horde* may be rendered 'pomp' here and in verse 18. The poem commences after the question of verse 2.

3. *Assyria*: the prophet could have been using Assyria as an example of a great nation but it seems more natural to assume

a textual error. The words 'pine-tree' or 'cypress' (translated 'box-wood' in 27: 6) may be read, and *it was a cedar in Lebanon* omitted as a secondary explanation of the difficult word. So the poem may originally have begun 'Look, a pine-tree whose fair branches . . .' *with its crown finding a way through the foliage*: the image is somewhat confusing. Read with the Septuagint, 'with its crown (or, top) in the clouds', and read 'clouds' for 'foliage' also in verses 10 and 14.

4. The source of growth was the inexhaustible cosmic deep. The word for *underground waters* is the same as for 'primeval ocean' (see on 26: 19).

9. This verse originally read: 'and all the trees of Eden envied it'. The ascription of the great tree's beauty to God is a pious addition not found in the Septuagint.

10–14. The interpretation of the allegory makes only incidental use of the poem's imagery. It is the destruction of the tree, of which there is no mention in the poem, that the prophet is concerned to portray. Nebuchadrezzar is the *prince* or 'mighty one' of verse 11.

10. *pride*: again the cause of human downfall (cp. the king of Tyre, ch. 28).

14. The first part of the verse is an instructive addition, warning other leaders of the dangers of pride and world domination. The second sentence reflects verses 15–18 and, like them, stresses the humble fate of all mortal rulers and their empires.

15–18. These verses are a later interpretation based on 32: 17–32. The tree not merely falls to the ground but descends to Sheol, the abyss or place of the dead. The subterranean waters grieve, together with other trees (or leaders of nations), at the felling of the great tree.

15. *Lebanon*: renowned for its fine, tall trees.

16. For the second half of the verse read simply: *From this all the trees of Eden. . .drew comfort in the world below*. The other trees mentioned are in mourning at the great tree's fall, but the jealousy of the trees in Eden was expressed in verse 9. The

consignment of all the trees to the underworld may derive from the same hand as verse 14.

17. *those who had lived in his shadow*: a reference back to the imagery of Egypt's widespread empire in verse 6.

18. The introductory question of verse 2 is repeated, though now a comparison is directly drawn with the trees of Eden. ✻

A DIRGE OVER PHARAOH

32 On the first day of the twelfth month in the twelfth[a] year
2 the word of the LORD came to me: Man, raise a dirge over Pharaoh king of Egypt and say to him:

> Young lion of the nations, you are undone.
> You were like a monster[b] in the waters of the Nile
>   scattering the water with its snout,[c] [d]
> churning the water with its feet
> and fouling the streams.

3 These are the words of the Lord GOD: When many nations are gathered together I will spread my net over
4 you, and you will be dragged up in its meshes. I will fling you on land, dashing you down on the bare ground. I will let all the birds of the air settle upon you and all the
5 wild beasts gorge themselves on your flesh. Your flesh I will lay on the mountains, and fill the valleys with the
6 worms that feed on it. I will drench the land with your discharge, drench it with your blood to the very mountain-tops, and the watercourses shall be full of you.
7 When I put out your light I will veil the sky and blacken

[a] Or, *with some MSS.*, eleventh.
[b] a monster: *so some MSS.; others* jackals.
[c] snout: *prob. rdg.; Heb.* streams.
[d] scattering. . .snout: *or* heaving itself up in the streams.

its stars; I will veil the sun with a cloud, and the moon shall not give its light. I will darken all the shining lights 8 of the sky above you and bring darkness over your land. This is the very word of the Lord GOD.

I will disquiet*a* many peoples when I bring your broken 9 army among the nations into lands you have never known. I will appal many peoples with your fate; when 10 I brandish my sword in the faces of their kings, their hair shall stand on end. In the day of your downfall each shall tremble for his own fate from moment to moment. For 11 these are the words of the Lord GOD: The sword of the king of Babylon shall come upon you. I will make the 12 whole horde of you fall by the sword of warriors who are of all men the most ruthless. They shall make havoc of the pride of Egypt, and all its horde shall be wiped out. I will destroy all their cattle beside many waters. No foot 13 of man, no hoof of beast, shall ever churn them up again. Then will I let their waters settle and their streams run 14 smooth as oil. This is the very word of the Lord GOD. When I have laid Egypt waste, and the whole land is 15 devastated, when I strike down all who dwell there, they shall know that I am the LORD.

This is a dirge, and the women of the nations shall sing 16 it as a dirge. They shall sing it as a dirge, as a dirge over Egypt and all its horde. This is the very word of the Lord GOD.

* This section is introduced as a dirge, but present disaster is referred to only in verse 2 ('you are undone') and it seems we have only the start of the dirge originally delivered. Verses 3–8 are a prophecy of judgement, taking up the figure of the

[a] *So Targ.; Heb.* vex.

monster in verse 2. The imagery is grotesque but appropriate to an event thought to involve the whole created order. A number of the words and phrases are paralleled elsewhere and this portrayal of the monster's fate is probably the work of Ezekiel's disciples. A series of additions, marked off by separate introductions or conclusions to the sayings, follows in verses 9–16. These relate to the people of Egypt and presuppose that Nebuchadrezzar's attack had not yet taken place.

1. The twelfth year was 586–585 B.C. (see on 1: 2), but in that case the date here is later than the one given in the next section (verse 17). There is evidence in the manuscripts and versions that the eleventh year is to be read in this verse, so the likely date is February–March 586 B.C., just two months after Ezekiel learnt of the fall of Jerusalem.

2. *Young lion*: an appropriate metaphor for the vigorous young Pharaoh Hophra, though precise application should not be attempted (cp. on 19: 3f.). *like a monster*: the abrupt change of metaphor, from *lion* to *monster*, also suggests the text of the dirge has suffered damage. In 29: 3 the image of a Nile crocodile is linked with that of a mythical sea monster. But here there is no reference to the Nile. For *in the waters of the Nile*, the literal 'in the seas' should be read, this being understood as a reference to the primeval waters of chaos (see on 26: 19), further identifying Pharaoh with the mythological forces of evil opposed to God.

3. *spread my net*: earlier it was Zedekiah who was to be caught in the divine net (19: 8).

4–6. Cp. 29: 5 and 31: 12f.

5. *the worms that feed on it*: this rendering of a difficult Hebrew word follows the Greek version of Symmachus. Another possible reading is: 'your carcass'.

7f. *put out your light*: that is, 'kill you'. There is, in 30: 18, the threat that daylight will fail and cloud will cover Egypt on the day of her judgement. But the obliteration of light from sun, moon and stars finds a closer parallel in Joel 2: 10 and 3: 15, which are from a later period much concerned about the signs of the end believed to be coming upon the known order of life.

9f. The first addition reverts to the common theme of a nation's destruction and the horror of those observing it (cp. 27: 35 and elsewhere). *broken army*: or read 'captives' with the Septuagint.

11–14. The word *sword* in verse 10 is taken up in terms of the sword of Nebuchadrezzar. The churning up of water (verse 2) is also referred to again, though now it is churned by the feet of men and cattle. The monster of the previous verses goes unmentioned, although the *waters* here are certainly those of Egypt's river Nile (cp. on verse 2).

16. With this verse cp. 19: 14 and 31: 18. For its author the word *dirge* may have had a broader sense than was normal among prophets since he classes the oracles of judgement in the chapter as dirges or laments which in the prophets are often anticipations of disaster (cp. on 19: 1–9). Women usually predominated among mourners. ✵

EGYPT'S DESCENT TO THE ABYSS

On the fifteenth day of the first[a] month in the twelfth 17
year, the word of the LORD came to me:

Man, raise a lament, you and the daughters of the 18
nations,
over the hordes of Egypt and her nobles,
whom I will bring down[b] to the world below
with those that go down to the abyss.

Are you better favoured than others? 19
Go down and be laid to rest with the strengthless dead.

A sword stands ready. Those who marched with her, 20
and all her horde, shall fall into the midst of those slain

[a] first: *so Sept.; Heb. om.*
[b] her nobles. . .down: *prob. rdg.; Heb. obscure.*

21 by the sword. Warrior chieftains in Sheol speak to Pharaoh[a] and those who aided him:

The strengthless dead, slain by the sword, have come
22 down and are laid to rest. There is Assyria with all her company, her buried around her, all of them slain and
23 fallen by the sword. Her graves are set in the recesses of the abyss, with her company buried around her, all of them slain, fallen by the sword, men who once filled the
24 land of the living with terror. There is Elam, with all her hordes buried around her, all of them slain, fallen by the sword; they have gone down strengthless to the world below, men who struck terror into the land of the living but now share the disgrace of those that go down to the
25 abyss. In the midst of the slain a resting-place has been made for her, with all her hordes buried around her; all of them strengthless, slain by the sword. For they who once struck terror into the land of the living now share the disgrace of those that go down to the abyss; they are
26 assigned a place in the midst of the slain. There are Meshech and Tubal with all their hordes, with their buried around them, all of them strengthless and slain by the sword, men who once struck terror into the land of the
27 living. Do they not rest with warriors fallen strengthless,[b] who have gone down to Sheol with their weapons, their swords under their heads and their shields over their bones,[c] though the terror of their prowess[d] once lay on
28 the land of the living? You also, Pharaoh, shall lie broken in the company of the strengthless dead, resting with

[a] *Lit.* him.   [b] *Prob. rdg.; Heb.* from strengthless ones.
[c] and. . .bones: *prob. rdg.; Heb. unintelligible.*
[d] their prowess: *so Pesh.; Heb.* warriors.

those slain by the sword. There is Edom, her kings and 29
all her princes, who, for all their prowess, have been
lodged with those slain by the sword; they shall rest
with the strengthless dead and with those that go down to
the abyss. There are all the princes of the North and all the 30
Sidonians, who have gone down in shame with the slain,
for all the terror they inspired by their prowess. They rest
strengthless with those slain by the sword, and they share
the disgrace of those that go down to the abyss.

Pharaoh will see them and will take comfort for his 31
lost hordes – Pharaoh who, with all his army, is slain by
the sword, says the Lord GOD; though he spread*a* terror 32
throughout the land of the living, yet he with all his
horde is laid to rest with those that are slain by the sword,
in the company of the strengthless dead. This is the very
word of the Lord GOD.

✶ The prophet is now told literally to 'wail', as distinct from
raising a 'dirge' (32: 2) or 'lament' (32: 18). That is to say, he
was to mourn the fate of Egypt, though not necessarily by
way of the regular style of funeral poem (cp. 19: 1–9). The
words of mourning are contained in verses 19–28, where the
fate, in Sheol, of other nations which lived by violence
prefigures Egypt's end.

The passage is complicated by a number of additions, but
the additions themselves are of considerable interest. Sheol, the
abyss or place of the dead, was for the prophet to some degree
a place of retribution. Those who died honourably received
recognition of the fact by the position of their graves in
Sheol. The concept of retribution after death was to be
developed markedly in later writings. And although the
prophet implies only that Sheol was a place of inanimate rest,

[a] *Prob. rdg.; Heb.* I have spread.

an addition to the lament in verse 21 indicates that at least those who had died honourably had the power of speech and a form of authority over others.

17. The month given in the Septuagint is suspect, but the date as restored by appeal to it is March–April 586 B.C. Even if a later month was originally read here the date is after the fall of Jerusalem.

18. *you and the daughters of the nations*: an addition dependent on verse 16.

19. *strengthless dead*: literally 'uncircumcised' (see on 28: 10).

20. The first part of this verse is an addition reaffirming that Egypt *shall fall* by the sword. The words of mourning in verse 19 originally continued: *into the midst of those slain by the sword*. The words *slain by the sword*, like the parallel term 'strengthless dead', signified dishonourable death.

21. The introduction of *Warrior chieftains* who speak to Pharaoh is the result of later reflection on the role of the 'warriors' mentioned in verse 27. As in Isa. 14: 9–11, those already in Sheol greet with scorn the mighty ruler who descends among them. The second half of verse 21 (*The strengthless dead* . . .) may be a note which once stood in the margin of the Hebrew text, giving the theme of the passage, and which was later copied into the text. The actual words of mourning continue in verse 22.

22. *Assyria*: her power, and the fear with which she was regarded, is much in evidence in the Old Testament. The Assyrian empire fell in 612 B.C.

23. *the recesses*: the place of greatest dishonour was the resting place of one of Israel's greatest enemies. *with her company . . . fallen by the sword*: a scribe has repeated part of the previous verse.

24. *Elam* lay east of Babylon. It was conquered by the Assyrians in 650 B.C.

25. Much of the verse repeats the previous one. The Septuagint has only: *In the midst of the slain*.

26. *Meshech and Tubal*: both were in Asia Minor and had

threatened Assyria in the seventh century. In chs. 38–9 they appear as a threat to the restored Israel.

27. A statement rather than a question should be read here: 'They do not rest. . .' The verse contrasts the fate of the dishonourable dead with the fate of warriors or heroes. *warriors fallen strengthless*: the Septuagint supports the change of *strengthless* (*mᵉrlm*) to 'of old' (*mᶜlm*) and the word for *fallen* (*nōphelīm*) may well be an allusion to the Nephilim of Gen. 6: 1–4. The Nephilim or 'giants' were semi-divine beings, the offspring of the sons of gods and daughters of men. The description of 'the warriors, Nephilim of old', lying with their weapons about them, implies that they rested in honour. And according to the addition in verse 21, these beings, honoured in legend, were honoured in death by their authority in Sheol, which enabled them to conduct the Egyptians about and then direct them to their resting place.

28. *Pharaoh*: the word does not appear in the Hebrew and the mourning-song is applied to the horde of Egypt (verse 18) rather than to Pharaoh.

29f. To the words of mourning for great nations of the past have been added these threats against the leaders of Judah's contemporary and future enemies. For *Edom* see on 25: 12–14. The *princes of the North* are those portrayed in chs. 38–9. The term 'Sidonian' could refer to Phoenicians in general, but since there is no mention of their kings or princes *all the Sidonians* may be a yet later addition.

31f. The first of these conclusions (verse 31) makes Pharaoh comfort himself as he realizes that Egypt's fate is not an isolated one. But the second counters the implication that Pharaoh, or anyone else, was able of his own accord to terrorize God's creatures. The Hebrew (see the footnote) should be read here, for this conclusion makes God himself say 'I have spread the terror of him (Pharaoh) throughout the land of the living.' Whoever added this verse was concerned to point out that Egypt, no less than Assyria (Isa. 10) and Babylon, was an instrument of the divine will and continually in God's control. ✶

The remnant of Israel in the land

✳ Early in the third major division of the book (chs. 33–9), news is brought to Ezekiel of Jerusalem's fall (33: 21f.). With the arrival of this news his dominant role appears to change from a proclaimer of doom to an encourager of hope. His appointment as a watchman or pastor to individual exiles (33: 1–20) may date from this time. There is still condemnation for those who remain impenitent (33: 23–33) and for Israel's negligent leaders (34: 1–16). But the dramatic symbolism of 37: 1–20 anticipates new life in a reunited nation, whose prosperous future is envisaged (36: 1–15) under the rule of both God and king (34: 17–31; 37: 21–8). Chs. 38–9 are treated separately in the N.E.B. ✳

APPOINTED A WATCHMAN

33₁,₂ THESE WERE THE WORDS OF THE LORD TO ME: Man, say to your fellow-countrymen, When I set armies in motion against a land, its people choose one of themselves 3 to be a watchman. When he sees the enemy approaching 4 and blows his trumpet to warn the people, then if anyone does not heed the warning and is overtaken by the enemy, 5 he is responsible for his own fate. He is responsible because, when he heard the alarm, he paid no heed to it; 6 if he had heeded it, he would have escaped. But if the watchman does not blow his trumpet or warn the people when he sees the enemy approaching, then any man who is killed is caught with all his sins upon him; but I will hold the watchman answerable for his death.[a]

[a] hold. . .death: *lit.* require his blood from the watchman's hands.

Man, I have appointed you a watchman for the Israel- 7
ites. You will take messages from me and carry my
warnings to them. It may be that I pronounce sentence of 8
death on a man because he is wicked; if you do not warn
him to give up his ways, the guilt is his and because of his
wickedness he shall die, but I will hold you answerable
for his death. But if you have warned him to give up 9
his ways, and he has not given them up, he will die
because of his wickedness, but you will have saved
yourself.

Man, say to the Israelites, You complain, 'We are 10
burdened by our sins and offences; we are pining away
because of them; we despair of life.' So tell them: As I 11
live, says the Lord GOD, I have no desire for the death of
the wicked. I would rather that a wicked man should
mend his ways and live. Give up your evil ways, give
them up; O Israelites, why should you die?

Man, say to your fellow-countrymen, When a righteous 12
man goes wrong, his righteousness shall not save him.
When a wicked man mends his ways, his former wickedness shall not bring him down. When a righteous man
sins, all his righteousness cannot save his life. It may be 13
that, when I tell the righteous man that he will save his
life, he presumes on his righteousness and does wrong;
then none of his righteous acts will be remembered: he
will die for the wrong he has done. It may be that when I 14
pronounce sentence of death on the wicked, he mends his
ways and does what is just and right: if he then restores 15
the pledges he has taken, repays what he has stolen, and,
doing no more wrong, follows the rules that ensure
life, he shall live and not die. None of the sins he has 16

committed shall be remembered against him; he shall live, because he does what is just and right.

17 Your fellow-countrymen are saying, 'The Lord acts without principle', but it is their ways that are unprin-
18 cipled. When a righteous man gives up his righteousness
19 and does wrong, he shall die because of it; and when a wicked man gives up his wickedness and does what is just
20 and right, he shall live. How, Israel, can you say that the Lord acts without principle, when I judge every man of you on his deeds?

✷ These verses need to be read in conjunction with 3: 16–21 and ch. 18. It has already been noted that none of these passages fits smoothly in its present context (see on 18: 1–9). The section 33: 1–20 introduces a new phase of Ezekiel's activity, but like the prophecies against the nations (chs. 25–32) it interrupts the natural connection between chs. 24 and 33: 21ff. For in ch. 24 the prophet was left dumb, to await the news of Jerusalem's destruction, which comes in 33: 21f.

This section is not a single composition. Verses 1–6 are a message for the exiles; verses 7–9 an address to the prophet; and verses 10–20 answer complaints of the exiles in words closely related to 18: 20–32. It appears that the second commission of the prophet (verses 7–9) has been explained by the subsequent addition of the watchman parable (verses 1–6) and the debate concerning divine justice (verses 10–20). But while verses 17–20 largely repeat 18: 25–30, verses 10–16 are a vigorous personal statement of God's own involvement in the judgement of his people. They stress the urgency of personal response to the prophet's warnings and emphasize above all the desire of God that men should repent and live.

The appointment of watchmen in the ordinary sense was commonplace in times of war. From a tower or some other vantage point a watchman would signal the approach of men to his city (cp. 2 Kings 9: 17). If they came to attack, men tending their fields beyond the city could take refuge within its walls and its defences could be manned. But it was not the watchman's responsibility to see that his warning was acted on. Ezekiel emphasizes this in verses 3–5. As long as the alarm had been sounded the watchman had fulfilled his duty. The figure of a prophet as a watchman was also a common one (Isa. 21: 8; Hab. 2: 1). Jeremiah had already spoken of God appointing watchmen to warn his whole people of the punishment God was bringing (Jer. 6: 17–19). But Ezekiel is to warn erring individuals, in terms of the laws of the sanctuary (see on 18: 1–9). The responsibility of the prophet as a pastor appears forbidding. Yet, following the analogy of the secular watchman's role, the responsibility for response to the prophet's warnings remained that of the individual himself.

2. *your fellow-countrymen*: the exiles, as in 3: 11.

6. *caught with all his sins upon him*: the transition is subtly made in this verse from the picture of a secular watchman warning men of an alien foe, to a man of spiritual vision warning men of punishment for sin. *but I will hold the watchman answerable.* . .: as the footnote indicates more clearly, the law of blood-vengeance (Gen. 9: 5f.) is invoked here. The watchman is treated as a murderer since he has allowed a man to die without warning and thus has virtually 'shed blood' himself.

7–9. The meaning of the parable lies in the commission to the prophet. But Ezekiel is made a watchman by God, the very one who threatens the guilty with death. The apparent illogicality of this situation is not explained until the address to the people resumes in verse 11. God wishes them to live, but must nonetheless punish them if they refuse to obey.

8. *sentence of death*: literally 'you shall surely die', the sentence of exclusion from the community which derived its life from God (cp. Gen. 2: 17 and on Ezek. 18: 1–9).

It was mentioned in dealing with 3: 16*b*–19 that those verses are verbally identical with 33: 7–9. Both deal with the appointment of Ezekiel as a watchman and give the example of his responsibility for warning a wicked man. Verses 20f. of ch. 3, however, go on to describe the prophet's responsibility in the case of a righteous man who begins to err. These two cases go together in 18: 21–4 and 33: 12–16. So it seems likely that words similar to 3: 20f. once followed verse 9 of ch. 33, but they were later omitted in error from the text. That is to say, if Ezekiel fails to warn 'a righteous man (who) turns away and does wrong' (3: 20), the man will die and the prophet will be held accountable. But if the man heeds the warning and corrects his ways both he and the prophet will live. In 3: 20 the words 'and I let that be the cause of his downfall' (literally 'and I put an obstacle, or stumbling-block, before him') are a later addition explaining the change of behaviour. Its author, who may have been responsible for inserting 3: 16*b*–21 in its present position, believed that a righteous man could sin only if God caused him to (cp. 14: 9; 20: 25f.; and Jer. 6: 21; Matt. 6: 13; although this idea is rejected in Jas. 1: 13).

10–20. The argument of these verses is discussed fully where the material appears in 18: 21–32. Whereas in that chapter the question is asked, 'Have I any desire ... for the death of a wicked man?' (18: 23), in this it is stated firmly, as a divine oath: *I have no desire for the death of the wicked* (33: 11). The reason for the people's complaint is likely to have been the weight of guilt they felt at the apparent hopelessness of their situation after the fall of Jerusalem. Verse 12 restates the general principle of judgement according to the deeds of each individual (cp. 18: 20). Verses 13–16 correspond to 18: 21f. and 24, although the case of the righteous man who errs is treated before that of the wicked. The two examples of repentance given in verse 15 – restoration of pledges and of money stolen – are extracts from the fuller lists of sins in 18: 5–20. Verses 17–20 are an abbreviated form of 18: 25–30, affirming the justice of God's actions. ✳

NEWS OF JERUSALEM'S FALL

On the fifth day of the tenth month in the twelfth*a* year   21
of our captivity, fugitives came to me from Jerusalem and
told me that the city had fallen. The evening before they   22
arrived, the hand of the LORD had come upon me, and
by the time they reached me in the morning the LORD
had given me back my speech. My speech was restored
and I was no longer dumb.

✳ These verses once followed directly after 24: 24 and marked
the start of the second major period of Ezekiel's activity. The
recovery of the prophet's power of speech is associated with
'the hand of the LORD' upon him (cp. on 1: 3; 3: 14f.). It
was no natural recovery but a divine sign that a new era was
opening. The prophecies that meant utter ruin had been
fulfilled. God would communicate with his people through
his prophet once more, and a new offer of grace would be
made. This passage is unique in the book in that it is a simple
narrative without any prophetic message. For the prophet's
experience of dumbness see on 3: 22–7.

21. *the twelfth year*: 'the eleventh year' should be read,
making the date December 587–January 586 B.C. The error
may have arisen because 32: 17 refers to the twelfth year and
an editor assumed these dates followed in chronological
succession. According to 2 Kings 25: 2f. and 8f., Jerusalem
was entered by Nebuchadrezzar's forces in the fourth month
of the eleventh year and burnt in the fifth month of that year
(July–August 587 B.C.). The fugitive is unlikely to have taken
eighteen months to reach Babylon, as the Hebrew 'twelfth
year' in this verse implies. But an individual evading pursuers
could reasonably have taken five or six months to travel from
Jerusalem to Babylon. *fugitives*: as mentioned in dealing with
24: 26, a single fugitive appears to be indicated. ✳

[a] *Or, with some MSS.*, eleventh.

CONTINUING DISOBEDIENCE

23, 24 These were the words of the LORD to me: Man, the inhabitants of these wastes on the soil of Israel say, 'When Abraham took possession of the land he was but one; now we are many, and the land has been granted to us in
25 possession.' Tell them, therefore, that these are the words of the Lord GOD: You eat meat with the blood in it, you lift up your eyes to idols, you shed[a] blood; and yet you
26 expect to possess the land! You trust to the sword, you commit abominations, you defile one another's wives;
27 and you expect to possess the land! Tell them that these are the words of the Lord GOD: As I live, among the ruins they shall fall by the sword; in the open country I will give them for food to beasts; in dens and caves they
28 shall die by pestilence. I will make the land a desolate waste; her boasted might shall be brought to nothing, and the mountains of Israel shall be an untrodden desert.
29 When I make the land a desolate waste because of all the abominations they have committed, they will know that I am the LORD.

30   Man, your fellow-countrymen gather in groups and talk of you under walls and in doorways and say to one another, 'Let us go and see what message there is from
31 the LORD.' So my people will come crowding in, as people do, and sit down in front of you. They will hear what you have to say, but they will not do it. 'Fine words[b]!' they will say, but their hearts are set on selfish
32 gain. You are no more to them than a singer of fine

[a] *Or* pour out.
[b] Fine words: *or* Love songs.

songs[a] with a lovely voice, or a clever harpist; they will listen to what you say but will certainly not do it. But 33 when it comes, as come it will, they will know that there has been a prophet in their midst.

✳ The first of these two prophecies (verses 23-9) concerns those who remained in Judaea after 587 B.C., while the other (verses 30-3) concerns the exiles. Both acknowledge that even the destruction of Jerusalem had not brought about the change of heart anticipated. Those who remained comforted themselves with their continued possession of the land. Those in exile listened willingly to the prophet, whose words had been vindicated by recent events, but their lives were unchanged. There is no indication of the source of Ezekiel's information about conditions in Judaea, but he reaffirms the complete destruction of the inhabitants. For those in exile, however, the seriousness of the prophet's words, which they take so lightly, will be seen when God effects his threats of death and his promises of restoration (verse 33).

24. The verse calls to mind the words of those who remained in Jerusalem after the exile of 597 B.C.: 'the land has been made over to us as our property' (11: 15). And again there is a basis to the claim in Israel's faith, namely God's promise of land to Abraham (Deut. 9: 5; 30: 20). Even though they were the poorest class in a ransacked land (2 Kings 25: 12), those who remained after 587 B.C. prided themselves on being God's favourites inasmuch as their lives had been spared.

25. *You eat meat with the blood in it*: literally 'you eat upon the blood'. This may reflect the Priestly law of Gen. 9: 4, prohibiting the consumption of blood in the belief that it contained the life-force of the animal and should be offered to God (see on 43: 18). But 'you eat upon the mountains' may have been the original reading. That and the following

[a] fine songs: *or* love songs.

practices are already familiar from ch. 18, as characteristic of unrighteous living. Idolatry and injustice are both still evident among the people.

27. Three-fold plagues are again invoked as in earlier prophecies (5: 12, etc.).

30–3. Such passages as 8: 1 and 14: 1 earlier portrayed representatives of the exiles sitting before the prophet; now everyone is eager to hear what he has to say. But there is here no message for the people. Rather, Ezekiel himself is encouraged not to despair when his words find little response. The fault will be in his listeners.

31. The second half of the verse is partly a repetition of verse 32 and partly a moralizing comment. The people are now condemned for their self-seeking, whereas Ezekiel was warned of their merely frivolous interest.

32. *or a clever harpist*: to render this phrase 'and beautiful music' would better emphasize that the prophet was not simply an instrumentalist. He spoke or sang as he played. The prophet Elisha called for a minstrel to play, and as he did so Elisha received and delivered an oracle from God (2 Kings 3: 15). So music seems to have had a place in prophetic inspiration. But the image of the minstrel should not be taken too literally here. It is intended as a sarcastic allusion to the people's desire for diversion or entertainment. They treat the prophet as they would a minstrel whose only message is of romantic feeling (see the footnote for the term 'love songs'). ✷

AGAINST THE SHEPHERDS

34₁,₂ These were the words of the LORD to me: Prophesy, man, against the shepherds of Israel; prophesy and say to them, You shepherds, these are the words of the Lord GOD: How I hate the shepherds of Israel who care only for themselves! Should not the shepherd care for the sheep?

3 You consume the milk, wear the wool, and slaughter the

fat beasts, but you do not feed the sheep. You have not 4
encouraged the weary, tended the sick, bandaged the
hurt, recovered the straggler, or searched for the lost;
and even the strong*a* you have driven with ruthless
severity. They are scattered, they have no shepherd, they 5
have become the prey of wild beasts.*b* My sheep go straying 6
over the mountains and on every high hill, my flock is
dispersed over the whole country, with no one to ask
after them or search for them.

Therefore, you shepherds, hear the words of the LORD. 7
As surely as I live, says the Lord GOD, because my sheep 8
are ravaged by wild beasts and have become their prey
for lack of a shepherd, because my shepherds have not
asked after the sheep but have cared only for themselves
and not for the sheep – therefore, you shepherds, hear the 9
words of the LORD. These are the words of the Lord GOD: 10
I am against the shepherds and will demand my sheep
from them. I will dismiss those shepherds: they shall care
only for themselves no longer; I will rescue my sheep
from their jaws, and they shall feed on them no more.

For these are the words of the Lord GOD: Now I 11
myself will ask after my sheep and go in search of them.
As a shepherd goes in search of his sheep when his flock 12
is dispersed all around him, so I will go in search of my
sheep and rescue them, no matter where they were scattered in dark and cloudy days. I will bring them out from 13
every nation, gather them in from other lands, and lead
them home to their own soil. I will graze them on the
mountains of Israel, by her streams and in all her green

[a] even the strong: *so Sept.; Heb.* strongly.
[b] *So Pesh.; Heb. adds* and they are scattered.

14 fields. I will feed them on good grazing-ground, and their pasture shall be the high mountains of Israel. There they will rest, there in good pasture, and find rich grazing on 15 the mountains of Israel. I myself will tend my flock, I 16 myself pen them in their fold, says the Lord GOD. I will search for the lost, recover the straggler, bandage the hurt, strengthen the sick, leave the healthy and strong to play,[a] and give them their proper food.

✶ The title 'shepherd' was used of rulers in both Babylon and Egypt. In Israel God was the great shepherd, as numerous passages illustrate (Gen. 48: 15; Jer. 31: 10; Ps. 23). But Jeremiah frequently referred to Israel's earthly rulers as shepherds and in Jer. 23 they are castigated for their neglect of duty in allowing God's flock to be scattered. Indeed, Jer. 23: 1f. appears to have been the model for the first part of Ezekiel's prophecy here. Verses 2–6 describe the shepherds' neglect of duty and the scattering of the flock. The judgement against the shepherds follows in verses 9f. Verses 11–15, however, go on to speak of God himself becoming a shepherd, seeking out and gathering once more those who were allowed to wander when beasts ravaged the flock. Verses 7f. and 16 can be readily distinguished from the original prophecy as later additions. Evidence of the impact of this and similar passages on the New Testament is seen in the references to people as sheep without a shepherd (e.g. Mark 6: 34) and the great parable of the good shepherd (John 10: 1–18).

3f. The shepherds' consumption of milk (or milk-products) and wool was not in itself reason for criticism. It was normal for shepherds to clothe and nourish themselves from their flocks. Even the slaughtering of fat beasts may have been acceptable. The charge is that, while the shepherds exploited their rights to the full, they utterly neglected their duties.

[a] leave . . . to play: *or, with Sept.*, tend the healthy and strong.

The list of duties can be summarized as the patient and gentle leading of the whole flock.

5. *wild beasts*: foreign nations.

6. The verse has been added to by a later hand. It should read: 'My flock is dispersed over the mountains and on every high hill and over the whole earth, with no one, etc.' The Assyrian exile of the northern kingdom is likely to have been in Ezekiel's mind too.

9f. The judgement announces God's rejection of the shepherds, whose treatment of the flock is now likened to that of wolves attacking the sheep with greedy jaws.

11. The theme of searching, of actively seeking out those who have strayed or been scattered (cp. verse 6), is an important feature of the passage. It has a correspondingly important role in the concept of pastoral responsibility in the church.

12. *in dark and cloudy days*: literally 'in the day of clouds and darkness', terms descriptive of the day of the LORD (see on 7: 7; 30: 3), and meaning days of divine judgement such as the time of Jerusalem's destruction (cp. 13: 5).

13. *from every nation*: numbers of Judaeans had also fled to Egypt to escape Babylonian authority (Jer. 43: 5–7).

14f. The imagery of Ps. 23 is most evident here. *I myself pen them in their fold* (verse 15): an attempt to vary the rendering of a verb which means 'to let or make lie down' or *rest*, as in verse 14 (cp. Ps. 23: 2). The verb is repeated in verse 15 to emphasize that it is God who gives his flock rest.

16. The faults of the shepherds listed in verses 3f. are the basis of this addition. None of the faults will be apparent when God acts as shepherd. *leave the healthy and strong to play*: the Hebrew verb in this phrase is 'to exterminate'. But the Septuagint (see the footnote) here renders a similar Hebrew word, which contrasts more appropriately with the strong being driven hard in verse 4. Now they will be tended or protected. The last words of the verse read literally: 'I will feed (the healthy and strong) with justice.' The word 'justice' affords

a link with the just judgements of God in the following
verses. ✲

JUDGING THE FLOCK

17 As for you, my flock, these are the words of the Lord
GOD: I will judge between one sheep and another. You
18 rams and he-goats! Are you not satisfied with grazing on
good herbage, that you must trample down the rest with
your feet? Or with drinking clear water, that you must
19 churn up the rest with your feet? My flock has to eat
what you have trampled and drink what you have churned
20 up. These, therefore, are the words of the Lord GOD to
them: Now I myself will judge between the fat sheep and
21 the lean. You hustle the weary with flank and shoulder,
you butt them with your horns until you have driven
22 them away and scattered them abroad. Therefore I will
save my flock, and they shall be ravaged no more; I
23 will judge between one sheep and another. Then I will
set over them one shepherd to take care of them, my
servant David; he shall care for them and become their
24 shepherd. I, the LORD, will become their God, and my
servant David shall be a prince among them. I, the LORD,
25 have spoken. I will make a covenant with them to ensure
prosperity; I will rid the land of wild beasts, and men
shall live in peace of mind on the open pastures and sleep
26 in the woods. I will settle them in the neighbourhood of
my hill*a* and send them rain in due season, blessed rain.
27 Trees in the country-side shall bear their fruit, the land
shall yield its produce, and men shall live in peace of
mind on their own soil. They shall know that I am the

[a] *So Sept.; Heb. adds* a blessing.

LORD when I break the bars of their yokes and rescue them from those who have enslaved them. They shall 28 never be ravaged by the nations again nor shall wild beasts devour them; they shall live in peace of mind, with no one to alarm them. I will give prosperity*a* to their planta- 29 tions; they shall never again be victims of famine in the land nor any longer bear the taunts of the nations. They 30 shall know that I, the LORD their God, am with them, and that they are my people Israel, says the Lord GOD. You 31 are my flock, my people, the flock I feed, and I am your God. This is the very word of the Lord GOD.

✻ Several sayings, more or less allied to the shepherd theme of the previous section, have been grouped here. Having dealt with the shepherds Ezekiel is now instructed to address the sheep (verses 17–22). There can be no question of them blaming their misfortune solely on their leaders. They are also responsible for their behaviour, and so they will be judged by God. The aggressive men of influence in the community are accused of selfish bullying, under two different figures in verses 17–19 and 20f. But the note of hope for the flock dominates the judgement of verse 22. Verses 23f., which envisage God setting as shepherd over the flock a new Davidic ruler, are in marked contrast to verses 11–15 and 31, which anticipate God himself shepherding his people. So they appear to be an addition, closely related to the fuller prophecy of David as king in 37: 21–8. The inclusion of verses 25–30 here may have resulted from their expectation of the wild beasts' removal from the land – wild beasts who might have ravaged the flock, although the figure of the people as sheep is not sustained in these verses. Verse 31, like verse 16, is the contribution of an editor who has attempted to unify the chapter by referring again to God as a dutiful shepherd.

17–19. 'Judgement' is here, and in verses 20 and 22, the

[a] prosperity: *so Sept.; Heb.* a name.

dominant feature of the good shepherd's care. *flock*: small cattle, that is, sheep and goats. *rams and he-goats*: the influential members of the community, who satisfy their own appetites and leave the remaining food and water unfit for others to consume. The verse recalls words of earlier prophets, concerning the rapacious greed of the powerful and their failure to consider the rights of others (Amos 4: 1; Mic. 2: 2), and it is later reflected in Jesus' parable of the sheep and goats (Matt. 25: 31–46).

20f. The prophecy of judgement and the reasons for it are now repeated. *I myself*: emphasizes God's participation in the judgement of the flock. *the fat sheep* (or goats) correspond to the 'rams and he-goats' of verse 17. They are even accused of having scattered the flock.

22. The combination of ideas of saving and judging recalls the role of Israel's earlier 'judges', who 'saved' or restored the rights of their people (Judg. 3: 9, 15). There can be no salvation without justice.

23f. That a descendant of the Davidic line should have had a place in Ezekiel's expectations of the future is natural enough. He would have been well aware of the divine promise, given through the prophet Nathan, to maintain David's family on the throne of Jerusalem (2 Sam. 7: 12–16). Ezekiel also regarded Jehoiachin as the rightful heir and ruler of his people and in the closing vision of the book a political head is envisaged, even though his powers in relation to the temple and worship are limited (see 43: 7–12; 45: 9–17). *one shepherd*: 2 Sam. 7: 8 recalls the tradition of David's humble origin as a shepherd lad. The single ruler implies the unity of the kingdoms of Israel and Judah once they are restored. *my servant David*: not David himself, risen from the grave, as has sometimes been supposed, but an ideal ruler of Davidic descent, who would rule as God's *servant* and so faithfully fulfil the duties of a shepherd. *prince*: the term is used in preference to 'king' (cp. Jer. 30: 9, 'the LORD their God and David their king', and see on Ezek. 37: 21–3).

25. Hosea also spoke of a future covenant of 'peace' (the literal rendering of *prosperity*), which God would establish between Israel and the *wild beasts* (Hos. 2: 18). Although Ezekiel appears to have been familiar with Hosea's concept, here it is God who is to be the covenant partner of the people, removing from them the fear of wild beasts. The effects of the covenant in this and the following verses are appropriately borrowed from a tradition of covenant blessings which Ezekiel knew in common with the authors of the Holiness Code (see on p. 7), particularly Lev. 26: 4–6. Faithfulness to the covenant with God would bring the blessings of security and material prosperity.

26. *I will settle them in the neighbourhood of my hill*: the word rendered *my hill* is not normally used in Ezekiel to allude to Mount Zion, the temple hill, and, in any event, such an allusion is out of place in a description of the whole land's fruitfulness. An alternative is to emend the Hebrew to read 'I will give showers in due time', understanding by this phrase the mild rain which precedes the heavier winter rain referred to later in the verse.

27. *the bars of their yokes*: cp. Lev. 26: 13. The prophecy of hope resumes after the formula asserting future recognition of God's power and purpose.

29. *plantations*: or arable land. *famine*: one of the plagues often mentioned earlier in the book. *the taunts of the nations*: cp. 36: 6f., 15. ✳

AGAINST EDOM

These were the words of the LORD to me: Man, look **35**1, 2 towards the hill-country of Seir and prophesy against it. Say, These are the words of the Lord GOD: 3

    O hill-country of Seir, I am against you:
        I will stretch out my hand over you
        and make you a desolate waste.
        I will lay your cities in ruins   4

and you shall be made desolate;
5   thus you shall know that I am the LORD.
For you have maintained an immemorial feud
and handed over the Israelites to the sword
          in the hour of their doom,
          at the time of their final punishment.

6   Therefore, as I live, says the Lord GOD,
I make blood your destiny, and blood shall pursue you;
          you are most surely guilty of*ᵃ* blood,
          and blood shall pursue you.
7   I will make the hill-country of Seir a desolate waste
and put an end to all in it who pass to and fro;
8   I will fill*ᵇ* your hills and your valleys with its slain,
and those slain by the sword shall fall into your
               streams.
9   I will make you desolate for ever,
          and your cities shall not be inhabited;
          thus you shall know that I am the LORD.

10   You say, The two nations and the two countries shall
be mine and I will take possession of them, though the
11   LORD is*ᶜ* there. Therefore, as I live, says the Lord GOD,
your anger and jealousy shall be requited, for I will
do to you what you have done in your hatred against
them. I shall be known among you*ᵈ* when I judge you;
12   you shall know that I am the LORD. I have heard all your
blasphemies; you have said, 'The mountains of Israel are
13   desolate and have been given to us to devour.' You have
set yourselves up against me and spoken recklessly against

[a] are most surely guilty of: *so Sept.; Heb.* most surely hate.   [b] *So
Sept.; Heb. adds* its mountains. [c] *Or* has been. [d] *So Sept.; Heb.* them.

me. I myself have heard you. These are the words of the 14
Lord GOD: I will make you so desolate that the whole
world will gloat over you. I will do to you as you did to 15
Israel my own possession when you gloated over its
desolation. O hill-country of Seir, you will be desolate,
and it will be the end of all Edom. Thus men will know
that I am the LORD.

* The reason for this chapter being placed here, rather than
among the prophecies against the nations (chs. 25–32),
appears to be its links with ch. 36. Within this prophecy
addressed to Mount Seir mention is made of the mountains
of Israel (35: 12), and within the prophecy addressed to the
mountains of Israel (ch. 36), Edom in particular is castigated
(verse 5). Chs. 35 and 36: 1–15 are intended by the editors of
the book to be taken as a single unit, the harsh threats against
Israel's enemies in the first half throwing into greater relief
the encouraging promises for Israel in the second. For the
background of these prophecies against Edom, see on 25:
12–14. The movement of Edomites into southern Judaea
after 587 B.C. naturally provoked Jewish animosity. Here four
originally independent sayings have been gathered to express
God's rejection of Edomite plans to possess the land (verses
3f., 5–9, 10–13 and 14f.). But the extent to which their imagery
is paralleled elsewhere suggests that, like some of the prophecies against Israel's neighbours in chs. 25–32, they are the
work of Ezekiel's followers rather than the prophet himself.

    2. *look towards. . .*: see on 25: 2. *hill-country of Seir*: or
Mount Seir, an extensive mountain range south-east of the
Dead Sea. In Num. 24: 18 the name Seir is equivalent to
Edom, traditionally the home of Esau (Gen. 32: 3).

    3f. For other judgements in terms of waste and desolation,
both here and later in this chapter, cp. 6: 14 and 12: 20.

    5. The second prophecy now begins – reading 'Because',
rather than *For* – with the reason for the judgement, which

is given in verses 6 and 9. The long-standing rivalry between
Israel and Edom was portrayed in the patriarchal stories of
Esau and Jacob (Gen. 25: 19–34). The subjection of the Edom-
ites under David and Solomon (2 Sam. 8: 13f.; 1 Kings
11: 14–25) gave good reason for their early hostility, and the
Edomites are accused by Obadiah (Obad. verses 10f.) of
complicity in Babylon's overthrow of Judah. *an immemorial
feud*: or 'age-long enmity', mentioned in relation to the
Philistines in 25: 15. *their final punishment*: the destruction of
Jerusalem.

6. *I make blood your destiny, and blood shall pursue you*: a later
repetition of the second half of the verse. *blood*: or bloodguilt,
demanding vengeance (see on 22: 3).

7f. Both verses betray themselves as part of a later expansion by speaking of Mount Seir and its inhabitants in the third
person. The N.E.B., under the influence of a further addition,
has rendered verse 8 as addressed to Seir. This addition included
a reference to *your hills*, *valleys* and *streams* alongside that to
'its mountains' (see the footnote) following the example of
6: 3; 36: 4 and 6. Verse 8 once read: 'I will fill its mountains
with its slain, and those slain by the sword shall fall on
them.'

9. *desolate for ever*: at this point the prophecy corresponds to
the exclamation of the Edomites over Judah's ruin (see on
36: 2).

10. *The two nations. . .*: Israel and Judah, cp. 37: 22. Edom
in fact attempted to settle only Judaean territory. *though the
LORD is there*: cp. 48: 35. This is probably an editorial
addition affirming that the land was God's alone to dispose of.

13. The subject of the address is in the plural, so the verse
appears to be a later expansion, elaborating the idea of God
hearing the Edomites' blasphemies.

14f. The first sentence of verse 15 does not appear in the
Septuagint, but seems to have been added originally as a note
in the margin of the text to explain the corrupt saying of verse
14, which reads literally: 'according to the gloating of all the

land, a desolation I will make for you'. Verse 15 indicates that 'all the land' was Judaea (reading literally 'the inheritance of Israel' for *Israel my own possession*), and those who gloated over it were the Edomites (cp. Obad. 12f.). Verse 14*b* may once have read: 'As you gloated because my land was desolate, so I will do to you.' ✳

ISRAEL'S PROSPEROUS MOUNTAINS

And do you, man, prophesy to the mountains of Israel **36** and say, Mountains of Israel, hear the words of the LORD. These are the words of the Lord GOD: The enemy has 2 said, 'Aha! now the everlasting highlands are ours.' Therefore prophesy and say, These are the words of the 3 Lord GOD: You mountains of Israel, all round you men gloated over you and trampled you down when you were seized and occupied by the rest of the nations; your name was bandied about in the common talk of men. Therefore, listen to the words of the Lord GOD when he 4 speaks to the mountains and hills, to the streams and valleys, to the desolate palaces and deserted cities, all plundered and despised by the rest of the nations round you. These are the words of the Lord GOD: In the fire of my 5 jealousy I have spoken plainly against the rest of the nations, and against Edom above all. For Edom, swollen with triumphant scorn, seized on my land to hold it up to public contempt. Therefore prophesy over the soil of 6 Israel and say to the mountains and hills, the streams and valleys, These are the words of the Lord GOD: I have spoken my mind in jealousy and anger because you have had to endure the taunts of all nations. Therefore, says 7 the Lord GOD, I have sworn with uplifted hand that the

nations round about shall be punished for[a] their taunts.
8 But you, mountains of Israel, you shall put forth your
branches and yield your fruit for my people Israel, for
9 their home-coming is near. See now, I am for you, I
10 will turn to you, and you shall be tilled and sown. I will
plant many men upon you – the whole house of Israel.
The cities shall again be inhabited and the palaces rebuilt.
11 I will plant many men and beasts upon you; they shall
increase and be fruitful. I will make you populous as in
days of old and more prosperous than you were at first.
12 Thus you will know that I am the LORD. I will make men
– my people Israel – tread your paths again. They shall
settle in you, and you shall be their possession; but you
shall never again rob them of their children.

13   These are the words of the Lord GOD: People say that
you are a land that devours men and robs your tribes of
14 their children. But you shall never devour men any more
nor rob your tribes of their children, says the Lord GOD.
15 I will never let you hear the taunts of the nations again
nor shall you have to endure the reproaches of the
peoples.[b] This is the very word of the Lord GOD.

* While the editors of Ezekiel have made these verses appear
as a counterpart to ch. 35, they are even more a counterpart
to ch. 6. There the prophet spoke against the mountains of
Israel. Here he is instructed to prophesy their imminent
prosperity, a prosperity never known before. The section is
full of introductions to separate sayings and it is extremely
difficult to distinguish the original core of the prophecy. The
solution suggested here is that the reason for the prophecy is

[a] be punished for: *or* bear.
[b] *So Sept.; Heb. adds* and you shall no more cause your tribes to fall.

to be found in the words of Israel's enemies in verse 2. The punishment for the enemies' self-satisfied taunts against the desolate land will be similar desolation of their own countries, brought about by God's hand (verses 6*b*–7). Israel's future prosperity is then described (verses 8f. and 11) and a later supplement asserts that the land will never be depopulated again (verses 13–15).

2. *The enemy*: a general term, variously referred to as 'the rest of the nations' (verses 3 and 5), 'nations' (verse 6) and 'the nations round about' (verse 7). *Aha!*: see on 25: 3; 26: 2. *the everlasting highlands*: the Septuagint reading, which repeats the words rendered 'desolate for ever' in 35: 9, is to be preferred here. The enemy exclaims with malicious delight: 'Aha! Perpetual desolation! It has become our possession.'

3–5. In this major addition, which may have evolved in several stages, the attitude of the new inhabitants of the land is first elaborated. The term *the rest* (or 'remnant') *of the nations* (verses 3 and 5) implies that the judgements earlier predicted have already fallen on the surrounding peoples. Verse 4 clarifies the subject of the address in terms which agree with 6: 3 (*the mountains and hills . . .*) and 36: 10 (*desolate palaces . . .*). The specific references to Edom are unlikely to have been original to verse 5, which may once have read: '. . . the nations, who, swollen with triumphant scorn . . .'

6f. An attempt has been made in verse 6*a* to continue the prophecy begun in verse 2. But the subject is not simply 'the mountains of Israel' (verse 1), but the *soil*, the *hills*, etc., as in verse 4, indicating that this half-verse is secondary material dependent on verses 3–5. The original continuation of the reason for the prophecy, and the judgement of verse 7, read: 'Behold, I speak my mind in jealousy . . . Therefore, says the Lord GOD, I swear with uplifted hand . . .' The enemy nations round about Israel will suffer the same fate as made Israel the object of their malice, for they will 'bear' (see the footnote) their taunts themselves.

8f. and 11. Following the pattern that has become customary in chs. 33 ff., the word of judgement is followed by a promise of well-being for Israel. Fruitfulness was a common sign of divine favour (17: 23; Lev. 26: 3–13), and here it is the prelude to the return of the exiles.

8. *for their home-coming is near*: Ezekiel had earlier prophesied the nearness of judgement (7: 7; 12: 23). These words may simply be a corresponding expression, affirming the imminence of restoration. Alternatively, they may be the addition of a disciple, written toward the anticipated end of exile, or reflecting some change in the political situation, such as the rise to power of Cyrus of Persia, which encouraged the hopes of the second prophet Isaiah (Isa. 40–55).

9. *I will turn to you*: cp. Lev. 26: 9 and see on 4: 3.

10. A later hand has endeavoured to stress that both kingdoms (*the whole house of Israel*) will experience the restoration of their fortunes.

11. *I will plant many men and beasts upon you*: 'I will multiply men . . .' is a more literal, and also a more natural, rendering. *they shall increase and be fruitful*: an addition based on Gen. 1: 22.

12. The second person singular is largely used in this verse, which leads on to the supplementary word of promise for the land, as distinct from the mountains of Israel. (In effect 'the mountains of Israel' already designated the whole land; see on 6: 2.)

13–15. The background is now given to the puzzling final clause of verse 12 ('you shall never again rob them of their children'). The land is said to have depopulated itself, like some cannibal monster, and rendered itself childless. Among the curses for breaking the covenant was the threat of being 'swallowed up' by an enemy's land (Lev. 26: 38). And the later Priestly account of the report of the spies who had explored Canaan states that the country 'will swallow up any who go to live in it' (Num. 13: 32). The land of Israel is thus accused of being an enemy to its own inhabitants, and is taunted for her humiliating state of childlessness. There

will be no grounds for either charge in future. The prophecy
may have been intended to relieve the exiles' fears that to
return to their homeland would be to risk a repetition of
previous disasters. ✶

THE HALLOWING OF GOD'S NAME

These were the words of the LORD to me: Man, when the 16,17
Israelites lived on their own soil they defiled it with
their ways and deeds; their ways were foul and disgusting*a* in my sight. I poured out my fury upon them 18
because of the blood they had poured out upon the land,
and the idols with which they had defiled it. I scattered 19
them among the nations, and they were dispersed among
different countries; I passed on them the sentence which
their ways and deeds deserved. When they*b* came among 20
those nations, they caused my holy name to be profaned
wherever they came: men said of them, 'These are the
people of the LORD, and it is from his land that they have
come.' And I spared them for the sake of my holy name 21
which the Israelites had profaned among the nations to
whom they had gone.

Therefore tell the Israelites that these are the words of 22
the Lord GOD: It is not for your sake, you Israelites, that
I am acting, but for the sake of my holy name, which you
have profaned among the peoples where you have gone.
I will hallow my great name, which has been profaned 23
among those nations. When they see that I reveal my
holiness through you, the nations will know that I am
the LORD, says the Lord GOD. I will take you out of the 24

[a] disgusting: *lit.* like filth.
[b] *So some MSS.; others* he.

nations and gather you from every land and bring you to
25 your own soil. I will sprinkle clean water over you, and
you shall be cleansed from all that defiles you; I will
26 cleanse you from the taint of all your idols. I will give you
a new heart and put a new spirit within you; I will take
the heart of stone from your body and give you a heart
27 of flesh. I will put my spirit into you and make you
conform to my statutes, keep my laws and live by them.
28 You shall live in the land which I gave to your ancestors;
you shall become my people, and I will become your God.
29 I will save you from all that defiles you; I will call to the
corn and make it plentiful; I will bring no more famine
30 upon you. I will make the trees bear abundant fruit and
the ground yield heavy crops, so that you will never
again have to bear the reproach of famine among the
31 nations. You will recall your wicked ways and evil deeds,
and you will loathe yourselves because of your wickedness
32 and your abominations. It is not for your sake that I am
acting; be sure of that, says the Lord GOD. Feel, then, the
shame and disgrace of your ways, men of Israel.

✻ Verses 16–38 of ch. 36 have sometimes been thought to
summarize Ezekiel's theology. In them several earlier themes
are enlarged upon, but in ways which imply that Ezekiel's
followers may here have been attempting to press certain
ideas to logical conclusions and tidy other loose strands of the
prophet's thought. Ezekiel had earlier mentioned God's
concern for the honour of his name as a motive for his actions
(see on 20: 9). Now concern for his name is portrayed as God's
sole reason for restoring Israel (verses 16–22 and 32), an idea
held in common with the author of Isa. 43: 25 in the late
exilic period. Ezekiel also foresaw the need of Israel's inward
renewal (see on 11: 19f.), but now ritual cleansing and

substitution of the divine for the human spirit in man is envisaged (verses 24–8). Certain words and phrases also stand out as distinct from those used elsewhere in the book in passages more likely to be from the prophet. This is particularly true in verses 24–38 and it suggests that at least those verses, if not the whole second half of ch. 36, represent a later development of Ezekiel's words.

17. The defilement of the land has already been amply illustrated. *foul and disgusting*: the behaviour is summarized as impure, 'like menstrual uncleanness' (Lev. 15: 19–33 contains the regulations governing this).

18. *because of the blood...*: these words are absent from the Septuagint. They are also superfluous after verse 17, but they recall Ezekiel's own summary of Israel's defilement in terms of violence as well as idolatry (22: 3f.).

20f. The distinctive feature of the passage lies here. *my holy name*: God's name represents his faithfulness and power (see on 20: 9); holy things had to be carefully distinguished from those which were common or profane (cp. on 22: 26). The relationship between god, people and land was an intimate one in the ancient world. Inasmuch as foreigners questioned the power of Israel's God to maintain his people on his land, they treated his name as a common thing. As the following verses go on to stress, it was concern for his name, not for his people, that made God act to restore Israel to its former land, and so demonstrate once more his power and the holiness of his name.

23. The N.E.B. has re-ordered the text for reasons of style, but the words: *When they see that I reveal my holiness through you*, should follow *says the Lord GOD*. Both phrases are part of an editorial link with the later material which follows. Here it is said to be God's holiness, not the holiness of his name, that is to be revealed.

24. Cp. 34: 13.

25. The first of three acts is now described, which will restore Israel and make obedience to God possible. Ritual

washings for purification (cp. Num. 19, especially verse 18) are likely to have been in mind. Ps. 51: 7 asks that God might symbolically cleanse the worshipper by sprinkling. This verse of Ezekiel has had a profound impact on subsequent religious thought. It is reflected in the baptism of new members entering the Qumran Community, according to the evidence of the Dead Sea Scrolls, as well as in the rite of sprinkling in Christian baptismal practice. But here the action is not so much a symbol of renewal as a prelude to it.

26. As in 11: 19, the *new heart* and *spirit* come unasked as gifts from God (cp. on 18: 31). For the significance of the human heart and spirit, see on 11: 19f.

27f. Identification of the new spirit as the spirit of God ensures that men will be empowered to obey the divine will. Indeed they will be directed in everything by the very power of God himself. The divine spirit was formerly a thing added to certain men, beyond their normal constitution, enabling them to perform special tasks (e.g. Judg. 3: 10; 1 Sam. 10: 6; 16: 13). Now it appears to replace the human spirit, ensuring the fulfilment of the covenant and preventing further expulsion from the promised land (cp. 37: 14). The post-exilic book of Joel looks for the outpouring of God's spirit on all mankind (2: 28f.). The phrase affirming the covenant relationship: *you shall become my people, and I will become your God*, follows as in 11: 20. But the Hebrew pronoun for *I* in this verse indicates that it is a later form of expression.

29f. Salvation here (cp. on 34: 22) means cleansing. The result of obedience will be material prosperity.

31f. The restoration of Israel's fortunes must never become a source of self-congratulation, as if the Israelites themselves have contributed anything toward it. Moreover, God has acted for his own sake, not for theirs, as if they have any claim upon his favour. Against the harshness of this conception must be set the heightened appreciation of God's power, and his refusal to be limited in action either by man's guilt or by the punishment man deserves. Verse 31 recalls 20: 43. Verse

32*a* links 24-32 with 16-23. With the command to feel *shame and disgrace*, cp. 16: 52. ✳

JERUSALEM A POPULOUS CITY

These are the words of the Lord GOD: When I cleanse you 33
of all your wickedness, I will re-people the cities, and the
palaces shall be rebuilt. The land now desolate shall be 34
tilled, instead of lying waste for every passer-by to see.
Men will say that this same land which was waste has 35
become like a garden of Eden, and people will make their
homes in the cities once ruined, wasted, and shattered,
but now well fortified. The nations still left around you 36
will know that it is I, the LORD, who have rebuilt the
shattered cities and planted anew the waste land; I, the
LORD, have spoken and will do it.

  These are the words of the Lord GOD: Yet again will 37
I let the Israelites ask me to act in their behalf. I will make
their men numerous as sheep, like the sheep offered as
holy-gifts, like the sheep in Jerusalem at times of festival. 38
So shall their ruined cities be filled with human flocks,
and they shall know that I am the LORD.

✳ For reasons already mentioned in the introduction to 36:
16-32, neither of these additions is likely to be from Ezekiel
himself. The first (verses 33-6) again describes the expected
restoration of the land and the surrounding nations' recognition of this as the work of God. The second (verses 37f.)
revokes the earlier refusal of God to respond to his people's
inquiries and stresses the size of the population, employing
once more the image of sheep from ch. 34.
  33f. Cp. 36: 10 and 9 respectively.
  35. The most significant parallel to the theme of a

wilderness become an Eden is Isa. 51: 3, from the late exilic period.

36. For *The nations still left*, see on verses 3–5.

37. *ask*: literally 'inquire of' or 'consult' (14: 3; 20: 3, 31).

38. *sheep offered as holy-gifts, like the sheep in Jerusalem . . .*: the two expressions are intended to signify large numbers, although the thousands of animals said to have been sacrificed at the temple in 1 Kings 8: 63, 1 Chron. 29: 21, and elsewhere, are ideal figures. Other prophecies envisaged a large population in the restored land (Isa. 49: 19; Zech. 2: 4). ✳

THE DRY BONES

37 The hand of the LORD came upon me, and he carried me out by his spirit and put me down in a plain full of bones.

2 He made me go to and fro across them until I had been round them all;[a] they covered the plain, countless

3 numbers of them, and they were very dry. He said to me, 'Man, can these bones live again?' I answered, 'Only

4 thou knowest that, Lord GOD.' He said to me, 'Prophesy over these bones and say to them, O dry bones, hear the

5 word of the LORD. This is the word of the Lord GOD to these bones: I will put breath[b] into you, and you shall

6 live. I will fasten sinews on you, bring flesh upon you, overlay you with skin, and put breath in you, and you

7 shall live; and you shall know that I am the LORD.' I began to prophesy as he had bidden me, and as I prophesied there was a rustling sound and the bones fitted them-

8 selves together. As I looked, sinews appeared upon them, flesh covered them, and they were overlaid with

9 skin, but there was no breath in them. Then he said to me, 'Prophesy to the wind, prophesy, man, and say to it,

[a] He made...all: *or* He made me pass all round them.
[b] *Or* wind *or* spirit.

These are the words of the Lord GOD: Come, O wind, come from every quarter and breathe into these slain, that they may come to life.' I began to prophesy as he 10 had bidden me: breath came into them; they came to life and rose to their feet, a mighty host. He said to me, 11 'Man, these bones are the whole people of Israel. They say, "Our bones are dry, our thread of life is snapped, our web is severed from the loom."[a] Prophesy, therefore, 12 and say to them, These are the words of the Lord GOD: O my people, I will open your graves and bring you up from them, and restore you to the land of Israel. You shall 13 know that I am the LORD when I open your graves and bring you up from them, O my people. Then I will put 14 my spirit[b] into you and you shall live, and I will settle you on your own soil, and you shall know that I the LORD have spoken and will act. This is the very word of the LORD.'

✻ Ezekiel's vision in the valley of dry bones is the most arresting passage of the book. Brief, vivid and speaking to man's deep concern about the end of life, it has been the subject of countless paintings and songs. Its symbolism thus extends far beyond its original meaning, as a prophecy of restoration for the exiled Israelites. The vision (verses 1–10) appears to have been of unusual intensity, for, like 11: 1–13, it is not qualified as a visionary experience. Ezekiel seems to have felt himself involved bodily in the removal to the scene of the events. Jeremiah had spoken of the bones of the unfaithful lying exposed to the elements, without the benefit of decent burial (8: 1–3). Corresponding to that prophecy of judgement is Ezekiel's portrayal of future hope by the revival

[a] our web...loom: *prob. rdg.; Heb.* we are completely cut off.
[b] *Or* breath.

of the bones. The first interpretation of the vision is to be found in verses 11 and 14. Verses 12 and 13 are a later addition extending the symbol of new life for the exiles to those Israelites who were literally dead and buried in their graves.

1. The abrupt introduction to the vision and the unusual form of the verb with which the verse begins in the Hebrew suggest that the chapter once began with a statement of the date. There is no indication of what that date may have been, except that the despair of the people reported in verse 11 implies that Ezekiel had not yet succeeded in encouraging them to share his hopeful outlook for the future. *he carried me out by his spirit*: literally 'he brought me out by the spirit of the LORD'. The term 'the spirit of the LORD' is unusual in Ezekiel, and this is the only instance in which the prophet has used it in relation to his own experiences (it has been added later in 11: 5). Normally a 'spirit' undefined, or 'wind', conveys the prophet from place to place (see on 2: 2). This fact further emphasizes the unusual character of the events described here, and suggests that the nature of the experience compelled Ezekiel to ascribe it, in the most direct way, to God himself. *a plain*: a broad valley-plain, possibly that in which the exile settlement of Tel-abib was situated (cp. 3: 22).

2. The large number of bones implies the widespread extent of death, while their dryness implies that death had long since taken place and they had been stripped of all flesh by wild beasts. It is interesting that there is no reaction on the prophet's part to the danger of impurity from contact with the dead, as in 4: 14. In 39: 11–16 ground is given for the burial of Gog and his forces to prevent contamination of the land.

3. *can these bones live again?* is a rhetorical question calling attention to the apparent hopelessness of the situation in view of the extent and finality of death. The prophet's reply – literally 'Thou knowest, Lord GOD' – does not anticipate the miracle to follow, but nor does it assume limitations to the power of God over death or life. The prophet is unlikely to have believed in any general resurrection of the dead, for that

only began to be glimpsed in a few later Old Testament passages (Isa. 26: 19; Dan. 12: 2). He would, however, have known the reports of earlier prophets reviving the dead (1 Kings 17: 17–24; 2 Kings 4: 31–7) and would have believed in the power of God even in the realm of Sheol (1 Sam. 2: 6; Ps. 139: 8).

5f. Prophesying to inanimate objects was not strange to Ezekiel (cp. 36: 1). The word rendered *breath* in these verses and in verses 8 and 10 is *rūaḥ*, alternatively rendered 'spirit' or 'wind' in verses 1, 9 and 14. The footnote explains this here, though such a note has not been added to every occurrence of the word 'breath'. For this important word see also on 2: 2 and 11: 19f. Here *rūaḥ* is the animating principle, received once the physical frame of man has been fashioned, as in Gen. 2: 7.

7. The startlingly prompt effect of the prophet's words within a vision is paralleled in 11: 13. *a rustling sound:* a somewhat louder and more disturbing sound is indicated by the text, like the sound of a commotion (cp. the 'fierce rushing sound' of 3: 12f.).

9. *every quarter*: literally 'the four winds'. For the winds as agents of God see Ps. 104: 4; Jer. 49: 36. *these slain*: the scene is represented as one of battle.

11. The interpretation by the prophet is straightforward. The real condition of the Israelites, of whichever kingdom and whether in exile or not, is a longstanding state of despair or death (see on 33: 8), as their own complaints indicate. *Our bones are dry*: they lack the good news and glad expectations that should warm the marrow of their bones (Prov. 15: 30); *our thread of life is snapped*: the same expression is rendered in 19: 5, '(her) hope was lost'; *our web is severed from the loom*: cp. Isa. 53: 8, 'cut off from the world of living men'.

12–14. The opening words of verse 12, which introduce the oracle for the people, originally went straight on to verse 14, foretelling the gift of God's spirit (see on 36: 27f.) and the restoration to the land of Israel; thus: *These are the words of the*

Lord GOD . . . I will put my spirit into you, etc. *O my people*:
these words are absent from the Septuagint in both verses
12 and 13. The remaining words of those verses: *I will open
your graves . . .*, are an over-literal interpretation of the symbol
of new life. The bones are no longer scattered in an open field,
as the figure of the earlier verses describes them, following
Jer. 8: 2f. This second interpretation is an attempt to answer
what must have become a pressing question for Ezekiel's
followers, namely the fate of those who had already died in
exile. ✳

UNITED IN GOD'S HAND

15, 16 These were the words of the LORD to me: Man, take one
leaf of a wooden tablet and write on it, 'Judah and his
associates of Israel.' Then take another*a* leaf and write on
it, 'Joseph, the leaf of Ephraim and all his associates of
17 Israel.' Now bring the two together to form one tablet;
18 then they will be a folding tablet in your hand. When your
fellow-countrymen ask you to tell them what you mean
19 by this, say to them, These are the words of the Lord
GOD: I am taking the leaf of Joseph, which belongs to
Ephraim and his associate tribes of Israel, and joining*b*
to it the leaf of Judah. Thus I shall make them one tablet,
20 and they shall be one in my hand. The leaves on which you
write shall be visible in your hand for all to see.

21 Then say to them, These are the words of the Lord GOD:
I am gathering up the Israelites from their places of exile
among the nations; I will assemble them from every
22 quarter and restore them to their own soil. I will make
them one single nation in the land, on the mountains of
Israel, and they shall have one king; they shall no longer
23 be two nations or divided into two kingdoms. They shall

[a] *Lit*. one.   [b] *Prob. rdg.; Heb. adds* them.

never again be defiled with their idols, their loathsome ways and all their disloyal acts; I will rescue them from all their sinful backsliding*a* and purify them. Thus they shall become my people, and I will become their God. My servant David shall become king over them, and they 24 shall have one shepherd. They shall conform to my laws, they shall observe and carry out my statutes. They shall 25 live in the land which I gave my servant Jacob, the land where your fathers lived. They and their descendants shall live there for ever, and my servant David shall for ever be their prince. I will make a covenant with them to 26 bring them prosperity; this covenant shall be theirs for ever.*b* I will greatly increase their numbers, and I will put my sanctuary for ever in their midst. They shall live 27 under the shelter of my dwelling; I will become their God and they shall become my people. The nations shall 28 know that I the LORD am keeping Israel sacred to myself, because my sanctuary is in the midst of them for ever.

✻ The acted prophecy of verses 16f. is interpreted in verse 19. It describes simply but vividly the re-unification of the two former kingdoms of Israel. A second interpretation is given in verses 20–3. Although there are parallels in these verses to other passages in the book, the reference to a future king (verse 22) suggests that Ezekiel himself contributed to this later assessment of the acted prophecy's implications. Verses 24*b*–28 are later material deriving from Ezekiel's followers. Their content is only remotely connected with the acted prophecy and the title for the future ruler reverts to 'prince'.

16. *leaf of a wooden tablet*: this phrase interprets a single Hebrew word meaning 'a piece of wood'. The N.E.B.

[a] backsliding: *so Symm.; Heb.* dwellings.
[b] *Prob. rdg.; Heb. adds* and I will put them.

understands the word to mean a writing tablet, as in Isa. 8: 1: 'Take a large tablet and write on it'. The Aramaic Targum supports such an idea, but the Septuagint translates the word in terms of the 'staves' of the tribal leaders mentioned in Num. 17: 1–11. In the latter passage the staff of the tribe of Levi is to be written on (verse 3). While either interpretation is possible, the Septuagint would appear to provide the more reliable guide to the meaning of the text, and the allusion in Ezekiel may be to a staff as a kind of ruler's sceptre (cp. 19: 11 and the two staves in Zech. 11: 7–14, which may be in part based on this passage). *and his associates of Israel*: these words do not appear after 'Judah' in verse 19. Probably the command was to write just 'Judah' and 'Joseph' on the pieces of wood. Those names alone signified the tribes of the southern and northern kingdoms respectively. *Joseph*: Ezekiel never refers to the northern kingdom as 'Israel', as if the name had a merely political connotation (see on 3: 4); rather he refers to it by using the name of its leading tribe (so too Amos 5: 6). *the leaf of Ephraim*: the name 'Ephraim' was more commonly used to designate all the northern tribes (Hos. 4: 17; Isa. 7: 8f.). These words are an addition, even later than the references to the associated tribes, intended to leave no doubt about the subject of the prophecy.

17. *a folding tablet*: this is not easy to visualize, whether 'staves' or 'writing tablets' were originally meant. The essential thing is that the two objects are to be held in such a way as to give the appearance of a single staff or tablet.

19. *which belongs . . . of Israel*: later material, see on verse 16.

20. The command to perform the acted prophecy is partly recapitulated before the second interpretation.

21–3. The words describing the gathering of the people from exile and their purification are strongly reminiscent of 36: 24ff. But verse 22 introduces a new element to the more general images of restoration with its reference to the *king*. Ezekiel elsewhere distinguishes between Jehoiachin the 'king' and Zedekiah the 'prince' (17: 12f.), but the latter term was not of itself derogatory. Ezekiel normally uses the term 'prince' for Israel's rulers (e.g. 12: 10; 19: 1, see on 7: 27). The choice of the word *king* here was probably suggested by the use of the word *kingdoms*. For the assonance of the two words is as marked in Hebrew (*melek–melākōth*) as it is in English, and we have already noted other examples of the prophet's liking for such devices. The term 'prince' or 'chief' earlier referred to the leaders of Israel's tribes (Exod. 22: 28) or to the leaders of other people (Gen. 34: 2). Ezekiel also used it of the rulers of other nations (e.g. 27: 21 and see on 26: 16). However, the rulers of Babylon and Egypt are usually called 'kings' (e.g. 21: 19; 29: 2) and the term 'prince' seems intended by Ezekiel normally to indicate the rulers of comparatively small kingdoms, as opposed to those of great empires.

24a. My servant David shall become king over them, and they shall have one shepherd: in this expansion of verses 20–3, Ezekiel or one of his followers has identified the king with the shepherd–prince of 34: 23f.

25f. for ever: the same words are used of the people's dwelling in the land, the rule of the servant prince, the enduring covenant and God's sanctuary among his people. Stability and permanence – appealing qualities to those who had been involved in the misfortune of exile – would characterize the restored nation. The everlasting covenant was unconditional, like the Priestly versions of the covenants made with Noah (Gen. 9: 16) and with Abraham (Gen. 17: 7). The *sanctuary* in the midst of the people anticipates the great vision in the closing chapters of the book, according to one part of which the temple is to be almost at the geographical centre of the land (48: 1–29).

28. While holiness was a requirement for approaching the presence of God, God's presence also confers holiness or sanctity on all round about (see on 48: 35). ✶

God's triumph over the world

✻ Isaiah had spoken of a far-off nation coming against Judah (Isa. 5: 26) and Jeremiah spoke at length of an enemy coming from the north (Jer. 4–6). Ezekiel takes up the idea of a powerful force of men from the distant north descending upon Israel. But instead of allowing them to punish his people further, God destroys the aggressors, so fulfilling the earlier prophecies and affirming the restoration of divine protection to the people and land. Although some scholars would deny both chs. 38 and 39 to Ezekiel, 38: 1–9, 39: 1–5 and 39: 17–20 are by no means out of character with Ezekiel's earlier prophecies. Later additions, however, have given the events of these verses a broader, even a universal, significance, suggesting the title given the section in the N.E.B. Subsequent writers, particularly the author of the New Testament book of Revelation, have seen prefigured in these chapters the final battle between the forces of good and evil, of God and Satan. ✻

AGAINST GOG

38 1,2   THESE WERE THE WORDS OF THE LORD TO ME: Man, look towards Gog, the prince of Rosh, Meshech, and Tubal, in the land of Magog, and prophesy against him.
3   Say, These are the words of the Lord GOD: I am against
4   you, Gog, prince of Rosh, Meshech, and Tubal. I will turn you about, I will put hooks in your jaws. I will lead you out, you and your whole army, horses and horsemen, all fully equipped, a great host with shield and
5   buckler, every man wielding a sword, and with them the men of Pharas, Cush, and Put, all with shield and helmet;
6   Gomer and all its squadrons, Beth-togarmah with its

squadrons from the far recesses of the north – a great
concourse of peoples with you. Be prepared; make ready, 7
you and all the host which has gathered to join you, and
hold yourselves in reserve for me.[a][b] After many days you 8
will be summoned; in years to come you will enter a
land restored from ruin, whose people are gathered from
many nations upon the mountains of Israel that have been
desolate so long. The Israelites, brought out from the
nations, will all be living undisturbed; and you will come 9
up, driving in like a hurricane; you will cover the land
like a cloud, you and all your squadrons, a great concourse
of peoples.

✻ 2. *Gog* has been identified as various historical figures
(including the Lydian king, Gyges, of the mid-seventh
century B.C.); as a mythical figure representing all the forces
of darkness and chaos opposed to God (cp. on 29: 3); and
collectively as barbarian people of Asia Minor, or even
Babylon, against whom Ezekiel nowhere prophesies openly.
While no definite conclusion may be reached on the specific
identification of Gog, he is portrayed as the leader, whether
actual or ideal, of a force deriving from nations which have
already been referred to in the book of Ezekiel, and which
played an important role in the history of Ezekiel's period.
the prince of Rosh: the word for *Rosh* may also be rendered
'head' or 'chief', so that 'chief prince of (Meshech and Tubal)'
should probably be read here and in verse 3. *Rosh* is certainly
not a cryptic allusion to Russia, as has sometimes been supposed. *Meshech and Tubal*: countries of north-west Asia
Minor mentioned in the trade list of 27: 12–24 and in 32: 26.
in the land of Magog: in the Hebrew these words intrude
between the name of Gog and his title as 'chief prince, etc.'.

[a] me: *so Sept.; Heb.* them.
[b] and hold. . .me: *or* and you shall be their rallying-point.

They have been added later to the text (see further on 39: 6).

4. *I will turn you about, I will put hooks in your jaws*: an addition, borrowing from 19: 4 and 29: 4 the image of animals led captive in a train.

5. *and with them the men of Pharas.* . .: Pharas and Put were probably north African tribes (see on 27: 10f.), while Cush was Ethiopia. That the verse is a later addition, emphasizing the extent and strength of the force, is evident from the third person reference (*with them*) to the subject of the address.

6. *Gomer and . . . Beth-togarmah*: both peoples inhabited the mountainous region south and east of the Black Sea. By the former name was meant the Gimirrai or Cimmerians, a war-like people who invaded Asia Minor in the eighth century B.C. and who continued to trouble Assyria in the seventh century. Beth-togarmah, said to be a trading partner of Tyre in 27: 14, is referred to as the son of Gomer in Gen. 10: 3.

7. The N.E.B. text gives the best rendering here. The point being made is that Gog and his allies are ultimately in God's control.

8. Preparation will give way to a united advance, once the restoration of Israel has taken place. *After many days. . .in years to come*: these words should not be taken as a reference to 'the end of this age' as in Dan. 2: 28, nor to the end of Christ's thousand-year reign in Rev. 20: 2–9. They imply the fulfilment of all that has been prophesied in chs. 34–7 (and 40–8). *undisturbed*: the same Hebrew word is rendered 'in peace of mind' in 28: 26 and 34: 25.

9. Jer. 4: 13 refers to the enemy from the north advancing 'Like clouds'. The second half of the verse, *you and all your squadrons. . .*, is a later repetition of part of verse 6. ✻

ALL SHALL BE SHAKEN

This is the word of the Lord GOD: At that time a thought 10
will enter your head and you will plan evil. You will say, 11
'I will attack a land of open villages, I will fall upon a
people living quiet and undisturbed, undefended by walls,
with neither gates nor bars.' You will expect to come 12
plundering, spoiling, and stripping bare the ruins where
men now live again, a people gathered out of the nations,
a people acquiring cattle and goods, and making their
home at the very centre of the world. Sheba and Dedan, 13
the traders of Tarshish and her leading merchants,*a* will
say to you, 'Is it for plunder that you have come? Have
you gathered your host to get spoil, to carry off silver and
gold, to seize cattle and goods, to collect rich spoil?'

Therefore, prophesy, man, and say to Gog, These are 14
the words of the Lord GOD: In that day when my
people Israel is living undisturbed, will you not awake*b*
and come with many nations from your home in the far 15
recesses of the north, all riding on horses, a great host, a
mighty army? You will come up against my people 16
Israel; and in those future days you will be like a cloud
covering the earth. I will bring you against my land, that
the nations may know me, when they see me prove my
holiness at your expense, O Gog.

This is the word of the Lord GOD: When I spoke in 17
days of old through my servants the prophets, who
prophesied in those days unceasingly, it was you*c* whom
I threatened to bring against Israel. On that day, when at 18

[a] leading merchants: *lit.* young lions.   [b] *So Sept.; Heb.* know.
[c] it was you: *so Sept.; Heb.* was it you . . .?

length Gog comes against the land of Israel, says the
19 Lord GOD, my wrath will boil over. In my jealousy and
in the heat of my anger I swear that on that day there shall
20 be a great earthquake throughout the land of Israel. The
fish in the sea and the birds in the air, the wild animals and
all reptiles that move on the ground, all mankind on the
face of the earth, all shall be shaken before me. Mountains
shall be torn up, the terraced hills collapse, and every wall
21 crash to the ground. I will summon universal terror*a*
against Gog, says the Lord GOD, and his men shall turn
22 their swords against one another. I will bring him to
judgement with pestilence and bloodshed; I will pour
down teeming rain, hailstones hard as rock, and fire and
brimstone, upon him, upon his squadrons, upon the
23 whole concourse of peoples with him. Thus will I prove
myself great and holy and make myself known to many
nations; they shall know that I am the LORD.

✻ Reflection on Ezekiel's words against Gog has given rise
to a series of additions from the prophet's followers. The first
(verses 10–13) establishes Gog's motive in assembling a force
to attack Israel. It is greed for Israel's great wealth. Verses
14–16 call Gog to reflect on the ultimate purpose of his action,
namely that God's power and holiness might be proved to
all. Verse 17 appropriately recalls that the prophecy against
Gog deals with unfulfilled prophecies of former times, concerning an enemy coming from a distant land. Verses 18–23
diverge considerably from the original theme of the prophecy,
drawing out the cosmic significance of the battle described by
Ezekiel himself in 39: 1–5.

11. *undefended by walls*: there were no walls to protect
Israel's towns immediately after the exile. Although fortifica-

[a] universal terror: *so Sept.; Heb.* for all my mountains a sword.

tions are envisaged in 36: 35, and Jerusalem was to be walled according to 48: 30-5, there must have been considerable debate among the returning exiles over whether to rebuild defensive walls or trust entirely to God's protection. The author of this verse appears to have opposed such rebuilding, as did Zechariah, with his description of Jerusalem as 'a city without walls' (2: 4f.). But there are marked similarities between Ezek. 38: 10f. and Jer. 49: 30f., in which Nebuchadrezzar plans to attack the unprotected Arabs of Kedar, and the image of defencelessness here may have derived from the Jeremiah passage.

12. The allusion to renewed prosperity in verse 8 is now elaborated. *the very centre of the world:* Jerusalem (see on 5: 5).

13. *Sheba and Dedan* together indicate the whole expanse of Arabia. They are mentioned separately in the trade list of 27: 12-24. The former was in southern Arabia, the latter in the north-west. *Tarshish*: a port, probably in Spain (see also 27: 12 and 25). Leading traders will inquire of Gog's intent, anxious to enter into business and profit themselves from the spoil of Israel.

14-16. Numerous expressions used in verses 1-9 are repeated here.

14. *awake*: or 'rouse oneself', as in Jer. 6: 22.

16. For the demonstration of God's holiness by the destruction of a foreign nation, see also 28: 22.

17. *my servants the prophets*: the language is that of the editors of the books of Kings (2 Kings 9: 7; 17: 13) and Jeremiah (e.g. Jer. 7: 25; 26: 5). The distance in time between the author of this verse, and Jeremiah and his younger contemporary Ezekiel, is evident from the words *in days of old . . . in those days* (cp. Zech. 1: 4). *unceasingly*: literally 'years'; an addition probably intended to emphasize further how long ago the prophets had foretold what was now happening.

18-23. Ezekiel himself did not describe divine judgements in terms of cosmic catastrophes, even in portraying the coming day of the LORD (ch. 7). The drying up of the Nile (30: 12), the failure of daylight (30: 18) and the darkening of the heavens (32: 7f.) are all found in secondary material. A complication that remains unresolved is the fact that these events centre on the land of Israel, and while Gog is destroyed, so too, presumably, are the people of Israel. Such imagery is more typical of post-exilic writings.

18. *On that day*: like the similar phrases in verses 10, 14, 19 and 39: 11, these words indicate that the succeeding verses are secondary attempts to elaborate earlier allusions. The *land of Israel* rather than Israel's 'mountains' (verse 8) is now the subject. *my wrath will boil over*: literally 'my wrath will rise in my nostrils'.

19f. For such an earthquake in other post-exilic prophecies, see Isa. 24: 18–20; Joel 2: 10; Hag. 2: 6f.

21. *universal terror*: or 'every kind of terror'. For allies attacking one another in their terror, cp. Judg. 7: 22.

22. *pestilence and bloodshed* are mentioned in the secondary material of 5: 17 and 28: 23; *fire and brimstone*, signifying a volcanic eruption, are divine punishments in Gen. 19: 24 and Isa. 30: 33. ✳

THE DEFEAT OF GOG

39 And you, man, prophesy against Gog and say, These are the words of the Lord GOD: I am against you, Gog, 2 prince of Rosh, Meshech, and Tubal. I will turn you about and drive you, I will fetch you up from the far recesses of 3 the north and bring you to the mountains of Israel. I will strike the bow from your left hand and dash the 4 arrows from your right hand. There on the mountains of Israel you shall fall, you, all your squadrons, and your allies; I will give you as food to the birds of prey and the 5 wild beasts. You shall fall on the bare ground, for it is I who have spoken. This is the very word of the Lord

GOD. I will send fire on Magog and on those who live 6
undisturbed in the coasts and islands, and they shall know
that I am the LORD. My holy name I will make known 7
in the midst of my people Israel and will no longer let it
be profaned; the nations shall know that in Israel I, the
LORD, am holy.

Behold, it comes; it shall be, says the Lord GOD, the 8
day of which I have spoken. The dwellers in the cities of 9
Israel shall come out and gather weapons to light their
fires, buckler and shield, bow and arrows, throwing-
stick and lance, and they shall kindle fires with them for
seven years. They shall take no wood from the fields nor 10
cut it from the forests but shall light their fires with the
weapons. Thus they will plunder their plunderers and
spoil their spoilers. This is the very word of the Lord
GOD.

In that day I will give to Gog, instead of*^a* a burial- 11
ground in Israel, the valley of Abarim east of the Sea.*^b*
There they shall bury Gog and all his horde, and all
Abarim will be blocked; and they shall call it the Valley
of Gog's Horde. For seven months the Israelites shall bury 12
them and purify the land; all the people shall take their 13
share in the burying. The day that I win myself honour
shall be a memorable day for them. This is the very word
of the Lord GOD. Men shall be picked for the regular 14
duty of going through the country and searching for*^c* any
left above ground, to purify the land; they shall begin
their search at the end of the seven months. They shall 15
go through the country, and whenever one of them sees a

[a] *Prob. rdg.; Heb. adds* there. [b] *That is* the Dead Sea.
[c] searching for: *prob. rdg.; Heb.* burying those who are passing
through.

human bone he shall put a marker beside it, until it has
16 been buried in the Valley of Gog's Horde. So no more
shall be heard of that great horde,[a] and the land will be
purified.

✶ The original prophecy resumes in verses 1–5. Gog is
addressed again and the defeat of him and his allies is foretold.
The description of the conflict is in marked contrast to 38:
18–23. There is no convulsion of the earth nor widespread
destruction. The aggressors' weapons are simply stripped from
their hands and their dead bodies fall on Israel's mountains
(as the Israelites had earlier fallen, 6: 1–7), becoming prey
for wild birds and beasts. The first of the subsequent additions
(verses 6–8) anticipates the visitation of judgement on the
homeland of Gog, and against the coasts and islands. Verses
9f. take up the idea of the weapons lying scattered on the
mountains, while the concluding verses of the section (11–16)
concern the disposal of the aggressors' remains. Here the
Priestly interest in purifying the land is quite pronounced.

1. *prince of Rosh*: see on 38: 2.

3. Israel takes no part in the battle. It is God alone who
opposes Gog's forces. Although bows and arrows are not
mentioned as weapons in 38: 4, they are associated with
mounted troops in Isa. 5: 28 and Jer. 4: 29.

6. Several times in Amos it is said that *fire* will be sent
against foreign nations (e.g. 1: 4, 7). *Magog*: in Hebrew the
letter 'm' prefixed to a word may indicate its source or origin.
Thus Magog may originally have meant the 'place or land of
Gog'. The name has been understood as that of a people in
Gen. 10: 2, while Gog and Magog appear as co-leaders of
forces opposed to the faithful in later Jewish literature and in
Rev. 20: 8. The inclusion of the coastlands and islands in the
judgement is difficult to understand. Possibly it was through
the association of coastal peoples with Tubal, Meshech and

[a] So. . .horde: *prob. rdg.; Heb. obscure.*

Togarmah, the allies of Gog, in the trade list of 27: 12–24, and of Tarshish with Gog in 38: 13.

7. Verses 6–8 correspond to 38: 14–16. Both passages provide comments on the sections of the original prophecy which precede them and underline the promotion of God's holiness. Here the charge against Israel of profaning God's name among the nations (36: 20–3) is reversed.

9. As people once emerged from Samaria to find their attackers dispersed by God and the enemy camp unprotected (2 Kings 7: 16), so the people now emerge from their cities to find the weapons of the enemy lying all about. The idea of destroying garments of war by fire was already established in prophetic tradition (Isa. 9: 5) and reference is made in the Psalms to the burning of weapons of war (Ps. 46: 9). The range of weapons is greater than in 38: 4. *seven years*: symbolic of completeness, suggesting the destruction of all means of warfare (cp. Isa. 2: 4; Mic. 4: 3).

11. *instead of*: it is difficult to justify such a rendering. We should probably read: '. . . I will give to Gog a place in Israel, where there is a grave for him; the valley of Abarim . . .' (cp. footnote). *Abarim*: the mountains in northern Moab overlooking the Dead Sea (Num. 33: 47f.). Although this territory had for a time been part of the united kingdoms of Israel and Judah, it had been lost again to Moab and was outside Israel according to the borders described in chs. 47–8. But the Hebrew reads 'Oberim'; the words rendered *east of the Sea* are ambiguous; and *the Sea* is not necessarily the Dead Sea as the footnote states. The burial place of Gog thus remains obscure although it is likely to have been in Israelite territory. *Abarim will be blocked*: the phrase represents a play on the word 'Oberim', interpreted as 'travellers', thus '(the way of) the travellers will be blocked', probably an allusion to the impurity of the place, which would prevent use of the valley as a thoroughfare.

12. *For seven months*: see on verse 9. *purify the land*: unburied bodies defiled the land (cp. Num. 19: 11–13).

13. *The day that I win myself honour*: the occasion of Gog's defeat and burial.

14–16. These verses may be a later addition, making even more thorough the purification of the land already mentioned. There is to be set up a permanent commission whose members will mark the sites of any remaining bodies, so that burial parties can find and dispose of the remains.

16. *So no more shall be heard of that great horde*: a more literal rendering would be 'moreover the name of one city is Hamonah', which may be an aside, explaining the name of an unidentified city, Hamonah, as 'horde (of Gog)'. ✷

THE GREAT SACRIFICE

17 Man, these are the words of the Lord GOD: Cry to every bird that flies and to all the wild beasts: Come, assemble, gather from every side to my sacrifice, the great sacrifice I am making for you on the mountains of Israel; eat flesh
18 and drink blood, eat the flesh of warriors and drink the blood of princes of the earth; all these are your rams and
19 sheep, he-goats and bulls, and buffaloes of Bashan. You shall cram yourselves with fat and drink yourselves drunk on blood at the sacrifice which I am preparing for you.
20 At my table you shall eat your fill of horses and riders, of warriors and all manner of fighting men. This is the very word of the Lord GOD.

21 I will show my glory among the nations; all shall see the judgement that I execute and the heavy hand that I
22 lay upon them. From that day forwards the Israelites
23 shall know that I am the LORD their God. The nations shall know that the Israelites went into exile for their iniquity, because they were faithless to me. So I hid my face from them and handed them over to their enemies,

and they fell, every one of them, by the sword. I dealt 24
with them as they deserved, defiled and rebellious as
they were, and hid my face from them.

These, therefore, are the words of the Lord GOD: Now 25
I will restore the fortunes of Jacob and show my affection
for all Israel, and I will be jealous for my holy name. They 26
shall forget their shame and all their unfaithfulness to
me, when they are at home again on their own soil,
undisturbed, with no one to alarm them. When I bring 27
them home out of the nations and gather them from the
lands of their enemies, I will make them an example of
my holiness, for many nations to see. They will know that 28
I am the LORD their God, because I who sent them into
exile among the nations will bring them together again
on the soil of their own land and leave none of them
behind. No longer will I hide my face from them, I who 29
have poured out my spirit upon Israel. This is the very
word of the Lord GOD.

✻ The insertion of verses 11–16, commanding the burial of
Gog's horde, before this last section of the original prophecy,
has effectively robbed the birds of prey and wild beasts of their
sacrificial meal. A great feast for the creatures was announced
in verse 4 and in verses 17–20 Ezekiel is told to invite them to
share in it. The first of the additions, in verses 21f., like 38:
14–16 and 39: 6–8, refers to the significance for the nations
of what is about to happen. They will recognize God's power,
while Israel will recognize his lordship. An attempt has been
made in verses 23–9 to summarize Ezekiel's prophecies of
restoration (cp. 28: 24–6). No further mention is made of
Gog and his forces, and this affirms that the prophecy concerning Gog was not regarded by Ezekiel as an unsurpassable,

sweeping-aside of the whole created order, but as one among a number of demonstrations of God's care for his people.

17. Jeremiah had spoken of God summoning birds and beasts to feast on the remains of Israel (Jer. 12: 9; cp. Ezek. 29: 5) and Zephaniah had spoken of the day of the LORD as a day of sacrifice (1 : 8). Ezekiel has taken up ideas such as these and, envisaging the meal as a sacrifice, symbolizes the attainment of peace through a great offering.

18. *all these are your rams. . .*: a later hand has specified the likeness of the warriors to sacrificial animals. Bashan (see on 27: 5–7) was famous for its cattle (Deut. 32: 14).

19. *fat* and *blood* were normally offered to God, not consumed (44: 7 and 15).

22. *From that day forwards. . .* implies the Israelites' perpetual awareness of their responsibility before God, marking the end of their history of rebellion.

23. Taking up the reference to the nations in verse 21, the justification for the exile is restated. The phrase *hid my face from them* is repeated in verses 24 and 29 (see also Ps. 13: 1; Isa. 54: 8). It is to be understood in terms of the Aaronic blessing (Num. 6: 24–6), in which it is asked that God might look upon his people (cp. on 4: 3).

25. For the 'restoration of (Israel's) fortunes' see 16: 53–8, which is also a later addition. For the names *Jacob* and *Israel* in apposition, see on 20: 5.

26. *They shall forget their shame*: the Hebrew reads 'they shall bear their shame', a thought which has already been encountered in 16: 54 (cp. 20: 43). Although they will live in peace of mind (34: 28), it is never suggested in the book of Ezekiel that the restored people will forget their shameful past.

29. The continued blessing of Israel is confirmed by the outpouring of God's spirit (cp. 36: 27; 37: 14), a theme developed further in the book of Joel where God's spirit is regarded as a gift for all mankind (2: 28f.). ✲

The restored theocracy

✻ The final division of the book is presented as an account of a single vision, in which the prophet is led about by an angelic being to view the ideal temple of the future. The most significant features of the vision are the return of the glory of God to the temple (43: 1–12) and the impressive symbolism of new life and hope which then begin to flood from it (47: 1–12). The original vision narrative, otherwise found only in parts of chs. 40–2, is interrupted at various points, sometimes to introduce further details of the temple, sometimes to list instructions about the conduct of temple affairs or to give orders concerning the priesthood. Finally a description is given of the division of the whole land among the tribes of Israel. ✻

THE FINAL VISION

AT THE BEGINNING OF THE YEAR, on the tenth day **40**₁*ᵃ* of the month, in the twenty-fifth year of our exile, that is fourteen years after the destruction of the city, on that very day, the hand of the LORD came upon me and he brought me there. In a vision God brought me to ₂ the land of Israel and set me on a very high mountain, where I saw what seemed the buildings of a city facing me.*ᵇ* He led me towards it, and I saw a man like a figure ₃ of bronze holding a cord of linen thread and a measuring-rod, and standing at the gate. 'Man,' he said to me, 'look ₄ closely and listen carefully; mark well all that I show you,

[*a*] *In chs. 40–43 there are several Hebrew technical terms whose meaning is not certain and has to be determined, as well as may be, from the context.*
[*b*] facing me: *so Sept.; Heb.* to the south.

for this is why you have been brought here. Tell the Israelites all that you see.'

☆ The scene is introduced with phrases familiar from earlier vision accounts. The setting is 'a very high mountain', like the ideal mountain prophesied in Isa. 2: 2 and Mic. 4: 1.

1. *At the beginning of the year, on the tenth day of the month*: the month itself is not indicated. The civil year began in the spring, on the first day of the month Nisan (see 29: 17). But the new religious year commenced in the autumn, on the tenth day of the seventh month Tishri (September–October, cp. Lev. 25: 9), and that is the likely date here. It was an appropriate date for this vision of a new centre for the nation's religious life. That the year was 573 B.C. is confirmed by the references to both the exile and the destruction of Jerusalem.

2. *In a vision God brought me*: the Hebrew states that 'the hand of the LORD' (verse 1) brought the prophet 'in visions of God'. For these terms see on 1: 3 and 8: 2f. respectively. Normally it is 'a spirit' which conveys the prophet about in visions (so 43: 5). *the buildings of a city*: the temple buildings, walled round like a city.

3. The man was a divine messenger and, as the vision goes on to relate (47: 3), the linen cord was a longer measure than the rod. A similar figure appears in the later vision of Zech. 2: 1–5. ☆

THE TEMPLE'S OUTER WALL AND EAST GATE

Round the outside of the temple ran a wall. The length
5 of the rod which the man was holding was six cubits,
reckoning by the long cubit which was one cubit and a
hand's breadth. He measured the thickness and the height
6 of the wall; each was one rod. He came to a gate which
faced eastwards, went up its steps and measured the thres-
7 hold of the gateway; its depth was one rod.[a] Each cell

[a] *So Sept.; Heb. adds* and one threshold, one rod in width.

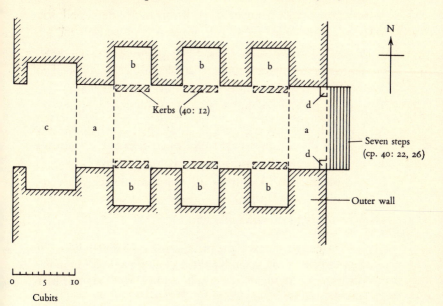

N

Kerbs (40: 12)

Seven steps (cp. 40: 22, 26)

Outer wall

0   5   10
Cubits

2. The outer east gate of the visionary temple (40: 5–16): *a* – thresholds (40: 6f.); *b* – cells (40: 7, 10, 12f.); *c* – vestibule (40: 8f.); *d* – gate posts.

was one rod long and one rod wide; the space between the cells five cubits, and the threshold of the gateway at the end of the vestibule on the side facing the temple one rod. He measured the vestibule of the gate and found it[a] 8 eight cubits, with pilasters two cubits thick; the vestibule 9 of the gateway lay at the end near the temple. Now the 10 cells of the gateway, looking back eastwards, were three in number on each side; all three of the same size, and their pilasters on each side of the same size also. He 11 measured the entrance into the gateway; it was ten cubits wide, and the gateway itself throughout its length thirteen

[a] facing. . .and found it: *so Sept.; Heb. repeats these words.*

12 cubits wide. In front of the cells on each side lay a kerb,
13 one cubit wide; each cell was six cubits by six. He measured the width of the gateway through the cell doors which faced one another, from the back[a] of one cell to the back[a] of the opposite cell; he made it twenty-five
14 cubits, and the vestibule[b] twenty[c] cubits, across; the gate-
15 way on every side projected into[d] the court. From the front of the entrance-gate to the outer face of the vestibule
16 of the inner gate the distance was fifty cubits. Both cells and pilasters had loopholes all round inside the gateway, and the vestibule had windows[e] all round within and palms carved on each pilaster.

✳ The eastern gate was the main entrance to the temple. The gate measurements resemble those of city gates of Solomon's period, but the square low wall, as thick as it was tall, is an unusual feature.

5. *the long cubit*: estimated to be 20.4 inches (518 millimetres). The *rod* was thus 10.2 feet (3.1 metres).

6f. *the threshold*: between the top step and the actual entrance gate. Beyond the threshold, on each side of the passageway, were three cells. Levites probably kept watch over the gates from these (44: 11). Beyond the cells lay a second threshold and then the vestibule opening to the outer court of the temple.

9. *pilasters*: square columns built into the walls.

11. The difference between the width of the entrance and the rest of the gateway suggests the existence of some kind of gate posts.

12. *kerb*: or barrier, like the 'rim' around the altar base (43: 13).

[a] So Sept.; *Heb.* roof.   [b] *Prob. rdg., cp.* Sept.; *Heb.* the pilasters.
[c] So Sept.; *Heb.* sixty.   [d] *Prob. rdg.; Heb. adds* pilaster.
[e] and . . . windows: *prob. rdg., cp.* Sept.; *Heb.* and so also the vestibules, and windows . . .

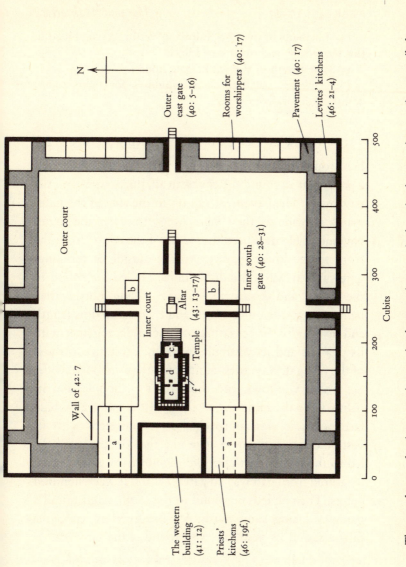

3. The temple complex (40: 17–27); *a* – priests' rooms (42: 1–14); *b* – priests' rooms (40: 44–6); *c* – vestibule (40: 48f.); *d* – sanctuary (41: 1–3) with its table (41: 21f.); *e* – Holy of Holies (41: 5); *f* – tiered arcades (41: 5–15).

271

14. Elements of the two following verses are combined in this secondary, and obscure, addition.

15. The length of the whole gate house.

16. *loopholes*: some form of windows for light. *palms*: common decorative features. ✲

THE OUTER COURT AND NORTH AND SOUTH GATES

17 He brought me to the outer court, and I saw rooms and a pavement all round the court: in all, thirty rooms on the
18 pavement. The pavement ran up to the side of the gate-ways, as wide as they were long; this was the lower
19 pavement. He measured the width of the court*a* from the front of the lower gateway to the outside of the inner gateway;*b* it was a hundred cubits. He led me round to
20 the north and I saw a gateway*c* facing northwards, belonging to the outer court, and he measured its length
21 and its breadth. Its cells, three on each side, together with its pilasters and its vestibule, were the same size as those of the first gateway, fifty cubits long by twenty-five wide.
22 So too its windows, and those of*d* its vestibule, and its palms were the same size as those of the gateway which faced east; it was approached by seven steps with its
23 vestibule facing them. A gate like that on the east side*e* led to the inner court opposite the northern gateway; he measured from gateway to gateway, and it was a hundred
24 cubits. Then he led me round to the south, and I found a gateway facing southwards. He measured its cells,*f* its pilasters, and its vestibule, and found it the same size as

[a] of the court: *so Sept.; Heb.* om.   [b] gateway: *so Sept.; Heb.* court.
[c] He led me . . . gateway: *so Sept.; Heb.* east and north, and the gate . . .
[d] those of: *prob. rdg.; Heb.* om. [e] like . . . side: *so Sept.; Heb.* and to
the east. [f] its cells: *so Sept.; Heb.* om.

the others, fifty cubits long by twenty-five wide. Both 25
gateway and vestibule had windows all round like the
others. It was approached by seven steps with a vestibule 26
facing them and palms carved on each pilaster. The 27
inner court had a gateway facing southwards, and he
measured from gateway to gateway;^a it was a hundred
cubits.

✷ 17. The outer court was where the people assembled for
worship. The thirty rooms were probably used by visitors
to the temple as places to meet and eat together.

19. Notice that the measurement is between the outer and
inner east gates only and not across the entire width of the
court.

22. *with its vestibule facing them*: better 'and its vestibule was
inside' (so the Septuagint). The vestibule was well beyond the
entrance steps (see on verses 6f.). The same correction is needed
in verse 26. ✷

THE GATES OF THE INNER COURT

He brought me into the inner court through the southern 28
gateway, measured it and found it the same size as the
others. So were its cells, pilasters, and vestibule, fifty 29
cubits long by twenty-five wide. It and its vestibule had
windows all round.^b Its vestibule faced the outer court; 31
it had palms carved on its pilasters, and eight steps led up
to it.

Then he brought me into the inner court, towards the 32
east, and measured the gateway and found it the same size
as the others. So too were its cells, pilasters, and vestibule; 33

[a] *So Pesh.; Heb. adds* southwards.   [b] *So some MSS.; others add*
(30) It had vestibules all round, and it was twenty-five cubits long
by five wide.

it and its vestibule had windows all round, and it was
34 fifty cubits long by twenty-five wide. Its vestibule faced
the outer court and had a palm carved on each pilaster;
35 eight steps led up to it. Then he brought me to the north
gateway and measured it and found it the same size as
36 the others. So were[a] its cells, pilasters, and vestibule, and
it had windows all round; it was fifty cubits long by
37 twenty-five wide. Its vestibule[b] faced the outer court
and had palms carved on the pilaster at each side; eight
steps led up to it.

✶ The inner court was entered only by priests. The design
of the inner and outer gates is essentially the same but the
order of vestibule and cells is reversed, the vestibule now
being nearest the entrance steps. The steps are now eight in
number. ✶

THE INNER COURT

38 There was a room opening out from the vestibule of
the gateway;[c] here the whole-offerings were washed.
39 In the vestibule of the gateway were two tables on each
side, at which to slaughter the whole-offering, the sin-
40 offering, and the guilt-offering. At the corner on the
outside, as one goes up to the opening of the northern
gateway, stood two tables, and two more at the other
41 corner of the vestibule of the gateway. Another four
stood on each side at the corner of the gateway, eight
42 tables in all at which slaughtering was done. Four tables
used for the whole-offering were of hewn stone, each a
cubit and a half long by a cubit and a half wide and a

[a] So were: *so one MS.; others om.*   [b] *So Sept.; Heb.* Its pilasters.
[c] the vestibule of the gateway: *prob. rdg.; Heb.* pilasters, the gates.

cubit high; and on them[a] they put the instruments used for the whole-offering and other sacrifices. The flesh of 43 the offerings was on the tables,[b] and ledges a hand's breadth in width were fixed all round facing inwards.

Then he brought me right into the inner court, and I 44 saw two rooms[c] in the inner court, one at the corner of the northern gateway, facing south, and one at the corner of the southern[d] gateway, facing north. This room facing 45 south, he told me, is for the priests who have charge of the temple. The room facing north is for the priests who 46 have charge of the altar; these are the sons of Zadok, who alone of the Levites may come near to serve the LORD. He measured the court; it was square, a hundred cubits 47 each way, and the altar lay in front of the temple.

---

* Verses 38–43 and 44–6 break into the description of the inner court with their details of slaughtering tables and priests' chambers. The vision narrative is taken up again only at verse 47.

38. The legs and intestines of whole-offering had to be washed before being offered (Lev. 1: 9).

39. *whole-offering(s)* were completely burnt, the others were eaten in part by the offerers and priests. *sin-offering(s)* were intended to restore the worshipper to purity, while *guilt-offering(s)* were originally fines imposed for damage done to people or property.

40f. The description of the tables in the vestibule is interrupted by the reference here to tables just outside the gate.

[a] So Sept.; Heb. adds and.
[b] The flesh. . .tables: or, with Sept., Roofs over the tables protected them from rain and from heat.
[c] Then. . .rooms: so Sept.; Heb. And outside the inner gate singers' rooms. [d] southern: so Sept.; Heb. eastern.

The gate seems to be the northern one (agreeing with Lev. 1: 11).

42f. The low stone tables were probably for the meat of the whole-offerings, not merely for the instruments. The N.E.B. has attempted to unravel the problems of these verses by re-ordering the two halves of verse 43. A more satisfactory solution might be to read what is now the last half of verse 43 before the last half of verse 42. Thus: '(the stone tables were) a cubit high, and ledges a hand's breadth in width were fixed all round facing inwards; and on them (i.e. the ledges) they put the instruments . . .'

46. The distinction between Zadokites and Levites will be dealt with later (see on 44: 15–31).

47. The altar was presumably in the middle of the court, in front of the temple proper. Ezekiel does not describe the altar, although a later addition in 43: 13–17 gives some details of it. ✵

WITHIN THE TEMPLE

48 Then he brought me into the vestibule of the temple, and measured a pilaster of the vestibule; it was five cubits on each side, the width of the gateway fourteen cubits and that of the corners of the gateway[a] three cubits in 49 each direction. The vestibule was twenty cubits long by twelve[b] wide; ten[c] steps led up to it, and by the pilasters rose pillars, one on each side.

41 Then he brought me into the sanctuary and measured 2 the pilasters; they were six cubits wide on each side.[d] The opening was ten cubits wide and its corners five cubits wide in each direction. He measured its length; it was 3 forty cubits, and its width twenty. He went inside and

[a] fourteen. . .gateway: *so Sept.; Heb. om.*
[b] *So Sept.; Heb.* eleven.   [c] *So Sept.; Heb.* which.
[d] *So Sept.; Heb. adds* the width of the tent.

measured the pilasters at the opening: they were two cubits; the opening itself was six cubits, and the corners[a] of the opening were seven cubits in each direction.[b] Then 4 he measured the room at the far end of the sanctuary; its length and its breadth were each twenty cubits. He said to me, 'This is the Holy of Holies.'

✻ Up yet another flight of steps, and through a gateway 14 cubits wide, was the first room of the temple proper, the vestibule.

48. The measurement of the *pilaster(s)* was the thickness of the wall at each entrance-way. The measurement of the *corners* of the entrance-ways was the distance from the side walls to the actual openings.

49. The vestibule was broader than it was deep. By length is simply meant the longer of the two distances. The *pillars* call to mind those of Solomon's temple (1 Kings 7: 15–22). Their diameter is not given, so the width of the gateway is uncertain.

41: 1f. *the sanctuary*: or nave, the main room of the temple. The length and width were the same as in Solomon's temple (1 Kings 6: 2, 17). No mention is made of the height, nor of any altar of incense, lamps, etc., that stood here in the former temple (1 Kings 7: 48f.).

3. Through the third of the progressively narrower doorways was a room which only the angel entered. As a priest Ezekiel could enter the nave, but he does not venture into the most holy of all places. After the exile the Holy of Holies was entered only by the high priest, and then only once a year, on the day of atonement (Lev. 16). ✻

[a] *So Sept.; Heb.* width.
[b] in each direction: *so Sept.; Heb. om.*

THE SIDE BUILDINGS

5 He measured the wall of the temple; it was six cubits high, and each arcade all round the house was four cubits
6 wide. The arcades were arranged in three tiers, each tier in thirty sections. In the wall all round the temple there were intakes for the arcades, so that they could be supported without being fastened into the wall of the
7 temple. The higher up the arcades were, the broader they were all round by the addition of the intakes,*a* one above the other all round the temple; the temple itself had a ramp*b* running upwards on a base, and in this way one went up from*c* the lowest to the highest tier by way of the middle tier.
8   Then I saw a raised pavement all round the temple, and the foundations of the arcades were flush with it and
9 measured a full rod, six cubits high. The outer wall of the arcades was five cubits thick. There was an unoccupied area beside the terrace*d* which was adjacent to the temple,
11*e* and the arcades*f* opened on to this area, one opening facing northwards and one southwards; the unoccupied
10 area was five cubits wide on all sides. There was a free
12 space*g* twenty cubits wide all round the temple. On the western side, at the far end of the free space, stood a building seventy cubits wide; its wall was five cubits thick all round, and its length ninety cubits.

[a] by. . .intakes: *so Sept.; Heb.* for the surrounding of the house.
[b] *Lit.* a broadening.   [c] from: *so Sept.; Heb. om.*
[d] beside the terrace: *prob. rdg.; Heb.* between the arcades.
[e] *Verses 10 and 11 transposed.* [f] *So Sept.; Heb.* arcade.
[g] There. . .space: *prob. rdg.; Heb.* Between the rooms.

He measured the temple; it was a hundred cubits long; 13
and the free space, the building, and its walls, a hundred
cubits in all. The eastern front of the temple and the free 14
space was a hundred cubits wide. He measured the length 15*a*
of the building at the far end of the free space to the west
of the temple, and its corridors on each side: a hundred
cubits.

✳ There follows now a series of passages intended to fill out
the bare description of the vision. The original vision account
is not taken up again until 42: 15.

5–7. The details of the *arcades* or side-chambers are obscure,
but they seem to follow the pattern of the temple of Solomon
(1 Kings 6: 5f, 8 and 10). They composed a three-storeyed
building round three sides of the temple. The lowest storey
was the narrowest and the top the broadest. The purpose of
the ninety rooms, thirty in each storey, is unknown. In verse 5,
the thickness and not the height of the temple wall is probably
meant by the measurement of 6 cubits.

8–11. The 6-cubits-high platform on which the temple was
built extended beyond the walls of the side-chambers. This
was the 5-cubits-wide *pavement* or *terrace*, and below it lay
an open space 20 cubits wide.

12. *a building*: another structure of unspecified purpose.
Again the length was the north–south measurement (see on
40: 49). The external dimensions of the building, together
with the free space in front of it, are given in verses 13 and 15.

13–15*a*. The measurements are of two squares each having
the same dimensions as the inner court: 'a hundred cubits
each way' (40: 47). ✳

THE DESIGN INSIDE

15*b* The sanctuary, the inner shrine and the outer vestibule
16 were panelled; the embrasures all round the three of them
17 were framed with wood all round. From the ground up
to the windows and above the door,*a* both in the inner
and outer chambers, round all the walls, inside and out,
18 were carved figures,*b* cherubim and palm-trees, a palm
between every pair of cherubim. Each cherub had two
19 faces: one the face of a man, looking towards one palm-
tree, and the other the face of a lion, looking towards
another palm-tree. Such was the carving round the whole
20 of the temple. The cherubim and the palm-trees were
carved from the ground up to the top of the doorway
21 and on the wall of the sanctuary. The door-posts of the
sanctuary were square.*c*

22   In front of*d* the Holy Place was what seemed an altar of
wood, three cubits high and two cubits long; it was fitted
with corner-posts, and its base*e* and sides also were of
wood. He told me that this was the table which stood be-
23 fore the LORD. The sanctuary had a double door, and the
24 Holy Place also had a double door: the double doors had
25 swinging leaves, a pair for each door. Cherubim and
palm-trees like those on the walls were carved on them.*f*
Outside there was a wooden cornice over the vestibule;

[*a*] the inner shrine...above the door: *prob. rdg., cp. Sept.; Heb. unintelligible.*
[*b*] carved figures: *prob. rdg.; Heb.* measures and carving.
[*c*] The door posts...square: *prob. rdg.; Heb. unintelligible.*
[*d*] In front of: *prob. rdg.; Heb.* The face of.
[*e*] base: *so Sept.; Heb.* length. [*f*] *Prob. rdg.; Heb. adds* on the doors of
the sanctuary.

on both sides of the vestibule were loopholes, with 26
palm-trees carved at the corners.*a*

✳ Back within the temple, the interior decoration is described.
Again the details are obscure.

15*b*–16. *The sanctuary, the inner shrine*: the Hebrew has 'the
inner sanctuary', probably meaning both the inner rooms.
It is remarkable that in this addition there seems no reluctance
to describe the interior of the Holy of Holies. *the embrasures*:
were the openings for windows and doors.

18. *cherubim* are known as guardians of sacred places (see
on 10: 2). *palm-trees* were decorative features of Solomon's
temple (1 Kings 6: 29).

21*b*–22. *the Holy Place*: presumably the Holy of Holies is
meant. The object that looked like an altar was the table on
which lay the Bread of the Presence – twelve loaves placed
on the table each Sabbath. Originally offered as food for God
(Lev. 24: 5–9), it later came to be thought of as a sign that God
provided for his people's needs. These verses may have been
part of Ezekiel's vision, once linked with 41: 4.

26. *loopholes*: see on 40: 16. ✳

THE PRIESTS' ROOMS

Then he took me to the outer court round by the north **42**
and brought me to the rooms*b* facing the free space and
facing the buildings to the north. The length along the 2
northern side was a hundred cubits,*c* and the breadth
fifty. Facing the free space measuring twenty cubits, which 3
adjoined the inner court, and facing the pavement of the
outer court, were corridors at three levels corresponding

[a] *Prob. rdg.; Heb. adds* and the arcades of the temple and the cornices.
[b] *So Sept.; Heb.* room.
[c] *The length . . . cubits: prob. rdg., cp. Sept.; Heb.* in front of a length
the hundred cubits, the northern opening.

4 to each other. In front of the rooms a passage, ten cubits wide and a hundred cubits long,[a] ran towards the inner

5 court; their entrances faced northwards. The upper rooms were shorter than the lower and middle rooms, because the corridors took[b] building space from them.

6 For they were all at three levels and had no pillars as the courts had, so that the lower and middle levels were

7 recessed from the ground upwards. An outside wall, fifty cubits long, ran parallel to the rooms and in front of

8 them, on the side of the outer court. The rooms adjacent to the outer court were fifty cubits long, and those facing

9 the sanctuary a hundred cubits. Below these rooms was an entry from the east as one entered them from the

10 outer court where the wall of the court began.[c] On the south[d] side, passing by the free space and the building,

11 were other rooms with a passage in front of them. These rooms corresponded, in length and breadth and in general

12 character, to those facing north, whose exits and entrances were the same as those of the rooms on the south. As one[e] went eastwards, where the passages began, there was an

13 entrance in the face of the inner[f] wall. Then he said to me, 'The northern and southern rooms facing the free space are the consecrated rooms where the priests who approach the LORD may eat the most sacred offerings. There they shall put these offerings as well as the grain-offering, the sin-offering, and the guilt-offering; for the

14 place is holy. When the priests have entered the Holy

[a] and a hundred cubits long: *so Sept.; Heb.* a way of one cubit.
[b] took: *so some MSS.; others* were able.
[c] began: *prob. rdg.; Heb.* breadth.
[d] *So Sept.; Heb.* east.   [e] *Prob. rdg.; Heb.* they.
[f] *Prob. rdg.; Heb. word unknown.*

Place they shall not go into the outer court again without leaving here the garments they have worn while performing their duties, for these are holy. They shall put on other garments when they approach the place assigned to the people.'

* The prophet is now led to view the rooms facing the free space and the building west of the temple described in 41: 12–15. Details are first given of the rooms to the north. The text is very difficult to interpret but it seems the rooms were in three parallel blocks, each set a little higher than the other on the slope between the outer court and the temple yard. The rooms of the block nearest the temple were twice as long as those adjacent to the outer court (verse 8). At the western end were the priests' kitchens (46: 19f.).

13f. The purpose of the rooms was threefold. There the priests ate, stored offerings in excess of their immediate requirements, and robed themselves for service of the altar. *the priests who approach the LORD* are later designated as the Zadokites. For the types of offering, see on 40: 39 and 45: 10–17.

An important feature of these verses is the portrayal of holiness as a semi-physical substance, from which the laity must be protected and which may not be contaminated by contact with people or things of a profane character (see further 44: 19). The sphere of holiness now includes the priests' rooms. *

THE OVERALL DIMENSIONS

When he had finished measuring the inner temple, he 15 brought me out towards the gateway which faces eastwards and measured the whole area. He measured the 16 east side with the measuring-rod, and it was five hundred

17 cubits.[a] He turned and measured[b] the north side with
18[c] his rod, and it was five hundred cubits.[a] He turned to[d]
the south side and measured it with his rod; it was five
19 hundred cubits.[a] He turned to the west and measured it
20 with his rod; it was five hundred cubits.[a] So he measured
all four sides; in each direction the surrounding wall
measured five hundred cubits.[a] This marked off the
sacred area from the profane.

✶ The style of the original vision is resumed as the prophet
sees the angel measure the outer wall of the temple area.
According to verse 20 this outer wall was the boundary of the
sacred area. ✶

THE GLORY OF GOD RETURNS

43 1,2 He led me to the gate, the gate facing eastwards, and I
beheld the glory of the God of Israel coming from the
east. His voice was like the sound of a mighty torrent, and
3 the earth shone with his glory. The form that I saw was
the same as that which I had seen when he[e] came to
destroy the city, and as that which I had seen by the river
4 Kebar,[f] and I fell on my face. The glory of the LORD
came up to the temple towards the gate which faced
5 eastwards. A spirit[g] lifted me up and brought me into the
inner court, and the glory of the LORD filled the temple.
6 Then I heard one speaking to me from the temple, and
7 the[h] man was standing at my side. He said, Man, do you

[a] *Prob. rdg.* (*cp. Sept. in verse 17*); *Heb.* rods.
[b] He turned and measured: *so Sept.; Heb.* round about. He
measured... [c] *Some MSS. place verse 18 after verse 19.*
[d] He turned to: *so Sept.; Heb.* round about.
[e] *So some MSS.; others* I. [f] *Or* the Kebar canal.
[g] *Or* wind. [h] *So Sept.; Heb.* a.

see[a] the place of my throne, the place where I set my feet, where I will dwell among the Israelites for ever? Neither they nor their kings shall ever defile my holy name again with their wanton disloyalty, and with the corpses[b] of their kings when they die. They set their threshold by 8 mine and their door-post beside mine, with a wall between me and them, and they defiled my holy name with the abominations they committed, and I destroyed them in my anger. But now they shall abandon their wanton 9 disloyalty and remove the corpses[b] of their kings far from me, and I will dwell among them for ever. So tell the 10 Israelites, man, about this temple, its appearance and proportions,[c] that they may be ashamed of their iniquities. If they are ashamed of all they have done, you shall 11 describe[d] to them the temple and its fittings, its exits and entrances, all the details and particulars of its elevation and plan; explain them and draw them before their eyes, so that they may keep them in mind and carry them out. This is the plan of the temple to be built on the top of the 12 mountain; all its precincts on every side shall be most holy.[e]

* The account of God's glory returning to the temple corresponds to the report of its departure in chs. 10–11. Ezekiel is brought to the east gate of the temple as the presence of God moves through it, just as it had formerly passed out to stand east of the city (11: 23). Other reminders of earlier

[a] do you see: *so Sept.; Heb. om.*   [b] *Or* effigies.
[c] its...proportions: *so Sept.; Heb.* and they shall measure the proportions.
[d] you shall describe: *so Sept.; Heb.* description.
[e] *So Sept.; Heb. adds* this is the plan of the temple.

visions are apparent in the sound of rushing water, the prostration of the prophet and a spirit lifting and bearing him about. The significance of the return can hardly be exaggerated. Just as his departure from the temple must have been a devastating sight to one of priestly descent, God's return must have filled the prophet with incredible joy and satisfaction. Its importance is explained in the speech of God from the Holy of Holies in verses 7–12. Some of these last verses are later additions, but others represent Ezekiel's own attempt to preserve the sanctity of the temple in the future. The instruction to inform the Israelites of the appearance and proportions of the new temple call to mind the command at the beginning of the vision (40: 4).

2. *His voice*: read rather 'Its noise' (cp. 1: 24; 3: 12).

3. The specific references back to earlier visions (cp. 3: 23 and 8: 4) are from the hand of an editor.

6–7*a*. The speaker is God, although Ezekiel is reluctant to name him. The angelic guide merely stands beside the prophet. Ezekiel combines older images of the temple as the throne of God (Jer. 17: 12) and as the place where God sets his feet (Ps. 132: 7), to emphasize the reality of the divine presence. But the ark of the covenant, which was thought of as the divine throne and footstool within the temple (see on 1: 4–14), is not mentioned. This agrees with Jer. 3: 16, 'men shall speak no more of the Ark of the Covenant'. The ark may have been taken as spoil to Babylon, but had possibly disappeared earlier.

7*b*. *wanton disloyalty*: idolatry. *the corpses of their kings*: it is uncertain where the graves of the kings were and it is preferable to read here 'the memorial stones of their kings'. These presumably bore some inscription concerning each king and his achievements. Their erection within the temple court may have been thought to have directed to the memory of unworthy men the respect and honour due to God. The same reading should be adopted in verse 9, where this half-verse is repeated.

8. An addition explaining the defilement as due to the king's palace standing beside the temple. That was the case with Solomon's temple, the palace being structurally independent of the temple but within the walls of the outer court.

10–11*a*. *that they may be ashamed. . .of all they have done*: a moralizing condition also added later.

11*b*–12. *all the details and particulars. . .*: the words *elevation* and *plan* represent Hebrew words usually translated 'statutes' and 'laws'. So these verses are best taken as an introduction to the regulations about worship in the sections following. *its precincts on every side. . .*: according to 42: 20 the outer wall 'marked off the sacred area from the profane'. Now the whole mountain top is said to be *most holy*.　　✳

THE ALTAR OF BURNT OFFERING

These were the dimensions of the altar in cubits (the cubit 13 that is a cubit and a hand's breadth). This was the height[a] of the altar: the base was a cubit high[b] and projected a cubit; on its edge was a rim one span deep. From the 14 base to the cubit-wide ridge of the lower pedestal-block was two cubits, and from this shorter[c] pedestal-block to the cubit-wide ridge of the taller[d] pedestal-block was four cubits. The altar-hearth was four cubits high and 15 was surmounted by four horns a cubit high.[e] The hearth 16 was twelve cubits long and twelve cubits wide, being a perfect square. The upper pedestal-block was fourteen 17 cubits long and fourteen cubits wide along its four sides, and the rim round it was half a cubit deep. The base of the altar projected a cubit, and there were steps facing eastwards.

[a] *So Sept.; Heb.* back.　　[b] the base. . .high: *prob. rdg.; Heb.* the base of the cubit.　[c] *Lit.* smaller.　[d] *Lit.* larger.　[e] a cubit high: *prob. rdg., cp. Sept.; Heb. om.*

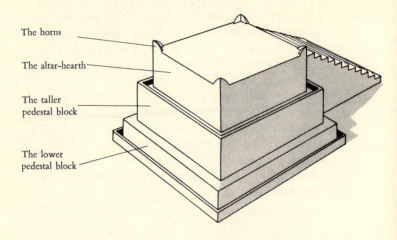

The horns

The altar-hearth

The taller
pedestal block

The lower
pedestal block

4. The altar of burnt offerings (43: 13–17).

✻ These verses are an addition describing the altar of the
inner court referred to briefly in 40: 47. The altar consisted
of three blocks. The *lower pedestal-block* (verse 14) was 2
cubits high and its horizontal surface 16 cubits square. The
taller pedestal-block was 4 cubits high and 14 cubits square,
while the topmost block (*the altar-hearth*) was the same height
but 12 cubits square. This gave the altar the appearance of a
series of steps (*the cubit-wide ridge(s)*), like a Babylonian temple-
tower, quite unlike the altar of unhewn stones that was
eventually used in the post-exilic temple. The bold use of a
Babylonian design is interesting. There appears to be no fear
felt at the use of such a foreign article in Israel's post-exilic
worship.

13. *a cubit and a hand's breadth*: or a long cubit, see on 40: 5.
the base was a cubit high and projected a cubit: the word *base* is a
technical term of uncertain meaning. Here it seems to indicate
a channel 1 cubit deep and 1 cubit wide, let into the ground to
collect the blood of the sacrifices. The height of the *rim*

around the outer edge of the channel is said to be *one span*, which was apparently equivalent to 'half a cubit' (verse 17).

15. *horns*: projections at the corners, common on altars of the time. They may originally have been symbols of divinity. A fugitive, by holding on to them, could find asylum from his enemies, protected by the god's holiness (1 Kings 2: 28).

17. The measurements of the lower pedestal-block (16 cubits square) may have dropped out of the text. For *the rim* and *the base* see on verse 13. *steps*: Exod. 20: 24–6 forbids the use of steps to ascend altars. The use of hewn stones was also forbidden by the same law, but it is evident that practices had changed over the years. ✻

THE CONSECRATION OF THE ALTAR

He said to me, Man, these are the words of the Lord 18 GOD: These are the regulations for the altar when it has been made, for sacrificing whole-offerings on it and flinging the blood against it. The levitical priests of the 19 family of Zadok, and they alone, may come near to me to serve me, says the Lord GOD. You shall assign them a young bull for a sin-offering; you shall take some of the 20 blood and put it on the four horns of the altar, on the four corners of the upper pedestal and all round the rim, and so purify it and make expiation for it. Then take the 21 bull assigned as the sin-offering, and they shall destroy it by fire in the proper place within the precincts but outside the Holy Place. On the second day you shall 22 present a he-goat without blemish as a sin-offering, and with it they shall purify the altar as they did with the bull. When you have completely purified the altar, you shall 23 present a young bull without blemish and a ram without blemish from the flock. You shall present them before 24

289

the LORD; the priests shall throw salt on them and
25 sacrifice them as a whole-offering to the LORD. For seven
days you shall provide as a daily sin-offering a goat, a
young bull, and a ram from the flock; all of them shall be
26 provided free from blemish. For seven days they shall
make expiation for the altar, and pronounce it ritually
27 clean, and consecrate it. At the end of that time, on the
eighth day and onwards, the priests shall sacrifice on the
altar your whole-offerings and your shared-offerings, and
I will accept you. This is the very word of the Lord GOD.

✶ These verses show clear evidence of later reworking. They
are an addition which is closely related to the Priestly material
of Exod. 29: 36f. Like Moses, the prophet is described as
receiving instructions for purifying the altar of the sin that
was believed to cling to all profane things.
   18. For *whole-offerings* see on 40: 39. The flinging of blood
against an altar was an early practice in covenant making
(Exod. 24: 6). It was believed the life-force of the animal
was in the blood and that it had to be offered back to God, the
giver of life, to bring cleansing from sin.
   19. For *the family of Zadok* see on 44: 15–31, and for *a sin-
offering* see on 40: 39.
   20. *expiation*: the covering-over or wiping-away of sin.
   21. Only the blood of the sacrifice was to be put on the
altar; the flesh was to be burnt outside the temple. Except that
the fat was usually burnt on the altar, this seems to have been
the regular custom with public sin-offerings (cp. Exod. 29:
13f.). It was only the flesh of private sin-offerings that the
priests received for their own use. *the proper place* is unknown.
   24. *salt*: its use with grain-offerings is mentioned in Lev.
2: 13. The meaning of the practice is not known.
   25. *For seven days*: should be 'for six days', since on the
first day only a single young bull was offered (verses 19-21).

27. Once the altar was consecrated by the week of special offerings, the regular sacrifices could be made. The flesh of *shared-offerings* or communion-offerings was eaten by the priests and the offerers, while the fat was burnt on the altar as God's share of the sacrificial animal. The fat, like the blood, was regarded as a life-giving part of the beast. ✳

LAWS OF THE SANCTUARY

He again brought me round to the outer gate of the **44** sanctuary facing eastwards, and it was shut. The LORD 2 said to me, This gate shall be kept shut; it must not be opened. No man may enter by it, for the LORD the God of Israel has entered by it. It shall be kept shut. The prince, 3 however, when he is here as prince, may sit there to eat food in the presence of the LORD; he shall come in and go out by the vestibule of the gate.

He brought me round to the northern gate facing the 4 temple, and I saw the glory of the LORD filling the LORD's house, and I fell on my face. The LORD said to me, Mark 5 well, man, look closely, and listen carefully to all that I say to you, to all the rules and regulations for the house of the LORD. Mark well the entrance to the house of the LORD and all the exits from the sanctuary. Say to that rebel people 6 of Israel, These are the words of the Lord GOD: Enough of all these abominations of yours, you Israelites! You 7 have added to them by bringing foreigners, uncircumcised in mind and body, to stand in my sanctuary and defile my house when you present my food to me, both fat and blood, and they have made my covenant void. Instead 8 of keeping charge of my holy things yourselves, you have chosen to put these men in charge of my sanctuary.

9 These are the words of the Lord GOD: No foreigner, uncircumcised in mind and body, shall enter my sanctuary,

10 not even a foreigner living among the Israelites. But the Levites, though they deserted me when the Israelites went astray after their idols and had to bear the punish-

11 ment of their iniquity, shall yet do service in my sanctuary. They shall take charge of the gates of the temple and do service there. They shall slaughter the whole-offering and the sacrifice for the people and shall be in attendance

12 to serve them. Because they served them in the presence of their idols and brought Israel to the ground by their iniquity, says the Lord GOD, I have sworn with uplifted hand that they shall bear the punishment of their iniquity.

13 They shall not have access to me, to serve me as priests; they shall not come near to my holy things or to the Holy of Holies; they shall bear the shame of the abominable

14 deeds they have done. I will put them in charge of the temple with all the service which must be performed there.

---

* Chs. 44–6 contain a variety of laws governing the rites and personnel of the sanctuary. All have been added later to Ezekiel's vision.

1–3. Here we return to the style of the original vision, with the prophet being led by the messenger from the inner court (43: 5) to stand in the outer court before the east gate. Since God entered the temple by the east gate, it is kept closed as a sign that he remains within the temple. Only the prince is allowed to eat sacrificial meals in the eastern gate-building, but as the gate itself is to remain closed he has to enter and leave from the outer court.

2. *The LORD said to me*: read rather 'then he (i.e. the messen-

ger) said to me'. *the LORD* is spoken of in the third person in the address to the prophet.

3. *when he is here as prince*: these words are an attempt to render a difficult text, in which the word *prince* has been repeated in error.

4f. These verses repeat earlier material with the intention of emphasizing the importance of the laws that follow. From the inner north gate the prophet again sees the glory of the LORD filling the temple and again he falls prostrate.

5. The instructions are based on 40: 4 and 43: 11. *The LORD said to me*: again read 'he' for *the LORD* as in verse 2.

6–8. These verses take the form of a prophecy to the people as a whole. But instead of them being addressed as a nation healed and restored, as Ezekiel prophesied in chs. 34–7, the people are reproached for their rebelliousness. Sin and guilt are again present realities and the return of God, to dwell among his people and restore holiness to them and to the land, is no longer the central theme. Instead there is a dominant concern in these chapters, as in the Priestly legislation of the Pentateuch, to protect holy things from contamination.

7. *foreigners*: Josh. 9: 23 and 27 record that Gibeonites were employed as servants of the altar of the Lord and Carites were used as temple guards according to 2 Kings 11: 4–8. It was commonly the practice to employ foreign slaves in temples and such slaves are likely to have been numbered among the 'temple-servitors' referred to in Ezra 2: 43–54 and elsewhere. *uncircumcised in mind and body*: foreign in ways of thought as well as of race. Spiritual circumcision, of the heart or mind, is mentioned in Deut. 10: 16 and Jer. 4: 4 and 9: 26.

9. Israel is now spoken of in the third person. What follows, though presented as a prophecy, is in fact a legal regulation. The attitude to foreigners in this verse is very different from that in Isa. 56: 3 and 6f., where their right to share fully in the faith and worship of Israel is plainly stated.

10–14. The attitude expressed here toward the Levites (apart from the family of Zadok, verse 15) can best be understood as the outcome of a struggle for dominance among rival priestly groups. The Levites are to undertake the tasks formerly entrusted to foreigners. The law code of Deuteronomy required that worship at all country sanctuaries should cease, and it made provision for Levites, unemployed by the closure of the 'high places', to act as priests in Jerusalem if they wished to do so (Deut. 18: 6–8). These verses of Ezekiel represent the reaction of those already employed as priests in the temple. Jealous of their position, they rejected, on the pretext of the Levites' apostasy, the right of the country priests to share their duties as equals. The Levites were to have charge of the gates and act as butchers of private sacrifices, but could not offer sacrifices on the altar.

14. *in charge of the temple*: a phrase distinguishing the service of the Levites from the service of the Zadokites, who were 'in charge of (the) sanctuary' (verse 15). See further in the next section. ✱

THE ZADOKITE PRIESTHOOD

15 But the levitical priests of the family of Zadok remained in charge of my sanctuary when the Israelites went astray from me; these shall approach me to serve me. They shall be in attendance on me, presenting the fat
16 and the blood, says the Lord GOD. It is they who shall enter my sanctuary and approach my table to serve me
17 and observe my charge. When they come to the gates of the inner court they shall dress in linen; they shall wear no wool when they serve me at the gates of the inner
18 court and within. They shall wear linen turbans, and linen drawers on their loins; they shall not fasten their clothes
19 with a belt so that they sweat. When they go out to the people in the outer court,[a] they shall take off the clothes they

[a] in the outer court: *so some MSS.; others repeat these words.*

have worn while serving, leave them in the sacred rooms and put on other clothes; otherwise they will transmit the sacred influence to the people through their clothing.

They shall neither shave their heads nor let their hair 20 grow long; they shall only clip their hair. No priest shall 21 drink wine when he is to enter the inner court. He may 22 not marry a widow or a divorced woman; he may marry a virgin of Israelite birth. He may, however, marry the widow of a priest.

They shall teach my people to distinguish the sacred 23 from the profane, and show them the difference between clean and unclean. When disputes break out, they shall 24 take their place in court, and settle the case according to my rules. At all my appointed seasons they shall observe my laws and statutes. They shall keep my sabbaths holy.

They shall not defile themselves[a] by contact with any 25 dead person, except[b] father or mother, son or daughter, brother or unmarried sister. After purification, they shall 26 count seven days and then be clean.[c] When they enter[d] the 27 inner court to serve in the Holy Place, they shall present their[e] sin-offering, says the Lord GOD.

They shall own no[f] patrimony in Israel; I am their 28 patrimony. You shall grant them no holding in Israel; I am their holding. The grain-offering, the sin-offering, 29 and the guilt-offering shall be eaten by them, and everything in Israel devoted to God shall be theirs. The first 30

[a] They. . .themselves: *so Sept.; Heb.* He. . .himself.
[b] any. . .except: *or* anyone else's dead, but only their own . . .
[c] and then be clean: *so Pesh.; Heb. om.*
[d] *So Sept.; Heb. adds* the Holy Place.
[e] they enter. . .they. . .their: *so Sept.; Heb.* he enters. . .he. . .his.
[f] no: *so Vulg.; Heb. om.*

of all the firstfruits and all your contributions of every kind shall belong wholly to the priests. You shall give the first lump of your dough to the priests, that a blessing

31 may rest upon your home. The priests shall eat no carrion, bird or beast, whether it has died naturally or been killed by a wild animal.

⋆ In dealing with 8: 16 it was said that Ezekiel probably accused the priests of Jerusalem of pagan worship. It is therefore unlikely that the prophet himself would have exonerated the priests in the fashion of verse 15. The Zadokite priesthood may in fact have been descended from the Jebusite priests who served in Jerusalem before David's capture of the city. The Zadokites probably claimed levitical descent even before Deuteronomy demanded that only Levites should act as Israel's priests. But as we have just seen in the previous section, this chapter declares all country Levites unfit for priestly service. It was under the influence of 44: 6–31 that a note of the exclusive rights of the Zadokites who 'may come near to serve the LORD' was added in 40: 46; 43: 19 and 48: 11. After the exile, the struggle for supremacy among the priests was resolved by allowing those who traced their descent from Aaron, the brother of Moses, the privilege of serving in the sanctuary. The Zadokites claimed to be of the line of Eleazar, an elder son of Aaron (1 Chron. 6: 3–8), while the other priests claimed to be of the line of Ithamar, Aaron's youngest son. The claim on the part of the Zadokites was a fiction, but it enabled them to preserve a leading role among the priests by reason of Eleazar's seniority of birth. The remaining Levites fulfilled a subordinate role such as that described for them in Ezekiel (see Num. 18: 1–7).

The question of priestly descent – which is really a matter of authority like the later claims to 'apostolic succession' – was one of the problems for the Jewish community in the last centuries B.C. The murder of the legitimate high priest

Onias III in about 172 B.C. (2 Macc. 4: 33–8; Dan. 9: 26) and
the appointment then and later of non-Zadokite high priests
are indications of deep rivalries in the struggle for power.

The meanings of the regulations in verses 17–31 are not all
fully understood, but most of them are paralleled in the
Priestly material from Exodus to Numbers.

15. *in charge of my sanctuary*: see on 44: 14.

16. *my table*: the table of the Bread of the Presence, see on
41: 21*b*–22.

19. See on 42: 13f.

24. Deuteronomy prescribed that difficult lawsuits should
be brought before priests (Deut. 17: 8f.), but the practice was
an ancient one. Priests had knowledge of civil and criminal
law, as well as of ceremonial law.

25. Contact with the dead was widely thought to incur
ritual impurity.

28. The idea of God being the inheritance of the priests was
clearly stated in Deut. 10: 9 and 18: 2. But it is contradicted
by the allotment to them of land in 45: 3f. and 48: 10–12.

29. *everything in Israel devoted to God*: things dedicated to
God by way of a vow. Formerly the spoils of war were
devoted to God and destroyed as a means of offering them to
him (cp. Josh. 6: 17).

30. *The first of all the firstfruits*: the best or choicest of the
firstfruits is meant. The same qualification was probably
intended to relate to *all your contributions* (tithes and first-
born animals), and it is likely that 'the best' rather than *the
first* lump of dough was meant.

31. Cp. 4: 14. Elsewhere the law against eating carrion is
to be observed by all Israelites (Lev. 7: 24). ✳

THE ALLOTMENT OF LAND

When you divide the land by lot among the tribes for **45**
their possession, you shall set apart from it a sacred reserve
for the LORD, twenty-five thousand cubits in length and

twenty[a] thousand in width; the whole enclosure shall be
2 sacred. Of this a square plot, five hundred cubits each
way, shall be devoted to the sanctuary, with fifty cubits
3 of open land round it. From this area you shall measure
out a space twenty-five thousand by ten thousand cubits,
in which the sanctuary, the holiest place of all, shall stand.
4 This space is[b] for the priests who serve in the sanctuary
and who come nearest in serving the LORD. It shall
include space for their houses and a sacred plot for the
5 sanctuary. An area of twenty-five thousand by ten
thousand cubits shall belong to the Levites, the temple
servants; on this shall stand the towns in which they live.[c]
6 You shall give to each town an area of five thousand by
twenty-five thousand cubits alongside the sacred reserve;
7 this shall belong to all Israel. On either side of the sacred
reserve and of the city's holding the prince shall have a
holding facing the sacred reserve and the city's holding,
running westwards on the west and eastwards on the east.
8 It shall run alongside one of the tribal portions, and stretch
to the western limit of the land and to the eastern. It
shall be his holding in Israel; the princes of Israel[d] shall
never oppress my people again but shall give the land to
Israel, tribe by tribe.

✲ This is a shortened form of the regulations given in 48:
8–22. Perhaps because of what was said in 44: 28: 'They shall
own no patrimony in Israel', it is here made clear that some
land is to be allotted to the priests. According to ch. 48, on
the re-entry of Palestine the whole length of the land was to be

[a] *So Sept.; Heb.* ten.   [b] *So Sept.; Heb. adds* holy.
[c] on this. . .live: *so Sept.; Heb.* twenty rooms.
[d] the princes of Israel: *so Sept.; Heb.* my princes.

Territory of Judah (48: 8)

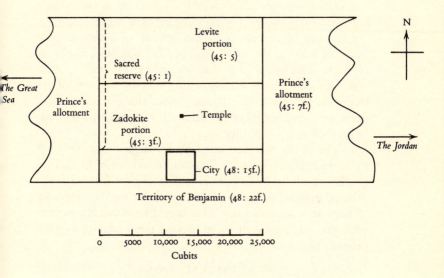

5. The sacred reserve and the city's holding (45: 1–8).

divided into horizontal strips of unspecified width (see p. 315). The strip described here lay between those allotted to Judah and Benjamin. Its central portion, 25,000 cubits square, was to compose a sacred reserve and a city reserve, while the remainder was the property of the prince. The sacred reserve was divided into two strips 10,000 by 25,000 cubits in area. The northern one was for the Levites' towns, the other for the priests' houses and the temple. To the south, beside the sacred reserve, was a strip of land 5000 by 25,000 cubits, in which the city was to stand, the property of all the people. The city thus no longer contains the temple. By this idealized scheme the place of the temple at the centre of national life was emphasized and the possibility of its defilement by contact with the palace or with the city was removed.

1. 25,000 cubits is about 8 miles (13 km). *length* is the east–west measurement, *width* the north–south.

2. The secondary addition of the sanctuary measurements here interrupts the train of thought between verses 1 and 3.

3. Notice again the different grades of holiness. The Israelites believed the entire land of God was holy, but at its centre was the *holiest place of all* (cp. on 43: 11*b*–12).

6. *each town*: the N.E.B. here associates the territory of the city with the area of the Levite towns. But this verse really deals with the city lying to the south of the sacred reserve: 'You shall give to the city . . .'

8. The prince was honoured by his large allotments next to the sacred reserve, and by the command later in the chapter to offer sacrifices. So this verse, with its critical attitude to the princes, may be an addition here, introducing the prophecy of verse 9. It appears from what is said here that the princes were given a large territory to prevent them taking away the people's land. ✻

THE PRINCES' TASKS

9 These are the words of the Lord GOD: Enough, princes of Israel! Put an end to lawlessness and robbery; maintain law and justice; relieve my people and stop your evictions,
10 says the Lord GOD. Your scales shall be honest, your
11 bushel[a] and your gallon[b] shall be honest. There shall be one standard for each, taking each as the tenth of a homer,
12 and the homer shall have its fixed standard. Your shekel weight shall contain twenty gerahs; your mina shall contain weights of ten[c] and twenty-five and fifteen shekels.
13 These are the contributions you shall set aside: out of every homer of wheat or of barley, one sixth of an
14 ephah. For oil the rule is[d] one tenth of a bath from every

[a] *Lit.* ephah.   [b] *Lit.* bath.   [c] *Prob. rdg.; Heb.* twenty.
[d] *Prob. rdg.; Heb. adds* the bath, the oil.

kor*a* (at ten bath to the kor*b*); one sheep in every flock of 15
two hundred is to be reserved by every Israelite clan.*c* For
a grain-offering, a whole-offering, and a shared-offering,
to make expiation for them, says the Lord GOD, all the 16
people of the land shall bring*d* this contribution to the
prince in Israel; and the prince shall be responsible for the 17
whole-offering, the grain-offering, and the drink-offering,
at pilgrim-feasts, new moons, sabbaths, and every sacred
season observed by Israel. He himself is to provide the
sin-offering and the grain-offering, the whole-offering and
the shared-offering, needed to make expiation for Israel.

* With the lessons of the past in mind, verse 9 warns the
princes against setting themselves above the law. Instead they
are to enforce it. Verses 10–12 specify the weights and
measures that are to be used in setting aside the people's
temple-offerings described in verses 13–15. And according
to verses 16f., the people are to give their offerings to the
prince, who then makes the offering on their behalf. These
last verses, which agree with verse 7 in referring to only one
prince, are a later attempt to assign the prince a place of
honour and responsibility in the restored community.

10f. *bushel*: a dry measure; *gallon*: the same amount by
liquid measure. There are quite wide variations in the equivalent present-day measures as calculated by different scholars.
However, the 'ephah' (see footnote) seems to have been
about half an imperial bushel (18 litres), and some pottery
remains suggest that the 'bath' (see footnote) held approximately 5 imperial gallons (23 litres). The meaning of the
regulation is plain. There are to be standard measures to avoid

[a] *So Sept.; Heb. adds the homer is ten bath.*
[b] *So Vulg.; Heb. to the homer.*
[c] clan: *so Sept.; Heb. unintelligible.*
[d] all. . .bring: *prob. rdg.; Heb. unintelligible.*

the unjust dealings of the past, such as are mentioned in Amos 8: 5 and Hos. 12: 7. The intention of setting verse 9 immediately before verses 10–12 may have been to imply that the prince was responsible for maintaining just standards. The word *homer* meant 'an ass' load', and is here said to be equivalent to the 'kor' (verse 14).

12. The *shekel* is taken as the standard unit of weight. The *gerah* was the smallest unit while the *mina* weighed 50 shekels. The unusual manner of calculating the weight of the mina suggests that there were intermediate weights of 10, 15 and 25 shekels. The shekel weighed approximately 0.4 ounces (11.4 gm). Again the meagre and sometimes conflicting evidence, and the variations in standards of measurement in different times and places of the ancient world, prevents precise calculation.

13–15. These offerings were additional to the tithes of 44: 30 but were probably meant to be paid in the first place directly to the priests.

17. *drink-offering*: libations were normally offered along with cereal and burnt offerings. Verses 14 and 24 suggest that libations of oil are meant here. For the festivals and their sacrifices see the following sections. *

TEMPLE PURIFICATION AND FESTIVALS

18 These are the words of the Lord GOD: On the first day of the first month you shall take a young bull without blem-
19 ish, and purify the sanctuary. The priest shall take some of the blood from the sin-offering and put it on the door-posts of the temple, on the four corners of the altar pedes-
20 tal and on the gate-posts of the inner court. You shall do the same on the seventh day of the month;[a] in this way you shall make expiation for the temple.

[a] *Prob. rdg.; Heb. adds* This comes from a man who is wrong and foolish. *Cp. Lev. 23: 24; Num. 29: 1. (For* on the seventh day of the month *Sept. has* on the first day of the seventh month.)

On the fourteenth day of the first month you shall hold $_{21}$ the Passover, the pilgrim-feast of seven days; bread must be eaten unleavened. On that day the prince shall provide $_{22}$ a bull as a sin-offering for himself and for all the people. During the seven days of the feast he shall offer daily as a $_{23}$ whole-offering to the LORD seven bulls and seven rams without blemish, and a he-goat as a daily sin-offering. With every bull and ram he shall provide a grain-offering $_{24}$ of one ephah, together with a hin of oil for each ephah. He shall do the same thing also on the fifteenth day of the $_{25}$ seventh month at the pilgrim-feast; this also shall last seven days, and he shall provide the same sin-offering and whole-offering and the same quantity of grain and oil.

✻ Verses 18–20 are related to 43: 18–27. Just as special sacrifices were ordered to make expiation for the altar, so special sacrifices must be made to purify the temple. But those for the temple are to be repeated annually. As blood was put on the altar in 43: 20, so it is to be smeared on various parts of the temple to remove the taint of guilt. Regulations for two annual festivals, to which all adult males were supposed to make pilgrimage, are dealt with in verses 21–5. But these regulations focus on the prince's part in the festivals and their emphasis lies more on the purification of the community than on joyful response to God's protection and providence (cp. Deut. 16: 11f.). Deuteronomy had required observance of Passover as a pilgrim-feast (Deut. 16: 1f.) where formerly it had been a family festival kept in worshippers' homes. Originally a lamb was sacrificed, reflecting an ancient rite of shepherds, intended to promote the increase of their flocks. But the rite became linked with the story of God passing-over the Israelite houses when he killed the first-born of the Egyptians (Exod. 12: 1–13). Thus Passover celebrated, at the beginning of each year, the exodus of Israel from slavery in Egypt. The feast of Ingathering, in the middle of the year, was the most important of all the festivals. In verse 25 it is called simply 'the pilgrim-feast'. It retained more of its earlier significance as an agricultural festival, marking the end of all harvesting for the year. But later it too was linked with an event in Israel's past, namely the dwelling in tents during the period of wandering in the wilderness (Lev. 23: 39-43).

20. As the footnote indicates, the sacrifice at the end of seven days was later thought to have been offered for sins committed in ignorance. The addition reflects such laws as are found in the Priestly material of Lev. 4: 13 and Num. 15: 22.

21. *the pilgrim-feast of seven days*: this rendering is based on the Septuagint and refers to the pilgrim-festival of Unleavened Bread (Exod. 23: 15), to which the Passover festival was joined in Deut. 16: 1-8. The Hebrew text has been altered to read 'the pilgrim-feast of Weeks', an obscure reference to the other great festival at the beginning of the harvest period (Exod. 23: 16), which is otherwise ignored in Ezekiel.

24. *hin*: one-sixth of a bath (see on 45: 10f.). ✶

REGULATIONS FOR WORSHIP

46 These are the words of the Lord GOD: The eastern gate of the inner court shall remain closed for the six working days; it may be opened only on the sabbath and at new
2 moon. When the prince comes through the porch of the gate from the outside, he shall halt at the door-post, and the priests shall sacrifice his whole-offering and shared-offerings. On the terrace he shall bow down at the gate and then go out, but the gate shall not be shut till
3 the evening. On sabbaths and at new moons the people also shall bow down before the LORD at the entrance to that gate.

The whole-offering which the prince sacrifices to the ₄ LORD shall be as follows: on the sabbath, six sheep without blemish and a ram without blemish; the grain-offering ₅ shall be an ephah with the ram and as much as he likes with the sheep, together with a hin of oil for every ephah. At the new moon it shall be a young bull without ₆ blemish,*a* six sheep and a ram, all without blemish. He ₇ shall provide as the grain-offering to go with the bull one ephah and with the ram one ephah, with the sheep as much as he can afford, adding a hin of oil for every ephah.

When the prince comes in, he shall enter through the ₈ porch of the gate and come out by the same way. But ₉ on festal days when the people come before the LORD, a man who enters by the northern gate to bow down shall leave by the southern gate, and a man who enters by the southern gate shall leave by the northern gate. He shall not turn back and go out through the gate by which he came in but shall go straight on. The prince shall then be ₁₀ among them, going in when they go in and coming out when they come out.

At pilgrim-feasts and on festal days the grain-offering ₁₁ shall be an ephah with a bull, an ephah with a ram and as much as he likes with a sheep, together with a hin of oil for every ephah.

When the prince provides a whole-offering or shared- ₁₂ offerings as a voluntary sacrifice*b* to the LORD, the eastern gate shall be opened for him,*c* and he shall make his whole-offering and his shared-offerings as he does on the

[a] without blemish: *so many MSS.; others have a plural form.*
[b] as. . .sacrifice: *so Sept.; Heb. repeats these words.*
[c] the eastern. . .him: *or he shall open the gate facing east.*

sabbath; when he goes out the gate shall be closed[a] behind him.

13 You shall provide a yearling sheep without blemish daily as a whole-offering to the LORD; you shall provide
14 it morning by morning. With it every morning you shall provide as a grain-offering one sixth of an ephah with a third of a hin of oil to moisten the flour; the LORD's grain-offering is an observance[b] prescribed for all time.
15 Morning by morning, as a regular whole-offering, they shall offer a sheep with the grain-offering and the oil.

✶ Instructions for the prince's part in worship continue, together with regulations for the people.

1-3. Neither prince nor people were to enter the inner court. But whereas the east gate of the outer court was perpetually closed, the inner east gate was open on sabbaths and new moons. The prince was permitted to go through the gateway to the entrance of the inner court and watch the sacrifices being offered. But the people worshipped in the outer court. *new moon*: the first day of each month, measured as months were by a lunar calendar. Like the sabbath it was a day of rest and religious observance and its relative importance is evident in the additional offering of a young bull. *terrace*: see on 10: 4.

4-7. The offerings differ considerably from those of the Priestly regulations (Num. 28: 9-15).

8-10. To control the large crowds of pilgrims at the major festivals, the people are directed to go out through the opposite gate to the one by which they entered. Verse 10 suggests that on those occasions the prince entered the temple at the head of a procession. Certainly he is closely associated with his people in their worship. *festal days*: or 'appointed seasons'

[a] the gate ... closed: *or* he shall close the gate.
[b] *So many MSS.; others* observances.

(verse 9). The term could be used for a variety of religious assemblies, but should, like 'pilgrim-feasts', be distinguished in this chapter from the festivals of the sabbath and new moon, when attendance at the temple was voluntary.

11. An isolated regulation possibly intended to correct, in the light of verse 5, the omission of a sheep from the list of sacrifices in 45: 24.

12–15. Verse 12 deals with sacrifices which the prince could make beyond the minimum prescribed. Some manuscripts read in verses 13f., 'he shall provide . . .', as though the prince was also responsible for the provision of the daily sacrifices. But the N.E.B. rightly translates this regulation in the second person, as directed to the whole community (cp. 43: 18–27; 45: 18–20). Daily sacrifices were required both morning and evening by the Priestly legislation (Num. 28: 3–8), and they were important features of post-exilic worship. ✣

LAND LAWS FOR THE PRINCE

These are the words of the Lord GOD: When the prince 16 makes a gift out of[a] his property to any of his sons, it shall belong to his sons, since it is part of the family property. But when he makes such a gift to one of his 17 slaves, it shall be his only till the year of manumission, when it shall revert to the prince; it is the property of[b] his sons and shall belong to them.

The prince shall not oppress the people by taking part 18 of their holdings; he shall give his sons an inheritance from his own holding of land, so that my people may not be scattered and separated from their holdings.

[a] out of: *so Sept.; Heb. om.*
[b] the property of: *so Sept.; Heb. his property.*

✽ The rules concerning land transfers by the prince pre-suppose the distribution of land in 45: 1–8 and 48: 1–29. They aim to prevent him taking more than his already generous allotment. For he is only permitted to make gifts of his own land and such land is not to pass from the royal estate as perpetual gifts to royal servants.

17. *the year of manumission*: probably the year of Jubilee, every fiftieth year. According to Lev. 25: 8–17, all alienated property had to be returned to its original owners on the year of Jubilee. But it is doubtful whether the law was ever observed. ✽

THE TEMPLE KITCHENS

19 Then he brought me through the entrance by the side of the gate to the rooms which face north (the sacred rooms reserved for[a] the priests), and, pointing to a place on their
20 western side, he said to me, 'This is the place where the priests shall boil the guilt-offering and the sin-offering and bake the grain-offering; they shall not take it into the outer court for fear they transmit the sacred influence
21 to the people.' Then he brought me into the outer court and took me across to the four corners of the court, at
22 each of which there was a further court. These four courts were vaulted and were the same size, forty cubits
23 long by thirty cubits wide. Round each of the four was a row of stones, with fire-places constructed close up
24 against the rows. He said to me, 'These are the kitchens where the attendants shall boil the people's sacrifices.'

✽ These verses are a supplement to 42: 1–14. According to 42: 13 separate rooms were provided in which the priests were to eat their share of the offerings. Provision is now

[a] reserved for: *prob. rdg., cp. Sept.; Heb.* to.

made for a kitchen where the food of the priests could be prepared, and for four other kitchens where the Levites (*the attendants*) could cook the worshippers' share of the offerings. Again the thought predominates that contact with holy things is dangerous and holy things can be contaminated by contact with the profane. ✴

A LIFE-GIVING TORRENT

He brought me back to the gate of the temple, and I saw **47** a spring of water issuing from under the terrace of the temple towards the east; for the temple faced east. The water was running down along the right side,[a] to the south of the altar. He took me out through the northern 2 gate and brought me round by an outside path to the eastern gate of the court,[b] and water was trickling from the right side. When the man went out eastwards he had 3 a line in his hand. He measured a thousand cubits and made me walk through the water; it came up to my ankles. He measured another thousand and made me walk 4 through the water; it came up to my knees. He measured another thousand and made me walk through the water; it was up to my waist. Another thousand, and it was a 5 torrent I could not cross, for the water had risen and was now deep enough to swim in; it had become a torrent that could not be crossed. 'Mark this, man', he said, and 6 led me back to the bank of the torrent. When we came 7 back to the bank I saw a great number of trees on each side. He said to me, 'This water flows out to the region 8 lying east, and down to the Arabah; at last it will reach that sea whose waters[c] are foul, and they will be sweetened.

[a] *So Sept.; Heb. adds* of the temple. [b] the court: *so Sept.; Heb.* the outside, a way. [c] waters: *so Sept.; Heb.* sea.

9 When any one of the living creatures that swarm upon the earth comes where the torrent*a* flows, it shall draw life from it. The fish shall be innumerable; for these waters come here so that the others may be sweetened, and where 10 the torrent flows everything shall live. From En-gedi as far as En-eglaim fishermen shall stand on its shores, for nets shall be spread there. Every kind of fish shall be there 11 in shoals, like the fish of the Great Sea; but its swamps and pools shall not have their waters sweetened but shall 12 be left as salt-pans. Beside the torrent on either bank all trees good for food shall spring up. Their leaves shall not wither, their fruit shall not cease; they shall bear early every month. For their water comes from the sanctuary; their fruit is for food and their foliage for enjoyment.'*b*

✳ At this point the original vision account resumes, and also concludes, with a portrayal of paradise regained. From a position outside the eastern gate, Ezekiel sees water issuing eastward from the temple complex. It becomes so broad and swift-flowing a stream that it promises life for the barren desert and sweetening for the waters of the Dead Sea. For people aware of the constant threat of desert droughts, the symbolism is as remarkable as that of the reincarnated bones in ch. 37. The vision, contained in verses 2–6 and 8, has been enlarged upon as freely as the opening vision of ch. 1. The promise of life for all created beings; the abundance of food from the river's fish; and the trees along the river's banks, all stress the extraordinary fertility brought about by the water issuing from the temple. Ps. 46: 4 refers to 'a river whose streams gladden the city of God', and the Eden story of Gen. 2

[a] torrent: *so Sept.; Heb.* two torrents.
[b] *Or, with Sept.,* for healing.

records that the river of God gave rise to the four world rivers (Gen. 2: 10). The restored temple, with its river of life, is then a source of blessing, in a physical as well as a spiritual sense, for the whole world, just as God's garden was intended to be at the creation. The image of life-giving waters flowing from God's dwelling-place recurs in later prophecies (Joel 3: 18; Zech. 13: 1 and 14: 8) and in Rev. 22: 1-2.

1. The verse is probably an addition linking the source of the water with the temple itself. Unnecessary detail, such as *the temple faced east*, and the laboured description of the water's direction of flow, confirm this.

2. Since the outer east gate was perpetually closed (44: 1f.), the prophet is led from the outer court by way of the northern gate. *from the right side*: is also an addition. The word for *the right side*, both here and in the previous verse, is different from that used in ch. 40. Read simply 'and water was trickling out'.

3-5. 1000 cubits is approximately 568 yards (518 metres). The further east the prophet went the greater the 'trickle' was seen to be. It was a miraculous torrent in the midst of what had been desert. *it had become a torrent. . .* (verse 5*b*): a doublet, repeating the earlier part of the verse.

6-8. The original speech of the messenger, commencing in verse 6, continues and concludes in verse 8: '*Mark this, man*', *he said . . . 'This water flows out to the region lying east, etc.'* *the Arabah*: the deep valley of the Jordan in which lies the Dead Sea (*that sea whose waters are foul*). The Dead Sea is nearly 1300 feet (396 metres) below the level of the Mediterranean ('the Great Sea', verse 10), and it is so salty that no fish can live in it. How different things would be, when the temple was rebuilt and inhabited by God, is made explicit in verses 9f.

7. Trees also feature in the story of Eden (Gen. 2: 9). Their purpose as symbols of plentiful food is explained in verse 12.

9. The words *living creatures, swarm* and *fish* recall the Priestly creation story of Gen. 1.

10. *From En-gedi as far as En-eglaim*: the first place, 'the

spring of the goat', was half-way down the west shore of the Dead Sea. The location of the second, 'the spring of the calf', is uncertain, but recent discoveries suggest a site on the eastern shore implying that the whole breadth of the Sea will be fished.

11. Since salt was harvested from the Dead Sea, provision has been made in the additions for some marshy areas to remain salty.

12. The image of fruitful trees whose leaves never wither is paralleled in Ps. 1: 3. The idea of the leaves serving medicinal purposes ('for healing', see the footnote for the Septuagint rendering) is adapted in Rev. 22: 2, where it is said that 'the leaves of the trees serve for the healing of the nations'. ✳

THE BOUNDARIES OF THE LAND

13 These are the words of the Lord GOD: These[a] are the boundary lines within which the twelve tribes of Israel shall enter into possession of the land, Joseph receiving

14 two portions. The land which I swore with hand uplifted to give to your fathers you shall divide with each other;

15 it shall be assigned to you by lot as your patrimony. This is the frontier: on its northern side, from the Great Sea

16 through Hethlon, Lebo-hamath, Zedad,[b] Berutha, and Sibraim, which are between the frontiers of Damascus and Hamath, to Hazar-enan,[c] near the frontier of

17 Hauran. So the frontier shall run from the sea to Hazar-enan[d] on the frontier of Damascus and northwards;[e] this

18 is[f] its northern side. The eastern side runs alongside the

[a] *So many MSS.; others have an unknown word.*
[b] Lebo-hamath, Zedad: *prob. rdg., cp. Sept.; Heb.* Lebo, Zedad, Hamath. [c] *Prob. rdg., cp. Sept.; Heb.* Hazar-hattikon.
[d] *So Sept.; Heb.* Hazar-enon.
[e] *So Sept.; Heb. adds* northwards and the frontier of Hamath.
[f] this is: *so some MSS.; others* and.

territories of Hauran, Damascus, and Gilead, and alongside the territory of Israel; Jordan sets the boundary to
the eastern sea, to Tamar.[a] This is[b] the eastern side. The 19
southern side runs from Tamar to the waters of Meribah-
by-Kadesh; the region assigned to you reaches the Great
Sea. This is[b] the southern side towards the Negeb. The 20
western side is the Great Sea, which forms a boundary
as far as a point opposite Lebo-hamath. This is the western 21
side. You shall distribute this land among the tribes of
Israel and assign it by lot as a patrimony for yourselves 22
and for any aliens living in your midst who leave sons
among you. They shall be treated as native-born in
Israel and with you shall receive a patrimony by lot
among the tribes of Israel. You shall give the alien his 23
patrimony with the tribe in which he is living. This is
the very word of the Lord GOD.

✻ The remainder of the book concerns the division of the
land among the tribes of Israel. The whole scheme is highly
idealized. Some of the place names have not been identified
with certainty. The northern boundary line seems intended to
follow that of David and Solomon's kingdom, which
extended to Lebo-hamath (1 Kings 8: 65). But the location
of that place is much debated. Some scholars hold that Lebo-
hamath was a little north of Dan, while others consider it to
have been well to the north, near Riblah. The latter solution
agrees with Ezek. 6: 14, where Riblah is said to mark Israel's
northern border. The Mediterranean (or Great Sea) formed
the western boundary, and the line of the Jordan river the
eastern. The former Israelite territory east of the Jordan is
completely ignored. The southern border is again intended

[a] Tamar: *so Pesh.; Heb.* you shall measure.
[b] This is: *so some MSS.; others* and.

to copy the traditional limits of Solomon's kingdom. From Tamar, south-west of the Dead Sea, it first followed a line further south-west, through the oasis of Kadesh, and then turned north-west to 'the Brook' (48: 28) which marked the border with Egypt. Similar boundaries are set in the Priestly material of Num. 34: 1–12, but tribes are also settled to the east of the Jordan (Num. 34: 13–15).

Immediately following the instruction to distribute the land in verse 21, a special provision has been added on behalf of foreigners living within Israel's borders. Previously the rights of aliens were protected. They were not to be ill-treated and, though generally classed among the poor, they could become wealthy individuals (Lev. 25: 47). However, they did not have rights as full citizens and did not possess property in land. Later law codes command that aliens should be treated in the same way as native Israelites (Lev. 19: 34; Num. 15: 29). But only here is there explicit mention of those who have settled permanently with their families receiving land. This probably assumed that the aliens would become proselytes, or converts to Judaism (Exod. 12: 48f.). The small population of post-exilic Judah may have encouraged this liberal attitude toward foreigners.

13. *Joseph receiving two portions*: in the list of twelve tribes in 48: 1–7, 23–9, Levi is not mentioned since the allotment of the Levites is within the sacred reserve. But Manasseh and Ephraim (sons of Joseph and grandsons of Jacob) receive separate allotments of land so that the number of tribes remains twelve. An editor has added this explanation here.

18. *the eastern sea*: the Dead Sea. ✻

THE NORTHERN TRIBES

48 These are the names of the tribes: In the extreme north, in the direction of Hethlon, to Lebo-hamath and Hazar-enan, with Damascus on the northern frontier in the

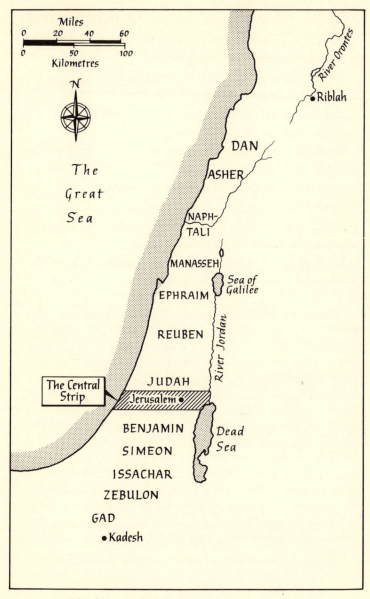

6. The division of the land among the tribes (48: 1–29).

315

direction of Hamath, and so from the eastern side to the western,[a] shall be Dan: one portion.

2   Bordering on Dan, from the eastern side to the western, shall be Asher: one portion.

3   Bordering on Asher, from the eastern side to the western, shall be Naphtali: one portion.

4   Bordering on Naphtali, from the eastern side to the western, shall be Manasseh: one portion.

5   Bordering on Manasseh, from the eastern side to the western, shall be Ephraim: one portion.

6   Bordering on Ephraim, from the eastern side to the western, shall be Reuben: one portion.

7   Bordering on Reuben, from the eastern side to the western, shall be Judah: one portion.

✻ The land is divided, by borders running east to west, into parallel strips of unspecified width. The allotments bear little relation to the earlier positions of the tribes, which were named after the traditional twelve sons of Jacob (Gen. 35: 22–6; or Jacob's grandsons in place of Joseph – see on 47: 13). Furthest north is Dan, whose territory was formerly at Israel's northern reaches, but the reason for Dan's northern-most position here is as much because Dan was a child of Jacob's concubine Bilhah. Asher and Naphtali were also sons of concubines, and the remoteness of these tribes from the sacred reserve (verses 8 ff.) may have been dictated by a notion of racial purity. There are seven tribes to the north and five to the south of the sacred reserve. Judah and Benjamin (verse 22) are in favoured positions on either side of the reserve, but Judah is now north rather than south of Benjamin. ✻

[a] from. . .western: *so Sept.; Heb.* the eastern corner is the sea.

THE CENTRAL STRIP

Bordering on Judah, from the eastern side to the western, 8
shall be the reserve which you shall set apart. Its breadth
shall be twenty-five thousand cubits and its length the
same as that of the other portions, from the eastern side
to the western, and the sanctuary shall be in the middle
of it.

The reserve which you shall set apart for the LORD 9
shall measure twenty-five thousand cubits by twenty[a]
thousand. The reserve shall be apportioned thus: the 10
priests shall have an area measuring twenty-five thousand
cubits on the north side, ten thousand on the west,[b]
ten thousand on the east,[b] and twenty-five thousand on
the south side;[c] the sanctuary of the LORD shall be in the
middle of it. It shall be for the consecrated priests, the 11
sons of Zadok, who kept my charge and did not follow
the Israelites when they went astray, as the Levites did.
The area set apart for the priests from the reserved 12
territory shall be most sacred, reaching the frontier of the
Levites.

The Levites shall have a portion running parallel to 13
the border of the priests. It shall be twenty-five thousand
cubits long by ten thousand wide; altogether, the length
shall be twenty-five thousand cubits and the breadth ten
thousand. They shall neither sell nor exchange any part 14
of it, nor shall the best of the land be alienated; for it is
holy to the LORD.

The strip which is left, five thousand cubits in width by[d] 15

[a] *Prob. rdg.; Heb.* ten.   [b] *So Sept.; Heb. adds* in breadth.
[c] *So Sept.; Heb. adds* in length.   [d] *Lit.* facing.

twenty-five thousand, is the city's secular land for dwellings and common land, and the city shall be in the
16 middle of it. These shall be its dimensions: on the northern side four thousand five hundred cubits, on the southern side four thousand five hundred cubits, on the eastern side four thousand five hundred cubits, on the western
17 side four thousand five hundred cubits. The common land belonging to the city shall be two hundred and fifty cubits to the north, two hundred and fifty to the south, two hundred and fifty to the east, and two hundred and
18 fifty to the west. What is left parallel to the reserve, ten thousand cubits to the east and ten thousand to the west,[a]
19 shall provide food for those who work in the city. Those who work in the city shall cultivate it; they may be drawn from any of the tribes of Israel.

20   You shall set apart the whole reserve, twenty-five thousand cubits square,[b] as sacred, as far as the holding of
21 the city. What is left over on each side of the sacred reserve and the holding of the city shall be assigned to the prince. Eastwards, what lies over against the reserved twenty-five thousand cubits, as far as the eastern side, and westwards, what lies over against the twenty-five thousand cubits to the western side, parallel to the tribal portions, shall be assigned to the prince; the sacred
22 reserve and the sanctuary itself shall be in the centre. The[c] holding of the Levites and the[c] holding of the city shall be in the middle of that which is assigned to the prince; it shall be between the frontiers of Judah and Benjamin.[d]

[a] *Prob. rdg.; Heb. adds* and it shall be parallel to the sacred reserve.
[b] square: *so Sept.; Heb.* fourth.   [c] *Prob. rdg.; Heb.* Some of the.
[d] *So Pesh.; Heb. adds* it shall belong to the prince.

✵ The sacred reserve, the city reserve and the prince's allotment have been described in the commentary on 45: 1–8.
Further details are given here of the city, which is to be a
square surrounded by a border of common land (see plan on
p. 299 and see also verses 30–5).

11f. This section originally distinguished between priests
and Levites, but these verses have been added to assert the
exclusive right of Zadokites to the priesthood (see on 44:
15–31) and to stress the special sacredness of the priest's
allotment.

14. The prohibition against the alienation of land covers the
priests' as well as the Levites' allotment since both are sacred
(verse 20).

16. 4500 cubits is approximately $1\frac{1}{2}$ miles (2.25 km).

21*b*–22*a*. *Eastwards, what lies over against the reserved* (land)
... *is assigned to the prince*: an intrusive supplement. ✵

THE SOUTHERN TRIBES AND THE CITY GATES

The rest of the tribes: from the eastern side to the western 23
shall be Benjamin: one portion.

Bordering on Benjamin, from the eastern side to the 24
western, shall be Simeon: one portion.

Bordering on Simeon, from the eastern side to the 25
western, shall be Issachar: one portion.

Bordering on Issachar, from the eastern side to the 26
western, shall be Zebulun: one portion.

Bordering on Zebulun, from the eastern side to the 27
western, shall be Gad: one portion.

Bordering on Gad, on the side of the Negeb, the border 28
on the south stretches from Tamar to*a* the waters of
Meribah-by-Kadesh, to the Brook as far as the Great Sea.

[*a*] to: *so some MSS.; others om.*

29   This is the land which you shall allot as*[a]* a patrimony to the tribes of Israel, and these shall be their lots. This is the very word of the Lord GOD.

30–31   These are to be the ways out of the city, and they are to be named after the tribes of Israel. The northern side, four thousand five hundred cubits long, shall have three

32 gates, those of Reuben, Judah, and Levi; the eastern side, four thousand five hundred cubits long, three gates,

33 those of Joseph, Benjamin, and Dan; the southern side, four thousand five hundred cubits long, three gates, those

34 of Simeon, Issachar, and Zebulun; the western side, four thousand five hundred cubits long, three gates, those of

35 Gad, Asher, and Naphtali. The perimeter of the city shall be eighteen thousand cubits, and the city's name for ever after shall be Jehovah-shammah.*[b]*

✻ The list of allotments continues, just as in verses 1–7. Gad, another son of a concubine, whose territory was formerly east of the Jordan, receives the allotment southernmost from the sacred reserve. Formerly only Judah and Simeon lay south of Jerusalem. Verse 29 concludes the section which began in 47: 13. The remaining verses are from a different source, for Levi is mentioned along with Joseph instead of Manasseh and Ephraim (see on 47: 13). Each side of the city has three gates and each gate is named after a different tribe (cp. Rev. 21: 12f.), so completing a picture of perfect order and harmony.

30f. The N.E.B. has reordered the text to correct a minor disarrangement in these verses.

35. 18,000 cubits is 6 miles (9 km) to the nearest whole figure. *Jehovah-shammah*: the new name is probably intended as a punning replacement of the old – Jerusalem (*yerushalaim* – *yahweh-shammah*). As the footnote indicates, the name signifies

[a] *So Sept.; Heb.* from.   [b] *That is* the LORD *is there.*

that God is present with his people. The wider implications of the name are specially significant within a series of chapters that stress the distinction between the sacred and profane, and firmly exclude the city from the sacred territory. For, somewhat as in the concluding verses of the book of Zechariah (14: 20f.), there is an intimation here that a day will come when every profane thing will be hallowed by the divine presence. ✻

✻   ✻   ✻   ✻   ✻   ✻   ✻   ✻   ✻   ✻   ✻   ✻   ✻

THE MESSAGE OF THE BOOK

The good news of the Old Testament was that God had rescued a handful of insignificant tribes from slavery in Egypt and offered to accept them as his people. Israel had gladly responded, joining in a covenant to serve the one who had brought them to new-found freedom. Although, in the course of time, justice had demanded that God punish those who had broken their agreement with him, he continued to hope for their return to life and freedom in his service. Despite the sometimes repulsive imagery of punishment, the telling of good news is the main point of Ezekiel's work as a whole. The God who had once given his people the opportunity of life again offered life to them, and desired that they should grasp it for themselves: 'I would ... that a wicked man should mend his ways and live' (33: 11). A new start was a real possibility with this God, for if only men would respond they would find they had the power to follow as they had never done before, because God would renew their heart and spirit (11: 19). And although the final vision stringently guards against the corruption of holy things, the nourishing of Israel holds the promise of divine grace for all the world (47: 1–12).

The extremely sensitive individual who saw this meaning in his people's suffering shared their experience of sorrow even before they did and anticipated new hope long before the restoration to their homeland became an actual possibility with the overthrow of Babylon by Cyrus of Persia in 539 B.C. All his hopes may not have been realized. The exiles were reluctant to return when the opportunity came and the temple was rebuilt spasmodically and hardly according to Ezekiel's design. But Ezekiel must have been a focus of hope for those concerned about the purpose of life in his deeply troubled times. He helped make people aware of the possibility of meaningful worship of God, beyond the boundaries of a particular holy land and without the benefit of participation in elaborate worship.

To Ezekiel, right worship unaccompanied by moral behaviour was unthinkable. He naturally associated the behaviour of the righteous man with appropriate religious observance. This may have been an oversimplified view. Ezekiel, unlike Amos (4: 5), did not concern himself with hypocrites who worshipped and then went about their works of injustice. Nor did he take account of the difficulties people have in breaking from the habits learnt in their homes when he called on sons to turn their backs on the bad ways of their fathers (18: 14–17). But the challenge comes to each reader of his words all the more clearly for their simplicity: it is that each should turn and follow the way God requires of us, to find life and freedom as his people. Such people are careful for others, particularly the less privileged of society; they are generous and just; in short, they are righteous. But they take no pride in this, for they remember their past and are thankful that God gives them the heart and spirit to follow him anew continually.

A NOTE ON FURTHER READING

There are fuller commentaries on Ezekiel by W. Eichrodt, Old Testament Library (S.C.M., 1970) and J. W. Wevers, Century Bible (Nelson, 1969); a shorter but useful commentary is by D. M. G. Stalker, Torch Series (S.C.M., 1968); all are based on the R.S.V. An English translation is awaited of the exhaustive German commentary by W. Zimmerli. Background material for the period may be found in P. R. Ackroyd, *Israel under Babylon and Persia*, New Clarendon Bible (Oxford University Press, 1970) and B. W. Anderson, *The Living World of the Old Testament* (2nd ed., Longmans, 1967), while R. de Vaux, *Ancient Israel* (Darton, Longman and Todd, 1961) will provide further details of the institutions referred to.

INDEX

abominations 42

abyss *see* Sheol

acted prophecies *see* prophecy, acted

aliens 88, 148, 291–4, 313–14; as judges of Judah 157; *see also* social responsibilities and evils

allegory 8, 110, 112, 137–8

altars 41–2, 53–4, 57, 59, 275–6, 280–1, 287–91

Ammon(ites) map p. 169; 107, 141–2, 144–5, 170–3

Amos, book of 44–5, 47, 168, 170, 322

angels 52, 58, 267–8, 277

apostasy and political alliances 153; *see also* prostitution

Ark of the Covenant 14, 17, 191, 286

arrogance or pride 188–90, 192, 209, 211, 322

Assyria(ns) map p. 169; 35, 98, 101, 136, 146, 152–7, 206, 214, 216–17, 256

augury *see* divination or augury

Baal 175; *see also* fertility cults; Tammuz

Babylon(ians) map p. 169; xi, 1, 10–11, 49, 75–6, 129, 136, 138, 142, 146, 154–9, 171, 189, 197–9, 203, 205, 217, 322; worship 14–15, 58, 87, 110, 288

bath or gallon (about 5 imperial gallons; 23 litres) 300n., 301; hin (one-sixth of a bath) 304; kor (10 baths) 301–2

Beth-togarmah *see* Togarmah

Beth-zur map p. 169; 173

blood: as life-force and in sacrifice 225, 266, 289–91, 294, 302–3; bloodshed and blood-guilt 46, 60, 96, 118–19, 146–8, 161–5, 221, 234, 236, 241

bones, as a figure for the exiles 246–50

Book of the Covenant 7, 116–17

branch or shoot, as a figure for the Davidic ruler 113–14, 124–5, 199–200

Bread of the Presence 281, 297; table of, site in temple p. 271; 280–1

breaking faith 89, 91–2, 94, 112

bride of God, a figure for Jerusalem and Samaria 94–108, 152–61

Brook of Egypt map p. 169; 314, 319

bushel *see* ephah or bushel

cedars, as figures for rulers 109–14, 206–10

Chaldaea(ns) map p. 169; 11, 76, 98, 101, 154–7

cherub(im) 14–15, 57, 60–4, 72, 190–1, 280–1

chosen of God 126–7

circling wheels *see* wheels

clean and unclean 33–5, 55, 150–2, 295

common or profane, as opposed to sacred or holy 35, 129, 150–2, 241, 243, 284, 290, 295, 309, 321; *see also* holiness

consulting God *see* prophecy, prophets as guides for the community

contributions 134, 136, 296–7, 300–2

covenant with God 7, 24, 94, 130, 233, 253, 290–1, 321; new covenant 71, 95, 107–8, 116, 233, 244, 251, 253; covenant between rulers 111–13

cubit, the long cubit (about 20.4 in.; 518 mm.) 268, 270

cup of judgement 158–9

Cush (Ethiopia) map p. 169; 196, 198, 200–3, 254, 256

cut off from God's people *see* death

Cyrus of Persia xi, 240, 322

Dan maps pp. 169, 315; 313, 316
Danel 89–91, 187, 189
dates xi, 1–3, 10–12, 51, 127, 162, 164,
    176, 178, 196–7, 199, 202–3, 205,
    208, 212, 216, 223, 248, 268
David, king of Israel 232, 236, 296,
    313; dynasty of 110, 114, 230–2,
    251, 253
day of the Lord 44–50, 200–4, 229
Dead Sea maps pp. 169, 315; 263,
    310–12, 314
Dead Sea Scrolls x, 244
death 88, 118–21, 130, 152, 161, 181,
    215–22, 246–50, 263, 295, 297
Dedan map p. 169; 172–3, 184, 257,
    259
deuteronomic reform 7, 41
Deuteronomy, book of 7, 88, 117,
    129, 135, 153, 294, 296–7, 303–4
dirge see lament or dirge
discount, lending at 117
divination or augury 78–81, 83–4,
    141–5, 151
doublets 3, 121, 311

eagles, as figures for rulers 109–13
Eden, garden of God 140, 189–92,
    206–10, 245–6, 310–11
Edom(ites) map p. 169; 106–7, 170,
    172–3, 184, 215, 217, 233–9
Egypt(ians) map p. 169; xi, 2, 101,
    111–13, 122–3, 126–30, 136, 152–7,
    168, 170, 176, 180, 189, 194–217;
    worship 55–6, 110, 126, 189, 197
elders 4, 47, 50–5, 57, 59, 72, 86–7,
    126–7
election see chosen of God
Elijah 6, 12, 59
Elisha 6, 12, 140
end, the coming 43–5; see also day of
    the Lord
ephah or bushel (about ½ imperial
    bushel; 18 litres) 300n., 301;
    homer (10 ephahs) 300–2
Ephraim 250, 252; allotment to
    tribe of map p. 315; 314, 316, 320
exiles in Babylon 1, 24–5, 69–72,
    86–8, 224–6; their hopelessness 19,

26, 116, 133, 135, 222; encouraged
    by Ezekiel 1, 26, 68–71, 116,
    133–6, 166, 194, 218–22, 227–33,
    237ff.; reluctant to return to
    Judaea 322
exodus 31, 58, 85, 126–30, 303–4,
    321; see also new exodus
expiation 108, 290
Ezekiel, book of: content and
    themes 1–2, 7, 27, 50, 73, 168, 170,
    218, 254, 267, 321–2; date 1–5; its
    order 2–3; collected sayings 3, 168,
    170; exposition and reinterpreta-
    tion 4–5, 31–2, 34–6, 38–9, 67, 75,
    103, 107–8, 112, 161, 178, 209,
    242–4, 250–3, 310–12; editing 3,
    11, 26–8, 41, 43, 52, 64, 105, 164,
    168, 170, 172, 194, 231, 235–6, 238,
    286, 314; style, text and history
    8–9
Ezekiel, the prophet: his name 25,
    167; addressed as 'Man' 20–2; age
    5, 10; priestly descent 5, 7, 10–11,
    286; his call and prophetic author-
    ity 1, 9–27; his life a sign 5, 28,
    31–2, 74–6, 166; visionary journeys
    6, 51–2, 66, 72, 248, 267–8, 284; his
    dumbness and seizures 5, 22, 28–
    31, 167–8, 199–200, 220, 223,
    284, 286; a bearer of iniquity 30–2;
    concerned for his personal purity
    33–5; his wife dies 5, 165–7;
    appointed a watchman or pastor
    26, 115–16, 218–22; his disciples
    4–5, 64, 170, 240–4

face of God see God, his face
false prophecy see prophecy, true and
    false
fat, as an offering 266, 290–1, 294
feasts see new moon; pilgrim-feasts;
    sabbath
fertility cults 53, 56, 100–1
foreign alliances see prostitution, as a
    figure for political alliances
foreigners see aliens
foundling's tale 94–108
fugitives 167–8, 223